ORGANISATIONAL CULTURE: ORGANISATIONAL CHANGE?

KV-531-207

Organisational Culture: Organisational Change?

PETER ELSMORE
East London Business School
University of East London

ASHGATE

© Peter Elsmore 2001

Published by
Ashgate Publishing Limited
Gower House
Croft Road
Aldershot
Hampshire GU11 3HR
England

Ashgate Publishing Company
Suite 420
101 Cherry Street
Burlington, VT 05401-4405
USA

British Library Cataloguing in Publication Data
Elsmore, Peter
    Organisational culture : organisational change?
    1. Organisational change 2.Corporate culture
    3. Organisational change - Case studies 4. Corporate culture
    - Case studies
    I. Title
    302.3'5

Library of Congress Control Number: 00-135327

ISBN 0 7546 1230 9

Reprinted 2004

Printed in Great Britain by
Antony Rowe Ltd, Chippenham, Wiltshire

Contents

Preface

When organisations change there seems to be anguish experienced by organisational members - and this is not necessarily confined to those people who occupy the lowest rungs on the status and power ladder. Anguish is evidenced in uncertainty about the future, for individuals and for whole groups of people. For example, amongst manual workers in the telecommunications industry, there is little demand for people whose work skills are based solely in line technologies in an age of fibre optics. The voice of pain is audible in a number of the interviews that led to the construction of chapter five of this book. So, a primary purpose in writing this was to give the room to make the voices more audible than they would otherwise have been.

This work is an empirical and theoretical investigation of the links between organisational cultures and organisational change, in two large businesses that have been privatised. The empirical work principally comprised the interviewing of seventy-two mostly middle ranking or more senior officials. The methodological approach has been largely rooted in interpretative theory. The theoretical argument ranges over issues in the social theory of work, and labour process. The orientation taken is largely critical, in sympathy with Willmott (1993).

The conclusions show that attempts to change corporate cultures on a massive scale are very difficult to achieve, in the organisations studied, certainly in the short and medium terms. So, what actually happens when culture change is instigated, from the perspective of middle and low ranking organisation members, is that there are unintended outcomes. Relatedly, then, the reality of day to day life may endorse the view that these new corporate cultures are the creatures of those who create and sustain them. Their sometimes baleful influences originate at the highest echelon of an organisation, but such influence pervades the working lives of all organisation members and this will include the members of sub-cultures and any anti-cultures existing within the organisation as a whole. When members of senior management groups attempt to change the culture of their organisation, more junior organisation members may see what they do as exploitative. This is in the sense that more demands are made of them in terms of hours at work and levels of skill and commitment required but the context is where rewards for most people are severely curtailed or halted altogether.

One part of this prevailing reality (as identified through the eyes of the middle and lower grades of white-collar workers) is that local anti-cultural groups may have power levels similar to supporters of the officially promulgated locally 'new' culture. However, in spite of almost everything, the evidence of this study indicates much loyalty to senior managements. The 'everything' just mentioned includes the lack of recognition by a number of the managers in post of the motivating power of non-pecuniary rewards and so their consequent under-emphasis of such rewards. Loyalty continues to be extended when senior managements seem to lack clarity in the messages they send about why their people fail to be promoted - and may even continue after the person has been severed from the organisation.

Acknowledgements

The two organisations studied in the empirical element of this work are British Gas (Eastern) Ltd. and British Telecommunications plc. Very sincere thanks are due to senior colleagues within each organisation for their 'sponsorship', and also to the many voices within each that kindly consented to speak to me and so made this study possible. Both are very large organisations and, of course, so much water has passed under each bridge between the time of executing the interviews and the middle months of this year, 2000, that substantial changes have taken place between that which is described and analysed and that which presently is. For example, British Gas (Eastern) no longer exists as a company, as the study was conducted before the wholesale national reorganisation of the gas industry. Similarly, in the case of BT, many of the working arrangements of that organisation bear only small resemblance to that which prevails today. I leave to the judgement of others the extent to which that detracts from this study.

Perhaps this is the point to offer equally sincere thanks to a large number of friends and colleagues. There are very many to name. Firstly, I must thank Christine my wife, and Helen my daughter. I understand that the conventional phrase at this point is typically 'without whose inspiration this work would never have been completed'. If that is the convention, then never has it been more appropriate than to apply it here. This book has grown from doctoral work supervised by Professor Hugh Jenkins. Hugh's scholarly outlook and zest for the topic were so important to this piece of research. Thanks also are due to a number of colleagues - Dr Jim Barry who convenes the Organisation Studies Research Unit within the University of East London; Mr Phil Knowles, until recently Dean of the East London Business School and Professor Kazem Chaharbaghi, Director of Research in the School.

The germ of the idea originated in the early years of the last decade when I was a manager in one branch of one part of the public services: to all my former colleagues another 'thank you' is due. Final thanks go to Avalon Associates of Chelmsford for final checking, formatting and preparation of camera-ready copy, and Anne Keirby and her colleagues at Ashgate Publishing Limited.

Academically, professionally and personally, in spite of the best efforts of a significant number of people - including many who are not identified above - errors of fact or judgement may be ascribed to this book. I take responsibility for all of this.

Peter Elsmore

1 A General Introduction

The Focus of the Study

This work has a clear objective: it seeks to examine and understand the organisational cultures of two large organisations. Coupled with this, it attempts also to examine and understand processes surrounding the ways that these organisations changed in the middle of the decade of the 1990s. In so doing, the study raises a number of significant theoretical, methodological and operational dimensions that arise directly from the study's empirical investigation. They are treated in more detail at appropriate places throughout the work as a whole, but their identification and exploration begins in this chapter. The cultural analysis of the two organisations is a worthwhile objective in the context of the middle and late 1990s in Great Britain, because the two organisations were formerly in the public sector. However, at the time of presentation of this study they have each been part of the private sector for more than ten years. In the early and middle years of the 1980s each organisation became subject to fundamental review as a consequence of the privatisation measures of the Conservative political administrations of that time. Each of these internal reviews, following on from the government statutory intervention, identified the need to render each organisation studied much more accountable to a number of constituencies (of course, a number of other organisations that were not part of this study faced a similar task as a consequence of similar privatisation measures). So, attempting to understand what happened as a result of the impact of enforced organisational change is judged to be an interesting task.

The first of these constituencies was to the new groups of shareholders (many of them with very modest holdings and who were, in many cases, equity holders for the first time). The second constituency was that of the service users. It was widely held at that time to be the case that consumers had rights, and here, for example, at the measurable level the quality or the value of the service and its delivery both to commercial and individual customers was regarded as problematic. At a more politically transparent level, issues around the relative levels of power and influence of the public sector trades unions of that time had also surfaced. A number of Conservative Secretaries of State for Trade identified over-powerful trades unions as a significant part of the explanation for relatively low standards of service to these corporate and domestic consumers. The third constituency to which attention seemed to be paid was the concept and practice of competition. Preceding notions about 'public service' may have had their origins in the post-war economic and social settlement. These ideas came to be regarded as old fashioned and inappropriate as a *modus vivendi* to underpin service delivery in the late century. Rather, the governments elected since 1979 were quick to replace such thinking with ideas of 'the market', 'the marketplace' and 'competition', and then attempt to realise or ground such aspirations by legislative intervention in the constitutions of what then comprised the public sector. In some cases where such economic and social phenomena as these were not easily observable, each was artificially created. However, where even a modest level of competition was not easy to fabricate, then, as a temporary measure, the office of 'the Regulator' was created to ensure that organisations that were monopolies or virtually monopolies would not be able to take undue advantage of their trading position. Subsequent reported comments about the Regulator contained in this work as interview data need to be understood within a context where this office was manufactured *in lieu* of a similar sized competitor.

One other highly noticeable element of the spirit of the 1980s in this respect was the view promulgated by successive governments of the period that, in words attributed to the then Prime Minister, Margaret Thatcher, 'there was no alternative'. What amounted to a battle cry from the political right of that time might have referred to the power of government to decide issues, or the perceived failings of public sector institutions, dependent upon usage and context. If, however, the nostrum is taken at its face value, then it seems reasonable to ask about its consequences. Hence, another key strand of this study examines the impact on organisational members of the initiation of widespread changes to the two existing organisational cultures. Such changes may have been initiated by organisational senior managers and/or other equity holders (including institutions) in the organisations, or 'businesses', as they eventually came to be understood. The study is not about either 'leadership' or 'leadership styles'. Such an individualistic focus would endanger full recognition of the group and processual elements of organisational life. Explicitly, such a concentration would move uncomfortably close to a view of organisational power relations which identifies individuals as solely responsible for outcomes.

The Justification For the Study

The related purpose of the balance of this chapter is to open up the significant theoretical, methodological and operational dimensions of the above issues, as mentioned in the opening lines of this study. To achieve this will require a reflection upon the nature of the term 'organisational culture' itself, and this is attempted shortly. It will be the first of a number of times that the concept will be addressed throughout this study. In this first chapter, the objective of the addressal is to consider the notion in a general way and so to use the idea as an organising proposition that will help to identify other, key, propositions in the study. Hence, a reading of some of the available scholarly literature in the interrelated fields of organisational culture and organisational change is an early area of interest for the study. In the next chapter there is an account of the methodology, but also contained within it is a second consideration of the concept of organisational culture. The purpose of that is to turn the phrase from a notion into one that can be measured or considered in a systematic way; it is operationalised. An overview of some of the relevant organisational culture literature is the subject matter for chapter three of this study. Hence, in the third chapter, the concept of organisational culture is considered again. There, the orientation is different again. It is to set out a broad understanding of the idea, but in the particular context of the theorising developed in this research. What follows in this chapter is an attempt to furnish a clear but general statement of some of the inadequacies and/or shortcomings of the existing material in the areas of organisational culture and organisational change that has been produced from within the discipline of management studies.

Overall, the study as a whole is intended to be a significant contribution to knowledge on two interrelated fronts. Firstly, it contributes by identifying empirically and then analysing some key dimensions and outcomes of change processes set underway by senior managers in two large organisations. It has not been possible to trace any similar study of the two organisations concerned. Secondly, it goes on to demonstrate and apply a relatively new method of data analysis through the use of an information and communication technology package generated as a means of helping to analyse the data developed by such empiricism. The package attempts to make sense of qualitative data through a logic not normally associated with qualitative research. Similarly, then, such an Information and Communications Technology (ICT) approach is believed never to have been attempted before in respect of the analysis of 'soft' data from the organisations studied as a pair.

The genesis of the project was in its author's own experiences of organisational/workplace cultural change, as a manager approximately half way up the organisational hierarchy in one branch of the public services, in two sequential employments in two separate locations. Sometimes these workplace organisational changes could be judged to be effective by a number of performance measures, and at other times other changes could be judged to be ineffective using the same or similar performance measures. On further occasions still, it was possible to perceive that organisational effectiveness had simultaneously seemed to improve and deteriorate: some indicators suggested effective change had occurred and others the opposite. In every effective case, personal experience appeared to suggest that it was the strategies with which the leaders led, and the areas where they directed their energies, that appeared to make a significant difference in terms of the quality and consistency of the outcomes. However, this study is not directed towards an understanding of leadership *per se*, rather a main concern of the work is to make sense of the impact of some of the strategies and behaviours exercised by organisational leaders on organisation members. The central argument of this research is that managers and organisational consultants need to recognise the all pervasive power and influence of an organisation's culture (as understood in the subsequent discussions of the meaning of the notion). There is no attempt to reify here; the central argument proposes that the deeply held attitudes, values and beliefs of organisation members have produced unintended consequences when such people are confronted with 'top-down' attempts to change the organisational *status quo* through the manipulation of an organisation's culture. Unless this recognition of complexity that may border on perversity in terms of members' responses is achieved, then strategies aimed at delivering organisational change to the constituencies identified in the first paragraphs of this chapter will not be successful. The whole issue of the nature and measurement of the cultural changes that senior organisational managers set in train is also, of course, another significant element of the overall study and it is properly considered both methodologically and theoretically in the next two chapters.

To make sense of the notion of organisational culture in an effective (and possibly even pragmatically useful) way, there seem to be at least two sets of problems. Firstly, there is the over-arching difficulty of generating an adequate understanding of the many speculations, hypotheses and observations that presently exist in the academic literature. Secondly, these diverse views of culture demand a new and more adequate analysis of them in the contemporary context of the empirically derived evidence generated from contemporary fieldwork. There is a long tradition of studying organisational cultures empirically and theoretically, each by various means. A significant amount of this literature originates outside of Britain, but there is also much written from within a British perspective. Collectively, and at the macro level of analysis, it amounts to an instrument to help understand British organisational life. However, at the more micro end of the research continuum, there remains a need to provide a contribution to the increasing volume of evidence generated from British cultural contexts that is both empirical and critical. So much of the literature identified both explicitly and more tacitly in the forthcoming literature search integral to this study comes from a deeply managerialist intellectual position, and in so doing seems to miss addressing simple but significant questions. One such question is: 'who benefits from organisational cultural change?' Paradoxically, major assistance for this aim was developed in the USA over thirty years ago. Garfinkel (1967) decided to attempt to disrupt the social order of the world of the taken-for-granted in order to render visible the previously invisible. His study, from a previous generation ago, allows this work to identify as crucial the role of organisational leaders in general and in particular the ways that their decisions are interpreted and implemented. Even though his fieldwork was derived from family and education networks in the USA, it is nevertheless a methodological approach that is attractive in other empirical contexts. Through developing an insight into how different activities of different managements facilitate and enable cultural change (or the opposite of these), it will still be possible to use Garfinkelian logic. He advocated that the best way to make sense of a *status quo* was to disrupt it. Through this cleavage of the social 'terrain' he argued that the processes would be visible by which social actors repaired fractures in the sets of rules, routines and taken-for-granted assumptions which guided social and organisational behaviour and this very visibility would also make meanings more transparent. The methodological orientation of this study is sympathetic to contemporaneous work by Berger and Luckmann (1966). They contributed to this elaboration of a new theoretical, and hence also methodological, paradigm. Both of these important works have a debt to the seminal work of Schutz (1932) who developed ideas around phenomenology in the inter-war period, and who was himself influenced by scholars such as Husserl (1931). All this thinking pointed to the way that members of social institutions actively collaborated in producing a version of social reality which, for its producers, was perceived as real and hence was real in its consequences. The supporting methodology of this study is largely sympathetic to this theoretical orientation. It is sensitive to individual differences between people, organisations and groups in those organisations. The methodology largely rejects the logic of positivism and a fuller account of methodology appears elsewhere in the next chapter.

A General Understanding of the Concept of Organisational Culture

An initial examination of the concept of organisational culture seems an appropriate next step. In the existing scholarly literature, while the term 'organisational culture' increasingly has become a dominant construct, it is difficult to argue convincingly that the meaning of the phenomenon is widely agreed and understood. It is more difficult to propose that it is uniformly handled, and impossible to assert that careful empiricism underpins the theorising in every case. No doubt as a result of such thinking, Pettigrew (1990) concludes:

> The most serious cause for concern [in the following respect] is the lack of empirical study of organisation culture in the 1980s.

This work from the following decade is an attempt to deliver such empiricism. Hence, it is judged that this makes this study both intrinsically interesting and also a useful one in terms of assisting the advancement of knowledge about how organisations work. Indeed, the present decade of the 1990s has now generated many different responses to Pettigrew's manifest anxiety, and some of these are considered in the literature overview chapter, chapter three of this study. This research aims to support the notion of organisational culture's academic validity by delivering an empirical investigation of the culture of two large-scale organisations. In so doing, it may perhaps prepare the ground for a subsequent and even more comprehensive national and/or international analysis. One of the two organisational cultures was examined in the context of a recognition of its national character, the second was examined in its own, regional, context.

To make sense, then, of the complexity of the concept of organisation culture is a central aim and activity of the whole of this study. Reflecting the proposition that achieving this will require the full length of the study, the task is handled in the incremental way set out above rather than as a matter that may be dealt with as an initial consideration then dismissed, more or less summarily. So, Schein (1985) supports the view that 'culture' is manifested in three major ways - through the language forms of its users, through their social, economic, political and other behaviours, and through the artefacts they produce. By adopting Schein's typologies of primary and secondary mechanisms, which enable leaders to create cultures, it becomes possible to examine the links between them. By 'primary mechanisms' Schein includes how leaders role model and coach; how they react to crises; how they allocate rewards including initial selection and subsequent promotion; and significantly, the matters to which they pay most attention. The exhortation adopted perhaps most notably by Peters and Waterman (1982) (*viz.*, that managers need to adopt the newer orientation of 'coach, cheerleader and developer of product champions') seems to derive from Schein's perspective. Schein's 'secondary mechanisms' concern how organisations are structured; how the physical reality of both building/artefacts and the organisational environment is handled; the impact - if any - of formally promulgated policy statements; and the impact - again if any - of stories and legends about the organisation upon the organisation. These are promising constructs insofar as they provide a helpful way of explaining and ordering the mass of acculturated behaviour which is such a significant part of the highly routinised everyday life of the members of the organisations. Some of these notions are a feature of latter parts of this study. In particular, some have been operationalised as interview questions, and chapter four of this study examines the responses to such questions whilst chapter five sets about analysing the replies.

Turning to the concept of organisational culture, its origins are unclear because of the multiplicity of meanings with which the concept is presently imbued. It is likely that its origin is set in the cultural anthropology of North America, in particular from the work of Kluckhohn, and her associates (see, especially Kroeber and Kluckhohn (1952), or her collaboration (1961) with Strodbeck). This lack of definitional clarity is clearly reflected in the development of the notion provided in Brown (1995). He identifies Jacques (1951) as the first user of the term and a full account of its development is reserved for chapter three of this study, the literature search proper. For the present purposes, there can be little controversy in identifying the roots of the idea of 'culture' from a social scientific perspective. The greater part of the current spread of meanings though is to be found in more recent scholarship. In particular, the publication by Deal and Kennedy (1982) seems to have been influential in setting the term in one of its more enduring meanings in Britain. Since then, Schein (1985, also 1990, 1992, and 1994) has developed the term in both a theoretical and empirical fashion in the North American context. Contemporaneously Hofstede (1984, 1988, 1992) has examined the notion quantitatively in the context of national cultures on the mainland of Europe and elsewhere.

It is necessary to make sense of the usage of the idea in this study, recognising that such usage is in the context of two of the large-scale players in the telecommunications and energy industries. The organisations studied were British Telecommunications plc and British Gas (Eastern Region) plc. Consequently, it is to the history of the usage of the concept that we must now turn, recognising that a review of its academic development is in the province of the literature search chapter.

The confused applications and meanings of the term 'organisational culture' is a significant issue. These vary along a continuum, and at one pole a definition might be 'those patterns of behaviour, which some or all organisation members have in common'. This loose and social scientific insight contrasts with the opposite pole, that which has been developed and elaborated by (frequently also expensively funded by) attempts by senior managers to set not only the organisational agenda for action, but also its *modus operandi*. Perhaps an illustration of the latter is the number of possibly apocryphal accounts of the 'Bill and Dave way' to deliver a task within the (William) Hewlett and (David) Packard Corporation. Referencing such observations is made more difficult because they are relatively rarely written down in conventional, academic ways. The most important aspect of this part of this discussion, then, is the recognition that high volumes of reports about such matters is of itself interesting, whether or not such reportage is verifiably accurate beyond doubt. There are clear differences, then, in the way that the concept has been handled - clearly demonstrated in the next chapter - and these originate in the differing parent social scientific perspectives from which they are initially generated; sociology, social psychology and anthropology. It is equally evident that they spring from a managerialist rhetoric which has overtones of a form of cultural imperialism, given the 'top down' emphasis of much of the current usage. This issue itself features later in this study, where empirical enquiry attempts to assert that there is indeed evidence of managerialist thinking in each of the organisations studied. Schein (1990) partly resolves the matter when he recommends the use of an ethnographic approach in order to isolate those cultural features of organisational life. Such an approach requires empirical investigation of observed data, so that firstly they may best be understood and then secondly cast into a more helpful theoretical context than those already extant. Such cultural features might include an examination of the ways that management practises may attempt (or not) to inform and influence the basic and underlying values of the members of an organisation. These management practices may attempt (again, or not) to 'fix' stories, practises and rituals in the routinised and taken for granted daily lives of organisation members. Schein's advice reflects his relatively catholic perspective in the contexts of culture and change. In this work, Schein (1990) identifies the historical linkage between the concept of organisational culture and other related notions such as 'organisation climate' and 'group norms' since the decade of the 1940s but asserts confidently: '...as a concept [it] has a recent origin...' He describes the growing and greater emphasis on the study of how organisational norms, attitudes and values are patterned, and hence seem to cut across the social relations of the workplace, in particular over the last fifteen years or so. The work of Trist and Bamford (1963) and his colleagues at the London Tavistock Institute was especially significant here in isolating 'socio-technical systems' as part of the foundations of individual and group orientations to workplace relations. One reading of that work is that the notion of socio-technical system forms part of the parentage of the concept of organisation culture that is presently under consideration. Echoing Pettigrew (1990), Schein (1994) concludes here with the remark: 'We need to find out what is actually going on in organisations before we rush in to tell them what to do about their culture'.

Other attempts to do this are now reviewed in broad terms. Immediately we acknowledge the validity of propositions asserting the complex nature of the idea of penetrating organisational cultures to make sense of them, we must confront the nuances that Kroeber and Kluckhohn (1952) provided. In their last analysis, culture is about 'a complete design for living...a blueprint...'.

Given the intended (but now rather anachronistically expressed) complexity of 'complete designs' and 'blueprints', it becomes difficult to assume that the behaviour of organisation members can always and unambiguously be easily understood in a detailed and thoroughgoing way as a result of every investigation intended to elicit this. Furthermore, it is just as difficult to infer meanings about the way the behaviour was intended to be understood by the social actors who perpetrated it, without the careful mapping exercises that an ethnographic approach presupposes. It is for this reason that the cognitive-mapping-led research strategy was elaborated for the empirical work associated with this study. There are significant methodological implications which derive from such a position, and these are considered elsewhere, in particular in chapter two of this study, which discusses methodology. There may also be similar difficulties in appreciating the notion of 'organisation'. What counts as such for one putative person or group may be interpreted as something rather different by another, say research-focussed person or group. For the present, the potential analytical power of the idea of organisational culture is recognised, and the beginnings of a working definition of the concept of organisational culture may, perhaps, now be attempted in the light of all the above.

Returning to Schein (1990), he casts the idea in a peculiarly American and structural functionalist manner itself derived from the 'functional prerequisites' of Parsons (1951). These are those basic activities which must exist before the group in question - or even society in the Parsonian scheme - could be said to be able to survive. It follows, then, that Schein seems to propose that organisational cultures may be initially understood as prerequisites for the effective establishment and maintenance of work groups. For Schein:

> Culture [is about]... (a) a pattern of basic assumptions, (b) invented, discovered or developed by a given group, (c) as it learns to cope with its problems of external adaptation and internal integration, (d) that has worked well enough to be considered valid and, therefore (e) is to be taught to new members as the (f) correct way to perceive think and feel in relation to those problems. The strength and degree of internal consistency of a culture, are, therefore, a function of the stability of the group, the length of time the group has existed, the intensity of the group's experiences of learning, the mechanisms by which the learning has taken place, (i.e., positive reinforcement or avoidance conditioning), and the strength and clarity of the assumptions held by the founders and leaders of the group. (Schein, 1990, p.1)

It will now be apparent that there appears to be an inconsistency or even contradiction in the Scheinian view developed thus far. That is to say, in adopting the former orientation of supporting an approach to the study of organisational cultures which itself derives from an interpretative or ethnomethodological framework, a reasonable assumption might be that the social world in which organisations are situated is barren and empty. There, people collaboratively create a social world of their own. Authorities such as Garfinkel (1967), Berger and Luckmann (1966) and Goffman (1968) would be sympathetic to this interpretation of Schein's thinking. However, by also adopting the Parsonian language (and therefore logic), we meet a view of the world which presupposes that social institutions create and sustain the social order, both in organisations and across wider society. In short, part of Schein's thinking seems ambiguous. On the one hand he seems to adopt an interpretivist set of opening premises, that individual organisation members create their own social world. He then seems to reify his expression of culture by arguing that it is the social institutions that shape individual behaviour. Of course, these appear to be mutually exclusive possibilities.

Ogbonna (1992) circumvents this problem by declaring that organisational cultures are the outcomes of:

> ...the interweaving of an individual into a community and the collective programming of the mind that distinguishes members...it is the **values, norms, beliefs and customs** that an individual holds in common with other members of a social unit or group... . (emphasis added)

Here, the basket weaving metaphor serves to underline the link between the individual and the organisations to which s/he belongs. Making sense of all these values, norms, beliefs and customs is the job of the ethnographer, or as Morgan (1993) put it, it is the role of 'the cultural stranger', with all the potential that this suggests for misinterpretation, misperception and other inaccuracy. The phrase is particularly interesting given the fundamental weakness of the symbolic interactionist perspective on organisational (and social) life. This weakness is that any validity attaching to accounts of the organisational world appears to be generated from the researcher having access to the meanings only available from the cultural details that arrive with organisational memberships. However, it is axiomatic that only organisation members, through their experience of organisational socialisation, may have insight into these most valid understandings of available meanings by and through organisational members. Membership is only available for neophytes (rather than scholarly researchers). On the other hand, given the fluid and complex nature of the social reality of organisational cultural life that is under discussion, there seems to be little alternative but to ask the questions that seem germane and court the consequent risks of misinterpretation, misperception and/or plain inaccuracy.

At the operational level, the study ends with some brief conclusions and recommendations that emerge from the detailed analysis and discussions of the preceding chapters.

So, this study attempts to understand what is behind and underneath the workaday behaviour of a number of employees in two commercial and industrial settings. It has already been suggested that gaining an understanding of each organisation's culture will be more likely to help achieve the goal of making sense of organisational change. The next chapter of this work examines in more detail the methodological underpinnings that derive from the theoretical heritage identified (but not fully elaborated) above.

2 The Penetration of Large-Scale Organisations

Introduction

This methodology discussion appears before the review of the associated literature as a means of helping to sort the high volume of scholarship that presently comprises writings about organisational cultures in the English speaking world (as well as elsewhere). Through identification of the means of analysis, some theorising, for example, is selected in and other work (including theorising) is selected out. After all, as Schattschneider (1960) observed: 'Organisation is the mobilization of bias'. As a result of adopting an interpretativist position, considerable work in the field of methodology was brought sharply into focus, and of course a deal was sidelined.

The chief focus of the overall research programme is bound up in making sense of the linked notions of organisational change and organisational culture. This was found attractive as the basis for a research activity by most of the organisations that were approached to participate in the empirical study. Without access to the organisations, there could not have been a study of this type, and so it was clearly a priority for this to be arranged; and yet, 'gate-keepers' in large organisations may typically reasonably be said to work to a rather different agenda compared with that of the researcher. So, the development of elements of enquiry of mutual interest seemed to be the most likely means of making any kind of entry to organisations. The approach here is, of course, one elaborated in the light of a range of ethical objectives: a genuinely mutual shaping of a research agenda appears more rather than less likely to lead to mutually satisfactory outcomes. This chapter seeks to ground the selected research methods in a context that is partly theoretical and partly pragmatic.

One of the central weaknesses of the interpretativist methodological position is that the approach adopted to data analysis does not always seem as rigorous as that developed by positivist research (see for example, Bryman 1988, or especially May, 1993). One novel aspect of this study has been the attempt to confront that potential problem by the utilisation of a computer software package, known as Graphics COPE. The package was first published in 1992 in Scotland and was developed by scholars in a collaboration between the University of Strathclyde and the University of Bath. The package is subsequently introduced.

Six organisations were approached as likely partners in the programme, and the basis for their selection was that each had received widespread and prolonged mass media coverage as organisations about to undergo rapid and far reaching change. This chapter of the study identifies the strategy used to gain entry to both of the large-scale organisations that actually agreed to assist in the work. Also, of equal interest, is what can be gleaned about the thinking of the other four sets of organisational officials who felt unable to open their organisations for analysis. This refusal was 'only at the time the request was made', according to senior members of two groups within the four organisations that felt unable to participate in the study. To make this part of the discussion meaningful, it is necessary to develop and elaborate the discussion further about the nature of organisational cultures. So, as has already been suggested, much of the preceding thinking about organisational cultures is designed to be a context in which the justification for the methodology for this research is set. That crucial thinking which operationalises the concept of organisational culture therefore follows on as the second strand of the chapter.

Presently, there remains little or no commercial secrecy attaching to the findings detailed in subsequent chapters. Therefore, for reasons of convenience, the participating organisations have already been named above, in chapter one of this study. In the case of British Telecom, the organisation was studied using the national basis as a sampling frame, but in the case of British Gas (Eastern) as a regional company, the study was necessarily from a whole organisation sampling frame, in its entirety. There was modest involvement with central British Gas institutions but these were not included as locations for study because industry organisation until the middle 1990s was characterised by its strongly regional flavour in terms both of funding and legal constitution. Even though the organisations are now named, it is not felt appropriate to furnish further details where individual work locations are named, because this might facilitate the identification of individual respondents. Naturally, this is regarded to be highly undesirable as each respondent was promised anonymity in the sense that the organisation of data reportage would be done in such a way that responses could not be linked to the individual people who made them.

The geographical reach of the empirical work comprised London and a segment of the South East of England between the east Kent coast and as far west as Portsmouth; Cardiff to the west and Manchester and Bradford respectively in the English north west and north east. In the English eastern counties, geographical limits ranged from London to Peterborough and Norwich.

The Research Approach and Philosophy

In this research project, the interpretative/action learning orientation to empiricism has been favoured. This recognises the primacy of dyadic and small-group interaction in the quest to understand organisation members' behaviours in the organisations in which they have become acculturated; that is to say, why 'Person x' advocated 'y' strategy, or why 'Person a' conducted herself in the meeting in 'b' fashion. Contemporaneously, attempts at understanding organisational realities solely through large-scale and hence typically quantitative analyses are seen largely as non-preferred methodologies because they may derive from flawed thinking. The central proposition here is that post-structural methodologies at least attempt to address the complex methods that organisational members use collaboratively to construct their view of the world. Here, reality is understood as complex and elusive (rather than merely an outcome of positivist interventions and hence available for inspection in a simplistic and rather taken for granted way). In short, the research strategy was designed to 'reach the parts...that objectivist and structuralist approaches don't reach'. The opening assumptions of wholly positivist organisational research strategies (that, for example, it is possible to make sense of social behaviour by unintentionally reifying it) seem deeply questionable. Clearly then, looking at behaviour in organisations through a perspective which both satisfactorily acknowledges the foundations of the psychology of individual differences and which seems to be able to produce meaningful accounts of organisational life is necessary. This is especially so where validity can further be buttressed by the addition of an ability to comb data rigorously for meanings through the use of an information and communication driven mechanism.

However, the relatively narrow research methodology that is further outlined and examined later in this chapter also has its weaknesses. Not least amongst these is the problem of replicability; as replication is impossible, verification of research that is only of an interpretative nature also becomes problematic. In an attempt to manage this matter, a questionnaire was included in the initial research strategy. The original and overt purpose has just been elaborated. It is interesting to note that there appeared to be an unintended benefit bound in with opening an interview sequence with a brief questionnaire. This benefit was that the respondents became better attuned to the broad issues at hand and this in turn seemed to facilitate an easier articulation of their understanding of the reality of their organisational lives with reference to the main thrust of this work. The questionnaire element was, however, ultimately rejected as a tool of research in this study. It was felt that the underlying positivist philosophy sat too uncomfortably beside the ethnographic posture of the main research tool, the interview. Yet, some triangulation of findings was possible. This was undertaken through the use of the non-participant observation data generated in the study.

The introduction to this work commenced an initial consideration of the concept of organisational culture, and it showed that attempts from a psychodynamic or social-psychological perspective to make sense of it by grounding it in management practises are not new. Jacques (1951) illustrates this. In 1983, for example, the *Journal of Organisational Dynamics* featured the concept in a series of articles. One of them, by Martin and Siehl, identifies the potential impact of the concept of organisational culture as a tool for managers to consider and perhaps attempt to manipulate in search of increased quality and/or gains in productivity. In another publication, Wilkins (1983) pointed to initially eccentric understandings of the idea, before touching on the centrality of the matter:

> ...in one organisation, all the men wore a particular kind of garter...in another a company song was 'chanted' each morning...culture consists of the notably outlandish things that organisational life gets people to do.

Perhaps more valuably, he adds:

> Poking fun at what seems ludicrous to us focuses on our interpretation of the quirks rather than on a sincere effort to understand how a group of people see their world and what it consists of.... (Pondy *et al.*, 1983, pp.81 and 92)

Perhaps of greatest value is a concluding thought here:

Over-whimsical treatments miss the powerful and sometimes overwhelming impact [that] organisational culture can have on the organisation's performance and decision-making. (Wilkins, 1983)

It is, naturally, the last comment which appears to be the most central and to have the most enduring interest, and the whole of the rest of this study addresses the point that is made. However, this is from the perspective of the organisations' members in their different hierarchical positions rather than from the managerialist focus that Wilkins *et al.* seem to imply. Wilkins goes on to argue that the idea in question is both 'people's customary behaviour' as well as 'their taken-for-granted ways of seeing the world'.

Whilst this is helpful it captures a different approach compared with, say, the more positivist orientation of Martin and Siehl (1983). These writers propose:

Four sentences capture the essence of much of the recent organisational research [i.e. research conducted in the late 1970s and early 1980s]. First, cultures offer an interpretation of an institution's history that members can use to decipher how they will be expected to behave in the future. Second, cultures can generate commitment to corporate values...so that employees feel that they are working for something they believe in. Third, cultures serve as organisational control mechanisms, informally approving or prohibiting some patterns of behaviour. Finally, ...some types of organisational cultures...[may be] associated with greater productivity and profitability.

The Martin and Siehl proposition about 'profit and profitability' is particularly interesting because it suggests that not all cultures have optimal performance judged from the perspective of the senior manager or equity stakeholder. The interpretativist perspective is certainly interested in multi-faceted ideas. Here, the view that for some organisation members what they say, think and feel is not entirely optimal in some way may well be considered news to senior managers! Certainly, all the criticism of the senior managers elaborated in subsequent chapters of this study seems entirely rational and appropriate to the critics themselves.

This introduces the notion of counter-culture and it becomes accessible through this interpretative perspective. The oppositional character of the concept of 'counter culture' in relation to the mainstream culture distinguishes it and so defines the term. By paying some attention to the idea of counter-culture, this study will assert (and even celebrate) the impact of the influence of the less senior managerial as well as the clerical and manual grades on members' experience of day-to-day life in the organisation. That is to say, the view of organisational culture set by senior managers is potentially only one amongst many. There may be at least one pragmatic-empirical explanation of the dearth of organisational culture analyses that capture something of the breadth and richness of the reality of organisational life. This is because officially appointed and hence salaried researchers and consultants with a substantial contract signed are simply not given the necessary access to this middle and also lower level of organisational insights. Typically, expensive consultant time may well not be deemed to be well spent if it is used in this way. In certain types of organisation, counter-cultural manifestations will be likely to be hidden from line managers. For example, where a publicly stated expression of anxiety may be interpreted as either a covert tilt at the *status quo*, or a not so covert personal criticism of senior management. They will be, perhaps, even less visible to senior management and any imported consultancy team. A provisional speculation here is that such behaviours that indicate the existence of a semi-permanent or permanent counter-cultural set of values will be more likely to be exhibited in interaction with a neutral new arrival to an organisation such as a research student. They will be less likely to be exhibited in front of a consultant hired by senior management. Put succinctly, the proposition is advanced that organisation members may be more likely to admit behaviours indicative of counter-culture in front of an independent research student than in front of a proxy for their senior management.

Consequently, a hope resides in the positioning of the incoming researcher/consultant. Such a person is a stranger (also see Schutz, 1972) at the human level and furthermore will be sponsored by the senior managers at the organisational level. The researcher/consultant will be given a sufficient set of behaviours by organisation members themselves to identify and then understand any aspect(s) of organisational counter-culture. It is therefore axiomatic that something expressed merely as hope cannot then be relied upon to form a central plank of a methodology for research. This is an entirely separate matter compared with whether access to the organisation is granted at all; this is always in the gift of the senior management. Furthermore, the impact of counter-culture may be quite free-standing and is thus a separate manifestation of organisational life compared with, say, the ways that managers may attempt to influence their staff's on the job performances. Schein's view of the nature of organisational culture is in contrast with the previously cited literature, but it has already been argued is not quite complete. He recognises the extent of the effects organisation members may produce, on the day-to-day life of the organisation, no matter whether their work-role is situated nearer the bottom than the top of the hierarchy. Perhaps it is the case, however, that Schein's position is in sympathy with those others that are rooted in social scientific understandings (rather than managerialist ones that may seem to carry overtones of a certain now dated political rhetoric).

> I will argue that the term 'culture' should be reserved for the deeper level of basic assumptions and beliefs that are shared by members of an organisation, that operate unconsciously, and that define in a basic, taken-for-granted fashion an organisation's view of itself and its environment. These assumptions and beliefs are learned responses to a groups problems of survival in its external environment, and its problems of internal integration. (Schein, 1985, p.6)

Schein's perspective needs to be recast so that it will explicitly recognise the impact of counter-culture on the formation of the organisational culture as a whole. It may then be possible to get to the heart of the more subtle managerial practices and tacit processes that are generated in and then reflected by the organisational cultures that these practices and processes seem to play such a large part in producing; we return to the question of whether senior managers create cultures or whether they merely respond to them. This task is the *raison d'être* for the study. The investigative tools aimed at delivering these ambitious objectives were principally non-participant observation; semi-structured, non-random interviewing; and also a brief structured questionnaire. The main use of the latter appeared to be as has already been identified, to help set the social and organisational milieu in which the other parts of the research strategy could take place. Interviewing was conducted in a semi-structured style to enable respondents to provide cultural insights which an even more structured approach may have hindered; perhaps the chief problem with the formal structured interview tool is that it can be said to assume that which it seeks to clarify or examine. That research strategy rests entirely upon the perceptions of the researcher as to the nature of the social reality s/he wishes to understand: to that extent it is irredeemably flawed. It will be clear now that what was gained in validity in the empirical work may have been lost in scientificity. That is to say, interpretative work will do no more than produce a 'snapshot' of the social relations prevailing within an organisation at a finite moment. They cannot be regarded as 'facts' in the Durkheimian sense (Durkheim, 1938) or 'fish on the fishmongers' slab' (Carr, 1964) ready for dissection. However, it should be equally apparent that the methodological discussion is about more than simply polemic between competing research paradigms. What is at question here goes to the heart of how best the researcher/consultant can make sense of the organisational reality s/he meets. The concomitant orientation out of the social science disciplines but in the discipline of management studies is how may the outcomes (or perhaps even 'findings') be fed back to the organisations to produce an authentic action learning experience for the people who are members of those participating organisations.

Wilkins (1983) wrote that organisational cultures have an impact that is 'overwhelming'. If an organisation's culture is as compelling and as significant as this, it surely demands consulting and research time. With this in mind, communications were addressed entirely speculatively to the directors of research in four large concerns and to two more, having taken advice from persons known socially who earned their respective livings in these latter two organisations. The names and job titles of these people were elicited from published material by the organisations, and were then verified for accuracy by switchboard operators at the chief offices of the organisations concerned. The earliest initial approaches may be called the contract-building stage, and this was where an attempt was made by both sides to develop a mutually attractive package of research objectives. Each organisation was promised anonymity whether or not its officers consented to participate in the research/consultancy programme. Therefore, the organisations that had senior management that chose not to participate are not identified by name.

Summer 1993: the Organisations Approached For Entry

Organisation One - the Finance House

This is a large subsidiary of a major British financial institution. The author wrote to the Chair and the Director of Training and Development. The letter, on a single sheet of paper, contained a brief outline of the sort of activities required to be carried out to conduct a cultural audit, mentioned the potential benefits accruing to the company by participating, then sought an interview with an appropriate organisation member to progress the planning. The reply arrived by return of post, under private and confidential cover, politely declining to take part and requesting that the exchange of letters should not receive publicity. One week later, several hundred redundancies were announced in that part of the company's operation. Of course, this brief experience speaks loudly about the need for mutuality in timing as well as in objective setting.

Organisation Two - the Office Equipment Corporation

This is a major supplier of high-technology office equipment and is owned by an American parent company that changed its President in the USA immediately before the London subsidiary was approached. Judging from insights gleaned from then current background data in the business press this new person at the top produced remarkable results in terms of changes to the company's culture. It was of course this press coverage which prompted interest in the first instance. A similar pair of letters to those referred to above produced a rapid and polite hand-written note advising that the company had recently undergone a similar audit conducted by a consulting practice, and the senior official felt that there was little to gain from participation, but offered good wishes for the success of the research project. Again, timing of the initial approach seems to be the chief lesson available for learning from this experience.

Organisation Three - the Manufacturing Company

This organisation is a leading manufacturer of non-fabric materials. It has two manufacturing centres in Britain, one each in the north and south, and has an administrative headquarters in the English home counties. The manager of the southern manufacturing centre received the 'opening bid' letter - and a preliminary meeting was arranged during a telephoned reply. During this, the organisation's Training Manager plus the Plant Manager showed considerable enthusiasm and spoke at great length about their company's training attainments. The meeting ended with their joint promise to approach Chief Office to arrange a subsequent Board level discussion to progress the initiative. After this conversation came five phone calls spaced at two weekly intervals, seeking to expedite the meeting and yet this meeting did not happen. Of course, it seems likely that the idea met with opposition at some point in the organisational hierarchy. The idea of 'resistance' seems germane, and perhaps it may also be legitimate to speculate that the prevailing organisational culture had some difficulty with saying 'No' to its admirers!

Organisation Four - the Local Police Service

This is one of the police services with a territory in the south of Britain. The names of both its Chief Officer and Training Director were obtained through means already described and the customary 'opening bid' letter was posted to each person. It produced an initially favourable response and subsequently several meetings in its headquarters building with a number of senior ranking organisational members. In the meetings, it was clear that the *bona fides* of researchers not employed as officers needed to be established early on if outcomes of use were to be achieved. The taken-for-granted framework only around which were senior officers prepared to collaborate seemed to centre on dimensions of personal appearance, social class adduced by accent and educational attainment. Above all else, co-operation with and assent to values which sat comfortably with those of the English middle classes in general and upholders of the *status quo* in particular, were sometimes assumed. At other times they were tested by direct but polite interrogation. Once all this was established, interest and intellectual curiosity was shown by many of those organisation members; and it is suspected that this was done in a relatively unguarded manner. If that was the case it seemed to underline the importance of being graded as 'the right sort of chap', prior to the desired and relevant conversation being given the room to take place.

Entry thus far into the police seemed already to bear out the rather more substantial analyses of police culture (from perspectives outside that of the disciplines of business and management studies). Such work includes Hall *et al.* (1979). To enter the higher echelons of this police service seemed to involve making a self-presentation appropriate to that of a serious yet pro-organisation person, i.e. someone who would not subsequently, for example, embarrass the organisation. The 'contract' that developed was a tacit one. After some weeks of negotiations, an agreement was reached which produced unspecified levels of access to serving officers and civil staff grades in their places of work in return for unspecified amounts of free management training activities. Before these details could be finalised and a proposed programme developed the announcement of a new chief officer was made public, and the potential vacuum of interregnum seemed to produce a sufficient level of uncertainty to unseat the precarious foothold in the institution. Shortly after, a letter was received which politely asked for an end to the professional interest in that organisation, 'in the circumstances, due to the untimeliness'.

The changed circumstances comprised the need of the new Chief Officer to use Training Department people as staff aides, and this naturally deflected them from their regular management activities. One other contact of interest was the only full-time postgraduate research student currently on that organisation's payroll; a Chief Superintendent interested in researching the leadership practises of middle ranking and senior police colleagues, and a number of informal meetings occurred. Ironically, six weeks later, the Chief Superintendent who was researching leadership commented that his sabbatical was close to its end and that he had been led to expect a role in the training area upon resuming normal duties. A number of informal meetings took place, and this person offered, in a telephone conversation, to reverse the decision made on this research project when he took up duties as the leader of the Training Department and permit participation if it would be of assistance. The offer was declined, with some reluctance, because more positive developments took place in contacts with other organisations at that time.

Organisation Five - BT plc - the Communications Company

Contact here was contemporaneous with Organisation Four, and it was facilitated by the existence of an organisational guide who provided expertise in the information filtering process from contacts made within the organisation. He is a personal friend of this researcher, with eighteen years experience in a number of managerial roles. Organisation Five is a well-known and large competitor in the British and overseas telecommunications markets, it is British Telecom plc. Consequently, it was initially valuable to have the opportunities to discuss the organisation's constantly evolving structure with an organisational 'insider' (in the Becker (1963) sense of the term), as well as gather informed perceptions about how it 'works' in a cultural sense. In such a strategy discussion, it was agreed that an official who manages in a senior role in the organisation development sphere would be a suitable potential sponsor for the research. This person was approached with the durable letter referred to above and, in the preliminary meeting, the organisation's own attempts to recognise and manage its own culture were the main heads of discussion. This was, of course, the first time that the concept of organisational culture had been reflected back by an organisational manager in any kind of fashion and the meanings that underpinned the organisational use of the term were congruent with those used by the researcher.

The next major contact with Organisation Five required the use of a marketing strategy which would deliver a persuasive answer to the 'What's in it for us?' question. The opportunity to share in insights gleaned from the other (participating organisations, but anonymously so) was perceived as attractive by the potential sponsor for the project. This was coupled with the promise of the new perspective and understanding of organisational processes that a research student in a consultant role could bring; it was sufficiently persuasive for help to be offered in developing the project. In the first instance, this was an introduction to the organisation's official with responsibility for internal communications, so that a meeting could be arranged to generate a mutually attractive research agenda. The discussion was a methodological one and the official offered to attach some jointly devised questions to the annual Staff Satisfaction Questionnaire. However, this opportunity was subsequently withdrawn for no publicly stated reason. It may have been decided at a senior policy making level that non-members of the organisation were not eligible to utilise such a communications vehicle for extra-organisational purposes. In a further meeting with the Organisation Development Manager, the strategy that was ultimately found to be usable was devised.

The strategy was based on penetrating the operational arms of the organisation via the already-extant network of quality support workers and trainers. This had a twin benefit. It allowed the research (and the researcher) to 'borrow' on the carefully accumulated credibility of the individual quality workers and it seemed that these workers could also provide practical geo-cultural suggestions about where the most fruitful locations might be for the research to be conducted. That such a grade of management should exist at all is of itself interesting, revealing as it does a particular insight into the notion of organisational quality, against the wider academic and practitioner context of what was known as 'Total Quality Management' (TQM). One inference was that quality was the province of specialist fosterers of it (whatever the 'official' perspective on the ownership of the notion of 'quality' within the organisations). For this reason, the application and attempt at realisation of the notion in working practises was short-lived. In the course of the research within the organisation this approach was superseded by a more typical understanding of TQM which made quality the responsibility of all workers. For the purposes of this study, however, it was fortunate that such a grade of manager existed because these people were well placed to identify a sample of fellows for research purposes. In the research model developed this may count as the second level of the filtration activity. It was necessary, subsequently, to use the same strategy of persuasion with these middle managers as was used with their seniors. Four of the 'quality workers' saw the potential benefits that may accrue to the organisation and provided serviceable *entrees* to various parts of the company. Interestingly, a fifth quality worker felt that there was a substantial threat of loss to her personal credibility in the event of a catastrophically poor piece of interviewing or similar. Consequently, she was not prepared to risk a contact between the managers with whom she was associated on the one hand, and the research programme on the other. This view was respected, leaving as unattainable a number of other potentially valuable leads into the organisation at middle management level. All the interviews conducted within BT are outlined in chapter four and analysed in chapter five of this study. The work within BT took a total of thirty-two days in the field to complete.

Organisation Six - British Gas (Eastern) plc - the Energy Company

This is one of the regional energy companies in the south of Britain, its legal constitution at the time of the research had it known as British Gas (Eastern) plc. The organisation's initial contact with the researcher was a rapid response to a block mailing of the 'first bid' letter that was customised in the five sets of circumstances already outlined above. The revamped letter was sent to each regional headquarters of each of the recently privatised former public utility companies of electricity and gas in the south and east of England. A member of the training team at British Gas (Eastern) plc. asked a few, limited questions then proposed a subsequent meeting in her office further to develop the project. In this meeting the research objectives were outlined and the Training Manager supplied a detailed account of her organisation's attempts to put its senior management in closer touch with the clerical and manual employees working in the business. Within the company, this was known as 'SWOC' (Succeeding With Organisational Change). The exercise ran parallel with another initiative developed by the industry's national layer of management that emphasised the restructuring deemed necessary to improve on efficiency achievements already produced. This national level of intervention was known as the Regional Organisation Review (and referred to in conversation as 'RO[a]R'). In a second subsequent meeting with the Directors of Personnel and of Operations, a consultancy intervention was requested by them to examine the success (or otherwise) of SWOC, their local organisation development activity.

The 'contract' between researched and researcher was set out in a relatively explicit way. This provided that access would be permitted - even encouraged - in all the main geographical centres through its region where its people conducted the business of the company. Secondly, subsistence expenses would be provided; the original research objectives were agreed to be mutually supportive; and the opportunity to further these was tacitly taken to be an appropriate 'in lieu' of payment. Interestingly, it was gleaned some weeks later that an additional key qualification for the task was to have had some years of experience in a managerial setting (as well, of course, as sufficient personal funding to live from during the course of the exercise). From a theoretical perspective this research opportunity cast the researcher in a different role compared with that occupied during the empirical enquiry within BT. In the case of the latter activities, perceptions of the role by interviewees and the other related organisational contacts seemed to shape around 'researcher-as-independent-post-graduate-asking-questions-about-the-firm'. This was a role that was sought because it was self-perceived to offer the greatest potential for honest, reflective and maybe even self-critical responses to the research prompts when they were implemented. In the case of research work with British Gas, there was a danger that the research process might be perceived by the sample chosen as one too close to senior management to elicit answers that were not so carefully self-censored as to render them suspect. With this in mind, early contact with both potential sample members and their line managers always emphasised the academic research objectives and played down enquiries about SWOC. It was the case that each respondent was advised that attitudes to the SWOC process would be reported to the Regional Board, but the timing of this was at a point where it was perceived that the confidence of the respondent was already won. Some of the minutiae of the early interactions with respondents are considered in a subsequent paragraph.

Moving on to produce an action plan to deliver these tasks was aided greatly by the Board level support the organisational research was accorded. However, this kind of sponsorship is, inevitably, double-edged in terms of its utility. On the one hand, acting out the role of consultant commissioned personally by the Chairman and the Board provided a quasi-magical incantation which literally opened all doors, especially with the most senior managers working away from the regional main building. These people seemed most enthusiastic about demonstrating how they were 'on the same wavelength' (to quote one) as their own managers in the regional head office. However, on the other hand and as already discussed in terms of perceptions, there is a clear danger of not being given a 'real' picture of organisational life by members towards the middle and bottom of the hierarchy because of this possibility of misperception as an 'agent' of the Board. The danger is exacerbated when the research in question seeks both to emphasise the organisational counter-culture as much as the culture and highlight the complexity of organisational life, as seen from the perspectives of organisation members at their different levels within the organisational hierarchies. Hence, the research is about how members seek to introduce their own insights and their own understandings either as a tension-reducing strategy, or as a means simply of making sense of it all. The added objective of examining the impact of the SWOC initiative seemed to fit well with the questions devised to address the researcher-led themes.

Yet, these apparent difficulties were judged to be mitigated by a number of factors. These include taking careful charge of how personal introductions were made, at the symbolic interactionist level, in order to highlight the acting out of the 'independent student' role and thereby focus away from the more threatening 'consultant-from-regional-office' role, or the rather more austere 'university-teacher's-doctoral-research-programme' role. They also include taking advantage of the usual breakdowns in communications in geographically well-scattered enterprises, by operating conventional non-verbal cues. As occasion demanded on meeting a potential respondent organisation member for the first time, this included smiling warmly and choosing not to provide all the detail requested beyond that necessary both to establish legitimacy, and not permanently damage the possibility of creating rapport. Thirdly, recognising and conforming to unwritten rules about what counts as appropriate dress may have helped smooth entries into a number of different organisational settings. This may have been especially significant in British Gas (Eastern) plc. as in each of the centres within the region, one full day was spent in the administrative block and one full day was spent outside, in customers' premises and in employees' vehicles whilst travelling to them. The work in this company took nineteen days in the field to complete.

Developing Theory, Developing Methodology

So, the two organisations studied had effectively selected themselves. The conclusion was immediately available that a very different piece of research may have resulted from an investigation which considered issues from any combination of the six organisations already identified, rather than the two which were studied because they agreed to participate. Each of these two was a privatised former publicly-owned utility. In the ontological and epistemological realm of 'what everyone knows about', was 'knowledge' about the telephone company and the energy company valid? Such knowledge said that each organisation was cautious, engineering led, and traditionally its senior managers were 'risk averse'. It also said that it would be more likely that preserving the anonymity of its officials would be regarded as a higher priority than openly proving its accountability to the public it was obliged to serve. However, as a result of joining the private sector, entrepreneurship, aggressive marketing and competition looked to be potential replacements for deeply held existing values. Such values included the public service ethos of 'service-delivery at all costs' with the actual costs incurred by the organisation considered as a secondary and quite separate issue. So, the existing value system might also have included an 'engineering-led' view of organisational priorities rather than a customer-led one. The choice of the two organisations which had allowed entry would thus be an interesting organisational context in which to examine the validity and veracity of such 'what everyone knows' thoughts about the two companies whose people participated in this work. Both organisations are highly recognised in the lives of many, if not most, people in modern Britain; the opportunity to research within them thus provided a chance empirically to consider the extent of the gap between 'what everyone knows' and the organisational realities of at least some organisation members.

The Chosen Methodology

All the foregoing preliminary thinking raised substantial questions about why the methodology that was used in the research was selected, at the expense of all other possible methods. This is the appropriate place to consider this important matter. The opening page of this chapter refers to 'the interpretative/action frame of reference'. In justifying the methodology, one starting point that has resonance is Max Weber's seminal definition of the sociological enterprise:

> Sociology...is a science which attempts the interpretive understanding of social action... In 'action' is included all human behaviour when and

insofar as the acting individual attaches a subjective meaning to it. Action in this sense may be either overt or purely inward or subjective; it may consist of positive intervention in a situation, or of deliberately refraining from such intervention or passively acquiescing in the situation. Action is social insofar as, by virtue of the subjective meaning attached to it by the acting individual (or individuals), it takes account of the behaviour of others and is thereby oriented in its course. (Weber, 1964, quoted by Carr and Kemmis, 1986, p.87)

So, three quarters of a century after his death, this summary of some of his theoretical insights freshly identifies the interior dimensions of meaning in the social sphere of reference. What was at the time of first publication his new paradigm of 'social action' extended the logic of the scientific approach to social behaviour. The logic grew on from that which was merely observable and hence easily recordable also to incorporate 'interpretive understanding' and the key aspect of individual or group action is, of course, the subjective meaning attached to it. That is to say, Weber opened up a strand of social theorising which could take account of differences between individuals and groups whilst at the same time offering powerful explanations of such behaviour. This view rests upon the logic that action has meaning to those who perform it, and that in order for others to understand it, they must see the action from the point of view of the actor him or her self. Carr and Kemmis (1986) offer the following illustration:

To say, for example, that 'metal expands when heated' reflects the way that the behaviour of heated metal is endowed with meaning by the causal explanation of the scientist. It is not to say anything about the way that metal interprets its own behaviour. (Carr and Kemmis, 1986, p.88)

Given that the identical piece of observable social action may be interpretable in a number of very different ways, the interpretation of the behaviour becomes the proxy for the behaviour itself. So, understanding the range of meanings attached to a further Carr and Kemmis (1986, p.88) illustration makes another serviceable example. They instance that the raising of a glass of wine can mean anything from a salute to a piece of Christian ritual. It is the social context that will usually allow the determination of meaning in the mind and social experience of the observer. Of course, this also is at the same time as the attempt by the observer to make sense of the meaning that the action has for the actor; its subjective meaning.

All human actions, then, have a social character. It follows that if an attempt is to be made to understand human individual and group behaviour, then a different account must be made of human behaviour compared with, say, the behaviour of natural objects such as metals or mountains as they move through time and space. Max Weber developed the notion of *'verstehen'* to explain how social actions have subjective meanings (see, for example, Gerth and Mills, 1948 or Bendix and Lipset, 1967 for an extended discussion). Of considerable importance is the set of sociological consequences of this. As societies (and so also organisations) comprise whole sets of subjective meanings interpreted by members, so the task of the sociologist is, in the first instance, identical to that of the social actor. The task is to clothe social action with meaning, then go on to document that meaning. Of itself this is problematic; it appears to make no distinction possible between participants and sociologist. One branch of social philosophy has used the label *'verstehen'* to help generate theoretical accounts of the subjective meanings of the social actions of group members (Carr and Kemmis, 1986). Walsh (1972) contributes to the debate. In a key part of his argument he sub-heads 'methodological rationalities: the management of explanation' he observes:

> The [sociological] observer is enjoined to treat the procedures of the everyday world as anthropologically strange. Secondly, the observer is enjoined to explicate systematically the role played by mundane or common-sense reasoning as a resource in his own explanations of the world. In terms of these injunctions [sociologists] have devised observational techniques.... (Walsh, 1972, p.31)

The seminal work of Schutz (1932), which has subsequently been elaborated and developed by Goffman (1968) and many others, was the intellectual parent of Walsh's argument. The notion of 'the stranger' is at the heart of the Schutzian idea of the discipline of phenomenology. This attempt to make sense of social behaviour centres around the opening proposition that social phenomena - simply what happens between people - are first negotiated then sustained through the development of intersubjective meanings already identified above. Husserl (1965) is helpful:

> A phenomenon is no 'substantial' unity; it has no 'real' properties, it knows no real parts, no real changes and no causality... To attribute a nature to phenomena...is pure absurdity. (Husserl, 1965, pp.106-107, quoted in Filmer *et al.*, 1972)

This logic continues so that the focus for attention for the social researcher becomes the recognition that all social interaction is problematic and therefore a proper focus for investigation.

Put another way, much is assumed in every piece of social interaction, so the role of the sociological observer is to render explicit the rules, routines, and the taken-for-granted-assumptions that underpin each piece of social interaction. The study or examination of the methods that social actors use to accomplish their memberships of their social situations has come to be known as ethnomethodology. Harold Garfinkel defines the activity of ethnomethodology in what has become a celebrated piece of sociological jargon. However, in the light of the above preparation it is hoped that his meaning is less opaque than without such preliminaries. For Garfinkel, ethnomethodology is about:

> ...the investigation of the rational properties of indexical expressions and other practical actions as contingent, ongoing accomplishments of artful practises of everyday life.... (Garfinkel, 1967, p.11)

The 'observational techniques' to which Walsh refers locate the link between theorising and methodological development. They comprise the systematic and detailed recording of interaction data from sequences of social interaction. Such data may be collected through a range of methods. These include participant observation, non-participant observation and also many points on the continuum that capture the various forms of interviewing. Here, at one pole is unstructured interviewing, at its opposite pole is formal and highly structured interviewing, and somewhere between them is situated the various shades of semi-structured interviewing. The interest of the interpretivist (or the phenomenologist or ethnomethodologist) will cease at some point around the middle of such a continuum.

The reasons for such a cessation of interest need to be explored. The simple explanation is that the interpretative researcher has no faith in either the logic or the methods of hitherto existing research in the social sciences. Silverman (in Filmer, 1972, p.2) has produced a succinct list of his dissatisfactions with what was then contemporary British sociological theorising. He criticised:

1. A view of theory as something constructed and negotiated from the armchair and presented...as something quite separate from...the everyday world.

2. A view of methodology as a set of techniques to be used to catch the unchanging properties of a 'solid' factual world.
3. A reliance on the unexplicated assumptions of common-sense knowledge expressed in a preparedness to impute 'reasonable' motives to [social] actors and to make phenomena non-problematic in terms of 'what everyone knows'.
4. An absence of philosophical sophistication in focusing on 'things' taken to be unquestionably obvious within a world through which our mind can roam at will.

Silverman's summary requires elaboration. In the first point he argues the egalitarian position already addressed above, that the theorising of the interpretivist researcher has no more value than that of the positivist ('scientific') researcher. This is so because the material that is studied - peoples' everyday lives - is deeply problematic as material. It is rather more complex than, say, matter in physics or chemistry because it has indexical properties. That is to say, social actors may treat and interpret their own actions in a characteristically different way compared with that which a 'reasonable' or 'common-sense' interpretation (by another person or persons) would interpret it. It is, after all, something of which they have the ownership. So if the social world does not contain unambiguous 'facts' then methods designed to study it as if it does seem doomed to miss more than they may be able to catch. Thirdly, already implied in this discussion, is the recognition that a readiness to assume the reasonableness of every social actor's motives on every social occasion, is a dangerous set of assumptions. Fourthly, Silverman expresses his dissatisfaction at the state of an academic discipline where so much is taken for granted. The scholarship of Karl Popper (1963, 1966) was a particularly significant plank in the theoretical debate surrounding how best social activities could be studied.

He argued that verification was the central task of research and that, in physics and in chemistry, this amounts to attempts to falsify previously gleaned 'facts'. Silverman summarises the issue clearly:

Proceeding from the rules of logic, [Popper] argues that an inductive argument of the form; 'if A then B therefore B' is a logically inapplicable one whereas an argument of the form 'if A then B, but if not B therefore not A' would be applicable. The denial of a consequence of a theory *ipso facto* denies the theory from which it originated. (Silverman, 1972, p.24)

It will be clear that, from within the ethnomethodological theoretical position, the taken-for-grantedness of the Popperian approach to the study of social behaviour is so great as to render it questionable as a basis for any research strategy.

If that is some of the theorising which explains the choice of methods used in this study, what of the methods themselves?

Blumer (1962) illustrates the problem of methodology for the interpretivist researcher in his consideration of the issue of the role of industrialisation and its links with the change in family structure from extended to nuclear. Without considering the views of the social actors themselves in this matter he finds it difficult to attribute cause to the former phenomenon and effect to the latter in the way that positivist research may be happy to do. So, the everyday social reality of the real people living in real families becomes constrained into the sets of procedures of the researcher. He/she may also be labouring under the additional misapprehension that it is necessary for all research in every discipline to copy the rules and procedures of natural science. In contrast to such an approach Blumer advocated an immersion in the real lives of the social actors that the researcher wishes to study. Blumer wrote about research methodology as follows:

> It is a tough job requiring a high order of careful and honest probing, creative yet disciplined imagination resourcefulness and flexibility in study, pondering over what one is finding and a constant readiness to test and recast.... (Blumer, 1962, p.122)

The classic positivist tool of social research, the detailed questionnaire placed in front of a large number of people, just would not do in place of such an immersion, for all the reasons already identified in this chapter.

There is a compelling need not to want to cast the researcher's own perceptions of the nature of the organisational realities onto the respondents to this research. Rather, the preferred perspective is situated in the wish to seek out these interpretations of elusive social and therefore organisational phenomena, with the organisational members, in a collaborative enterprise. The research strategy adopted in this research project is, then, necessarily non-positivist. It is also interpretative in that it is sympathetic in relation to much of the above theorising. Interviews were the main investigative tool used in this work. In terms of style they fell closer to the non-structured pole than the structured pole of the research interview continuum. In terms of content, the questions were developed from Edgar Schein's general orientation to making sense of organisational culture (see both the 1985 and the 1992 editions for a detailed account of this matter).

The Research Methods Used in This Study

This section lists the sub-issues around which the research strategy was framed and the same general orientation was adopted within each of the participating companies.

(i)   The Interview

The title of the third element of this chapter was designed to emphasise the unities that exist between theories and methods. In this rather briefer discussion, and in celebration of these fundamental unities, the justifications for each question asked in the schedule is placed alongside the written analysis and summary of responses. This is to be found in chapter five of this study. For the present purposes, interview questions were framed around the following areas, and the data recorded supports this. However the raw data also is characterised by a willingness to let the respondent open up supplementary issues and/or partially or even wholly to reject the questions in favour of the addressal of a different and self-chosen agenda. Of the total of seventy-two interviews conducted, fewer than half finished with the final questions asked in the way that they were planned; this reflects the willingness to let the respondent collaborate with the researcher in producing a version of the organisational realities under discussion. These, then, were the starting points for each interview.

- (a)   How do people in the organisation learn about senior management policy objectives?
- (b)   What do you say your leaders seem to pay most attention to?
- (c)   Tell me about when things go wrong (go right) in your organisation.
- (d)   Who are the opinion formers around you at work?
- (e)   What sorts of people in this company get promoted?
- (f)   What sorts of people do selectors look for, when they bring in new people?

(g)   Can you remember any really significant people from the past whose contribution to the organisation is still remembered?

(h)   Have you always worked in this particular building (or job for peripatetic manual workers)?

(i)   Has Information Technology changed your job (or role) in the recent past?

(j)   When did your organisation last restructure?
- what benefits accrued to you?
- and to your colleagues?
- were there any problems?
- if there were, were they anticipated, do you know?

(k)   What do you think your competitors say about your organisation?

Each interview was completed in the range of thirty-five minutes to an hour, and typically was preceded by a questionnaire of five to ten minutes duration.

No account of the setting out of interview questions could be complete without at least an initial thought appended concerning how best the responses could be analysed. These responses were written down, rather than tape-recorded or video-recorded. This was because the view was taken that if every scrap of data were to be collected then its sheer volume would possibly overwhelm at the analysis stage. In contrast it was decided to record a well-selected set of verbatim remarks. The basis for the selection was to be judged after some immersion in the local organisation's rules, routines and taken-for-granted assumptions. This decision continues to be regarded as a fine one. Clearly, not selecting from a complete record of events has its dangers. However, the possibility of losing key events under a welter of less important detail is also a matter of some significance.

(ii) Questionnaire

This piece of positivist methodology was initially identified as useful because it was expected that it would have a role as a common yardstick against which each interview could be understood. However, as has already been identified, both content and outcomes seemed to contradict the manifestly interpretative orientation of this study's underpinning theorising and associated methodology. On the other hand, this instrument did serve the useful if unforeseen purpose of 'scene-setting'. By asking a few written questions at the start of the interaction between respondent and researcher, there was an opportunity for the respondent to grasp something of the reach and extent of the subject matter deemed interesting. Secondly, this was done in a manner common to all the respondents; there was no question of some getting a more extended verbal or written introduction to the research process than others in the groups studied. Had that have occurred, then positivist logic would argue that the findings were flawed because of the lack of comparability between the measures used for each respondent. It is also worth noting that a deal of existing research uses both positivist techniques and interpretative techniques in order to make sense of behaviour. One celebrated example is Paul Corrigan's work (1981) in which he used a questionnaire simply to identify a smaller group for more intensive, qualitative study. In the questionnaire associated with this study, a Likert Scale was used with the neutral, middle column removed to encourage the expression of some attitude rather than none at all.

(iii) Non-Participant Observations (NPO)

Through use of this tool, it was possible to obtain some degree of triangulation in the analysis stage of the study. This research method is not so much 'joining in' which would make it full participant observation as 'looking on'. A significant number of these activities were conducted, with clerical, manual and managerial people in each organisation studied. Observed activities included attendance at four team briefings, heads of districts talking with their senior reports, telephone sales and service staff interacting with the public. In respect of manual staff, NPO activity included the observation of service engineers working in the homes of domestic customers, in the businesses of commercial customers and down holes of one metre plus in the street (a data observation template set of sheets was used to record/map the NPO work). Overall, this work took nineteen days in the field to complete in Organisation Five and a further thirty-two days in Organisation Six. It will be seen that a considerable amount of time was devoted to what Corrigan (1981) inelegantly termed 'hanging around... Doing nothing'. The purpose of this crucial aspect of the research was to assist in developing an 'insider' perspective on 'what was going on' inside each part of the organisation visited. At the simple level this meant knowing without needing to interrupt the flow of conversation that, for example, when someone spoke about 'the roar' it was actually the R[o]AR (the Regional Organisational Review) to which they were likely to be referring. At the more sophisticated level, this strategy meant knowing something of the local history of that part of the organisation from which a particular came. Here, for example, knowing that a District General Manager spent a weekend supervising the removal of walls inside a large building helps a researcher understand the full import of the use of a phrase by a respondent such as 'It's like Year Nought here, now'.

Corrigan's monograph (in Hall and Jefferson, 1975) was an examination of the street life of a group of adolescent young men. When they were asked by older people what they did on the street, they frequently replied that they were, in fact, 'doing nothing'. The account of all this proposes that 'doing nothing' was not actually nothing at all but rather it was a complex set of activities, actions and understandings. Only through observing it is it possible to recognise then understand such minute but sometimes significant behaviour. In conjunction with the interviews associated with this research, the NPO work always preceded interviewing. This gave the best opportunity affordable that a range of organisational insights were more rather than less likely to be agreed and understood between respondent and researcher. It must be added in conclusion here that only organisational 'insiders' (in the Becker 1963, *ibid.* sense) could have the full range of organisational common-sense meanings at their disposal, and of course this would take years to achieve. This contrasts somewhat with the total of only fifty-one days for the study overall and limits the achievable objective to little more than 'researcher knows enough about the organisation not to cause embarrassment by asking respondents questions that were too naïve'.

Action Research

This part of the overall research strategy rests upon the assumption that it will be effective to mirror back to an organisation outcomes and findings as the opening element in a dialogue between researcher/consultant and senior managers. This may begin a faster learning experience for the organisation than its members could manage without assistance of this kind. Certainly, a number of the relevant textbooks might argue this (see for example, Hannagan, 1995). From the point of view of the researcher, this method permitted some opportunity to test the validity and so accuracy of the insights gleaned with one of the constituencies identified in the opening paragraphs of this study. Perceptions from reporting to the two groups of senior managers are included in a subsequent chapter. The literature search in the next chapter provides some of the intellectual climate against which the research findings in chapter five may be set.

However, experience gleaned from the empirical process in this study suggests that the mirror metaphor is not as adequate as it may first appear: encouraging a process of critical self-reflection and self-evaluation is not something that will automatically commence as soon as any Organisation Development work ends. This early attempt at the generation of useful data for research purposes through the use of Organisation Development techniques was abandoned as unrealistic at an early stage. The section is included here merely to record that view. However, ironically, while the attempt to use the research strategy failed at an early stage, it was nevertheless pressed upon the researcher by the insistence of senior members of each organisation. That is to say, each organisation's senior members who were interested in this research exercise requested that a presentation should be made immediately the research activity itself was over, so that they could learn whatever was available to learn from the work. After the presentation, in each case, an extended discussion took place and it is contended that the half day in each organisation for reporting purposes amounted to the holding up to senior officials of the classic Organisation Development mirror.

Research methodology is one of the crucial elements of this study, and so, as a theme, it is visible as a strand in many other chapters of this study. If there is a sole aim in this chapter, it has been to set out the justification for the choices of methods used, and to place these methods within the wider context of research into organisational cultures. After the summary and chapter conclusion, chapter three gives an overview of the existing literature on organisational culture, and further develops the work on defining that term.

Summary and Chapter Conclusion

The introduction sets up the practical details of the research project by naming the organisations studied, locating the geographical sweep of the research and then beginning the discussion about the potential benefits that might accrue from it. The research approach adopted, and something about its underpinning philosophy, follows. The purpose of this is partly to develop an argument that highlights some of the key aspects of interpretative research. The second part of the purpose is to begin the discussion about the impact of the changes that organisational leaders initiate when they identify organisation culture as an area of legitimate interest with which they may concern themselves. So, this debate will necessarily include an account of counter cultural and anti-cultural evidence in a continuation of the discussion about the meaning of the term organisational culture. In this chapter, particular attention has been paid to the tasks of defining and operationalising the term. Subsequent thinking outlines the process through which the two organisations that participated came to be identified. This chapter's middle section touches a literature that seems fundamental to this part of the study; the authorities cited attach an indissoluble chain around theories and methods of research. The consequence of this linkage between them is that a treatment of one will always demand a treatment of the other. The last sections of this discussion identify the techniques of investigation actually selected with an associated commentary.

3 Some of the Wider Context

Introduction

The purpose of this discussion is to set the research issues within the wider context of the debate about organisational culture and to consider in a more detailed and thoroughgoing way the meaning and usage of the notion of organisational culture. To achieve these aims it will be necessary to construct a review of many of the landmark studies so that an analysis may be made of the theoretical underpinnings of the concept of organisational culture in the literature. This will indicate how the idea has been both altered and extended since its first use. This is helpful for three reasons. Firstly, the discussion will frame the account of fieldwork methodology and findings in the broader picture of key developments in the organisational culture area of interest within the interdisciplinary academic activity of organisation studies. Secondly, it will summarise several of the other recent theoretical developments and in so doing help codify the increasingly diffuse and burgeoning literature in the subject. This catholicism may be said to include importation from the sociology of education as well as the further development of an anti-managerialist critique of literature here. Both of these avenues are briefly explored in this chapter. Thirdly, it will permit a demonstration of some relatively recent theoretical avenues of enquiry. These concern the application of concepts such as counter-culture and anti-culture to the study of organisational cultures. This may, in turn, offer interesting avenues of exploration in the analysis of the culture of the two large organisations studied. Given the overall chronology of this study, the discussion of the more recent thinking is further developed in chapter seven. That is a research endpiece. It is appropriate in this chapter here, however, to begin that process of identification and discussion.

   The first of these strands begins with a brief chronology of the concept of organisational culture and then a more extended illustration of its present and diverse usages. There is a particular focus on the more recent contributions, particularly those from Brown (1995) and Bate

(1994). Brown helpfully provides a chronology and discussion. However, both are interesting references for a number of reasons; in terms of content the former examines linkages between culture, strategy and performance then considers the present state of certain aspects of organisational change theory. The latter work is concerned with looking at strategies for effecting organisational change, and in so doing presents a perspective which may appear managerialist. Both authorities deal with matters close to the forefront in the literature. Intriguingly, there is diversity indicative of the way that the notion of organisational culture seems now, on the one hand, to be increasingly politicised in one sense, by some management/ organisation writers. On the other hand, its meaning is sanitised and rendered neutral in the hands of other management/organisation academics and practitioners. It may be that the empirical evidence associated with this study will suggest that the concept of organisational culture can be understood as useful as an illustration of an ideological tool in the hands of both senior managers and equity holders in their organisations. It may be said presently to be a means of understanding something about the power relations of all the social constituencies which combine to produce organisation members, in their various class, gender and racial groupings. Of course, one potentially interesting line of enquiry not necessarily relevant to this study but of general interest is whether usage of the term organisational culture actually deflects interest away from the defining structuring of social life and hence also organisational life. This may demand analysis of some or all of the issues around social class, gender and race, or any other dimension of stratification.

So, here is one of the central questions that this research asks - is the concept of organisational culture little more than a stick with which organisationally powerful groups beat less favoured groups in the organisational hierarchy? The existence of the intra-organisational processes observed indicates that the notion of organisation culture may actually be no more than an intensely interesting means for some stakeholders to cloth realities about the real distribution and working of power in their organisations in a rhetoric. Such rhetoric may emphasise 'normalcy' in the C. Wright Mills (1959) sense and general organisation development that may be of benefit to all organisation members. This may be the case whether such an outcome is intentional or unintentional; a fuller discussion of this possibility is contained in another part of this work (and also elsewhere, see, for example Elsmore and Jenkins, 1994). Perhaps the soundest interpretation of the high degree of interest in the concept (by academics and practitioners) is generated out of the perceived potency of the notion to effect permanent organisation change. This will be perceived to be to the benefit of senior managers and other stakeholders in the organisation such as other equity owners. It is suggested that organisational changes such as these may well occur at the expense of the other, less powerful stakeholders in the organisation - and the medium and longer-term net consequences cannot be clearly accounted for at the outset.

Edgar Schein (1990) identifies the ideas of 'group norms' and 'climate' as something over half a century old. The period immediately following the Second World War was distinguished in this respect by the work of Lewin (1946, 1952b) and Schein (1992) asserts Lewin's usage of the term 'cultural island' as 'frequent' but, sadly for the present purpose, not 'explicit'. However, it is clear that Lewin's understanding is grounded in his own ideas of the importance of 'action research' which will encourage organisation members themselves to participate in the quest for valid insights and understandings into the social processes of their workplace. Lewin's (1952b) coinage of the term 'cultural island' seems to reflect a then increasingly well-established view of the phenomenon in the developing discipline of industrial psychology. This was that if a person at work was exposed to new thinking when in an unfamiliar social or work milieu, then the behaviours learned would quickly be unlearned when the person returned to his/her normal and established place of work. That is to say, the 'island' would be engulfed with a tidal wave of what later, phenomenological, literature referred to as 'thinking as usual' (see Schutz, 1972 in particular, but this idea is typical of a range of phenomenological work in both social theory and social enquiry).

The Concept of 'Organisation Culture' - a Brief Chronology

The earliest usage of the term 'organisation culture' that has been traced is by Jacques (1951), in his study *The Changing Culture of a Factory* (quoted by Brown, 1995, p.6). In the work, Jacques observed:

> The culture of the factory is its customary and traditional way of thinking and of doing things, which is shared to a greater or lesser degree by all its members, and which new members must learn and partially accept to be accepted into service in the firm. Culture in this sense covers a wide range of behaviour: the methods in production; job skills and technical knowledge; attitudes towards discipline and punishment; the customs and habits of managerial behaviour; the objectives of the concern; its way of

doing business; the methods of payment; the values placed on different types of work; beliefs in democratic living and joint consultation; and the less conscious conventions and taboos.

In particular it is interesting to note how modern is the 'feel' of Jacques' analysis in this orientation of the idea and hence, in a sense, how circular much of the subsequent intellectual development of the history of the idea may be said to be. This now dated set of propositions about the nature of organisational culture is judged sound in this study. This is because a deal of current academic understanding of the idea seems to be so close in meaning to that of Jacques. Clearly, however, the theoretical framework of the Jacques study is that of the strand of Durkheimian positivism which Parsons and later Merton developed into what became known as structural functionalism.

Schein's analysis of the concept moves also to the layer of meanings which seem to underpin the main planks of the Jacques view by also addressing 'basic assumptions...[and]...norms and values' as well as 'artefacts and rituals' (Schein, 1985). In keeping with one of the fundamental weaknesses of all functional analysis, however, there is clear evidence of the distorting effect of reification in both the Jacques approach, and also limitedly that of Schein. It therefore seems only partially helpful in terms of its potential to generate explanatory power. Alvesson (1993, p.25) supports such a view of Schein. He calls the Scheinian approach here 'a functionalist, narrative and conceptually biased conceptualisation of culture'.

In the literature of social theory, a number of works elaborate this problem (see, for example, Filmer *et al.* (1970) for a detailed discussion of the weaknesses of such analysis, or alternatively Berger and Luckmann (1966), Garfinkel (1967) or Goffman (1968)). Brown's (1995) chronology introduces a large gap by moving the focus forward from Jacques some twenty two years in a leap. However, other scholarship - notably Schein (1990) - is more helpful in permitting a consideration of the literature of the 1950s and 1960s in this field.

According to Schein (1990) the increasingly coherent academic interest in organisational analysis developed a psychological focus in the 1950s and this itself derived out of industrial psychology's characteristic and proper preoccupation with the behaviour of the (usually male) individual at work. The new interest in structures and processes throughout that and the succeeding decade became the foundation for recent work, as well as mirrored the interest in and contemporaneous growth and development of both industrial sociology and organisational sociology. Key works include Beckhard's (for example 1969) and also Bennis's (for example 1959) focus upon how organisations change. Socio-technical theorists such as Trist and Bamford (1963) and his fellows at the Tavistock Institute set out other significant signposts. Other research by Likert (1961) and Katz and Khan (1966) is valuable in this respect, but a discussion of the major positivist and highly quantitative contributions from Hofstede (1984), and then later from Trompenaars (1993), is a requirement of this account of the development and usage of the central notion.

Hofstede (1984) wrote of 'the collective programming of the mind which distinguishes the members of one human group from another' as the meaning of the term organisational culture. This seems an interesting way of understanding the notion. The computer metaphor is revealing, it points up as important group activity and difference, and group learning. He made a major examination of work related values at IBM, using a large sample of employees from over fifty country locations in three world regions. He 'discovered' four areas of work related value differences in all this. These are:

- Power distance - the extent to which hierarchy at work is seen to be an irreducible fact of life, or not

- Uncertainty avoidance - the degree of tolerance for rule breaking and the extent to which members feel threatened by behaviours which embrace (or reject) formal rules

- Individualism/collectivism - which entity is to predominate in the organisation; individual or group?

- Masculinity/ femininity - which goal is more important at work; pay and assertiveness or friendliness and good relations with the boss?

Hofstede (1984, 1992) imposed these structures of meaning upon his 100,000 plus sample responses and his work is highly respected in most journals. However, he is interested in something quite different to the stuff of this research. He comments himself that you cannot value values. That is to say, qualitative research is interested in the most deeply held and long lasting values that social actors hold in their work roles as members of organisations. This really is different compared with what people tick with a pencil, in boxes, on quantitative research schedules. Of course, such thinking sits atop fundamental issues in social theory and social research, some of which has been explored in this study's preceding chapter.

Trompenaars' (1993) has some interesting similarities with that of Hofstede. Hoecklin (1995) relates that over a ten year period he administered more than 15,000 schedules of questions to managers in twenty-eight different countries. Trompenaars' analysis produced the following dimensions of culture:

- Universalism versus particularism - how may what is good and right be determined? Is this best done through identifying abstract rules or is there always a set of absolutes that will apply?

- Individualism versus collectivism - which are more important; personal or group goals? The Hofstede thinking identified above also applies here.

- Neutral versus affective relationships - this relates to emotionality in terms of peoples' relationships with each other in the organisation. How are emotions expressed in work relationships?

- Specific versus diffuse relationships - this relates to the degree of involvement in work relationships. How far are people comfortable in sharing intimate levels of their own personality with their work mates?

- Achievement versus ascription - this concerns how power and status are legitimated within the organisation. Should these dimensions of power and status be based upon what someone does, or simply upon who someone is, in terms of, say, parenting?

Hoecklin (1995) attempts to integrate the pair of approaches by identifying power distance, uncertainty avoidance, collectivism and individualism, and finally universalism and particularism as aspects of the fieldwork which will be of most help in making sense of individual behaviour in different national contexts. However, her 'handy hints for managers' perspective does not grapple seriously with key theoretical problems concerning the difficulties with working with reified ideas, and the associated problems of defining in an operationalisable way the very concept of organisational culture itself, without assuming that which it seeks to explain.

Walsh (in Filmer *et al.*, 1972, p.21) contributes most usefully here. He observes:

> Phenomenological sociology...is concerned precisely with the notion of sharing and the manner in which an orderly social world is established in terms of shared social meanings (or common understandings).

There is a central problem with all large-scale and quantitative approaches to making sense of behaviour as intimate as cultural understandings. This is, that no matter how extensive the quantitative research is (Hoecklin calls Hofstede's methodology 'very deep' [1995, p.27]) in terms of the degree of detail in the analysis, there is always the space in time and meaning for a 'wait and see' quality to emerge. Garfinkel (1967) calls the same piece of phenomenon 'the etcetera clause'. Both Hofstede and Trompenaars deal in common understandings, but each authority seems separately to over-estimate the extent of the sharedness between organisational members. Walsh (in Filmer *et al.*, 1972, p.21) goes on to comment:

> Common understandings are not formal rules in the sense of actuarial devices by which members predict one another's future activities but agreements that can be used to normalize whatever the actual activities turn out to be. Action is never just the product of formal rules... What is important, therefore, is not formal rules, but the procedures by which members demonstrate that activities are in accordance with a rule... Social meanings, then, are the ongoing practical accomplishments of members achieved in situations of interaction.

If such a perspective as this can generate data that is interesting and rigorously analysed, then there seems rather less validity that can be generated from asking tens of thousands of organisational members to respond to sanitised questions that are written down for them to consider.

A common strand here between all the positivist organisational culture research is that it does not recognise the deeply problematic nature of the social order it attempts to explain. To a greater or lesser degree, it is concerned with the way that norms, roles and attitudes become integrated and then lock together to form a system. This seems to interrelate with the processual dynamics within the organisation in question to form what functionalist research has always come to address as a key cultural dimension. During the later part of the 1960s and into the early 1970s, interpretative social theory was developing in the USA and in Britain. It emerged partly out of the Schutzian tradition referred to earlier. Yet, one other part of its raison d'être seems to be pure pragmatism. This derives from an increasing degree of dissatisfaction on the part of scholars with the shortcomings of the ways that functionalist research attempted to make sense of social realities. In particular, the characteristic analytic style of Parsonian functionalist research seemed to distort through reification that which it sought to understand.

That is to say, at the theoretical level of analysis, there was an increasing realisation through the 1960s and early 1970s that functionalist perspectives which shone interesting light on problems around structure could not also, axiomatically, proceed to an examination of the detail of the stuff of the ethnomethodologist in organisational analysis. This perspective has been available to organisation research for approximately thirty years, and its influence is more or less visible in landmark studies since then. Turning to such work in the last couple of decades, it is appropriate to examine a brief summary of it emanating from both British and North American authorities. Deal and Kennedy (1982) provided a valuable and even landmark account of hitherto existing treatments of the concept of organisational culture. They furnished the usefully pragmatic working definition of the term organisational culture as, simply, 'the way we do things around here'.

They contribute to a debate about the nature of organisational culture and its impact that was increasingly well joined. So, for example, Morgan (1986, p.120) identified the notion as a metaphor:

> The culture metaphor points another means of creating organised activity: by influencing the language, norms, folklore, ceremonies and other social practices that communicate the key ideologies values and beliefs guiding action.

However, talk of 'creating' may not be helpful, suggesting as it does, the related notion of 'creator'. If, though, this is meant to be part of the metaphor and so not to be understood as a 'real' idea, then abstracting meaning from the approach becomes ambiguous and perhaps even tortuous. 'Creator' also carries connotations of 'controller' and this is further examined in a later chapter of this study, in the theoretical and empirical conclusions. The functionalism of Schein (1985, Ch.1) offers another approach to understanding the concept of organisational culture. For him, it is:

> A pattern of shared basic assumptions that a group learns as it solves its problems of external adaptation and internal integration, that has worked well enough to be considered valid and, therefore, to be taught to new members as the correct way to perceive, think and feel in relation to those problems.

'The way we do things around here' seems to involve multifaceted sets of understandings. Bound up in the idea will be phenomena such as organisational heroes, organisational mythology, and then a host of symbolic meanings, myths and rituals including the symbolic character of language itself. Cultural and social anthropology are academic disciplines that have provided helpful analytic tools, and the ideas of 'story' and 'myth' are illustrations of that proposition. 'Stories' are a part of the 'oral tradition' of an organisation. They may concern the organisations' founder or founders, or perhaps current chief executive, any combination of whom may also be understood as organisational heroes. The stories are embellished as they are told and retold, so that after a period of time they may contain a good deal that has no basis in fact. Their purpose is that they explain to new and existing members how and why things are done the way that they are. 'Myths', in part, contrast. They start from a position of untruth but serve the same purpose as stories. 'Organisational heroes' are not always founders. They may be unconventional thinkers or devoted (or even oppositional) charismatic personalities.

'Organisational symbolism' opens up a substantial toolkit of ideas within organisation studies, but a detailed account of this territory - sufficient, indeed, to cause the formation of a Standing Conference - would seriously skew this discussion. So, perhaps a simple statement that identifies something of the scope of the idea will suffice. The symbolic character of culture is bound up firstly in the way that language is used within the organisation. This includes jargon as well as specialist use, in for example, engineering or accounting vocabulary, within or outside the organisation. Secondly, it points the way that the means by which space and time are negotiated by organisational members is deeply symbolic in character. Here, what counts as, for example, 'early', 'late', 'close' or 'distant' between and within organisations will ultimately be a socially constructed meaning. Hofstede (1992) has used the term 'practices' to refer to social and cultural phenomena that are visible to people who are not members of the organisation but for whom the meanings of such phenomena are not similarly transparent. The Hofstede perspective, also properly it is judged, locates the deeply held values of organisation members at the very centre of the organisation's culture. This presupposes that they will be difficult to change and even that, for some organisation members, these values will be so deeply held they will not be possible to change at all, ever. The fieldwork associated with this study is very interested in this understanding.

'The way we do things around here' seems also to be understandable in terms of different typologies which illuminate how the idea has been interpreted by different authorities in the literature. So, Handy (1985) suggested that organisations may be understood as having one of four different organisation cultures:

- power culture
- role culture
- task culture
- people culture.

Power cultures are characterised by the web *motif* and the notion proposes that power resides at the centre of the web/organisation and that the 'spokes' are the functional organisational elements. The role culture is characterised by the 'Greek temple' structure. Here, power resides in the over-arching roof, and communication between the pillars (the functional areas of the organisation) is only possible by passing information through the heads of each department. The task culture is characterised by the lattice and it indicates a flexible structure that can be reinforced or denuded of resources dependent upon the demands of a particular project. Nodes in the lattice will thus be either 'big' or 'small' reflecting task importance/priority. The people culture is where individuals cluster within the organisation in a substantially autonomous way. They form what Handy (1985) called a 'galaxy of stars'. Power is shared and based on expertise.

Deal and Kennedy (1982) approach the operationalisation of the idea of organisation culture from a different position. They identify two elements in particular as significant:

...the degree of risk associated with the company's activities, and the speed at which companies, and their employees, get feedback on whether decisions or strategies are successful.

They plot a 2x2 matrix using the factors as axes, and insert four corporate culture types:

- the tough guy, macho culture
- the work hard, play hard culture
- the bet-your-company culture
- the process culture.

The tough guy culture is essentially entrepreneurial and is characterised by high degrees of risk taking and rapid feedback on the success or otherwise of such risk taking. In such cultures, Deal and Kennedy observe: 'Co-operation may be lacking and individuals who succeed may be immature and disruptive to the long-term maintenance of a strong culture'. The work hard, play hard culture is associated with high feedback and with low risk. Success here is typical for people who are good team workers and high achievers. Deal and Kennedy assert that such a culture may suit young people who are committed but maintaining senior staff who, presumably, 'have seen it all before' is more difficult. The 'bet your company culture' implies high risks with slow feedback on the risk taking. Technical expertise is respected and personalities of successful people have patience well developed.

Part of this approach to understanding organisation cultures through typologies (that echoes the Scheinian functionalism referred to and discussed above) is recognisable in the research instrument that is elaborated in succeeding chapters of this study. However, in the context of the broader theoretical discussion in which this study is lodged, the notion of organisational culture will also serve as an appropriate vehicle with which to demonstrate how micro-theorists have contributed to the available set of understandings about how organisations work.

Furthermore, since Deal and Kennedy (1982) and the other sources already identified and discussed, the accelerating rate of publication in the organisational culture field has reflected the extent of interest shared both by academics and practitioners. Brown (1995) illustrates the themes of organisation culture both in the British and European context and makes something of a contribution towards resolving a little of the totality of the theoretical difficulties inherent in the concept of organisational culture.

Within his eclecticism, key strands of thought comprise a review of material around the links between strategy and culture, and the implications of this for organisational performance. Secondly, he produces some thinking on what generates culture change and how the process proceeds. Both aspects of the study benefit from a critique. Brown proposes rather airily (1995, p.169) that in an assessment of the linkages between culture and strategy and performance the issue is beset by difficulties of definition but this can also be a source of:

> inspiration to us... This vagueness and these uncertainties, which in part reflect how little is known in this field are also a source of fascination... .

Nevertheless, in a characteristically managerialist and positivist fashion, Brown is able to discern no fewer than six ways in which the culture of an organisation impacts upon its mechanisms for strategy formulation, and ultimately organisational performance. The positivism is a sharply clear illustration of 'recipe knowledge'. This construct helps render problematic the ideas that count as 'knowledge' within organisations, and in the context of this study, the term refers to 'what everybody knows' about priorities in organisations. Further development of the idea is available in Young (1971) where he identifies social properties in the organisation of knowledge. For the present discussion, Brown's (1995, p.170) six ways of linking organisational culture with strategy formulation comprise:

1. Different organisations scan their market places differently, arriving at different conclusions about how best to proceed. This seems self-evidently to be a sound assertion.
2. During such scanning activities, organisational strategists will scan using different filters (or sets of working assumptions about priorities) and this will lead to selective perceptions. Even where scanning procedures are similar, differences in the breadth or extent of horizons scanned, or preferences between reliance on quantitative or qualitative data, or straightforwardly differences in ideology between organisations, will produce selective perceptions that differ. Again, this seems to be self-evident.
3. Once gathered, the way in which data will be interpreted is the subject of more cultural influence: linear deductive reasoning, Cartesian logic, pragmatism and inductive incremental reasoning are three national cultural stereotypes identified by Brown

(1995, p.170). Whether it is sensible to attempt to characterise all Fortune Five Hundred corporations as nearer one pole than another, or all those whose price is quoted on the Bourse, Hang Seng or the Stock Exchange, as of one type or another seems another over-simplified idea and hence less helpful.

4. Brown identifies the moral dimension of strategy formulation as significant. This appears to be another realistic *a priori* judgement, but his illustration of Volvo-Kalmar's decision to enhance the quality of their manual workers' lives as distinct from enhancing profitability seems naive as it appears that Brown sees no affinity here, only differences.

5. The manufacture of strategy as a consequence of agreeing how to interpret the data is also problematic. Brown asserts that managers rely on the 'thinking-as-usual' routines discussed earlier, but the empirical data associated with this research suggests differences (discussed elsewhere in this work).

6. Different sub-groups within an organisation will 'see' different priorities, each based upon its own, partial, perceptions of how best scarce resources within the organisation should best be allocated. Brown finally takes up the crucial issues about organisational power and its distribution, and the potential within an organisation for there to be different constituencies jockeying for positions of influence whilst power is in a constant state of flux between those groups (or sub-cultures or anti-cultures).

Whilst this is an interesting commentary on the impact of the idea of organisational culture, it seems to be characterised by its limited understanding of the proposition that, indeed, cultures are something that organisations are rather than something that they may be (see Pacanowsky and O'Donnell-Trujillo, 1982). As a result, analysis that is limited to merely one section of an organisation (in this case the management) will inevitably lead to a limited and hence inadequate understanding of the culture of the organisation. This is particularly clearly illustrated in the following definition of the idea of organisational culture:

'Culture' refers to the underlying values, beliefs and principles that serve as a foundation for an organization's management system as well as the set of management practices and behaviors that both exemplify and reinforce those basic principles. (Denison, 1990)

Denison seems to be suggesting that only the management may have 'values, beliefs and principles' that could serve as a basis for an organisation's culture. Furthermore, it appears to be only management people who develop practices and behaviours in response. This is a difficult notion to accept when one recognises the possibility that managements may choose to adopt a significantly different stance compared with their employees and indeed may fail to achieve its objectives because of this. In contrast, if one accepts the view that organisational reality is the outcome of a protracted series of minute negotiations between all the parties concerned who then deliver to each other and to themselves a shared version of reality, then Denison seems to be missing much. The forthcoming account of the fieldwork in this study highlights in many places the substantial gap between the value positions adopted by each side. So, the Denison expression seems closer to a wish from a managerialist position rather than an adequate account of an organisational reality.

Turning to Brown's second key theme; his view of what generates culture and how this process proceeds, there is another six point typology. The focus is described by Brown (1995, p.126) as '...practical approaches that have been devised for managing organisational culture...'. Several of the elements may be dealt with routinely, but others are worth a more extended consideration.

1. Brown locates the debate about whether it is possible to manage an organisation's culture - and as this matter is extensively discussed elsewhere in this work, it would not be proper to elaborate the arguments again here.
2. He develops 'a simple framework for managing culture'.
3. An examination is made of many of the chief areas of concern of Human Resource Management (HRM) with a view to deciding its overall role in the management of culture.
4. A review is conducted of the importance of 'symbolic leadership' and of how it may be possible to manage through the careful manipulation of symbols and organisational rites.
5. Brown examines an integrative model which endeavours to explain the management of culture change.
6. He attempts to synthesise the key issues identified throughout the above five areas of interest.

It may be of value to examine the last three of these elements in a little more detail. So, turning to the first of these - the import of 'symbolic leadership' - Peters (1978) is quoted by Brown to propose that senior managers in organisations 'do not synthesise chemicals or operate lift trucks; they deal in symbols...' (Brown, 1995, p.141).

According to Peters, executives can 'impose' on their own organisation's culture in a number of different ways. These include the precise ways they use their working hours, the ways they manipulate or circumscribe or develop the processes at meetings as well as the associated agenda and minutes, also the physical contexts in which organisational interactions take place are all in the 'gift' of such managers. Clearly, what organisational leaders actually do communicates whole rafts of meanings to subordinates.

Some More Recent Aspects of the Debate About Organisational Cultures

Brown asserts (1995, p.143) that if a chief executive promotes, for example, customer satisfaction surveys to the apogee of agenda, then chairs intensive *post-mortems* into them when the item appears under 'matters arising' in associated minutes:

> If the same customer satisfaction survey is repeated...and the chief executive pursues its findings with consistent enthusiasm,...over time this may...have an impact on the underlying beliefs, values and behaviours...throughout the organisation.

To this extent then, the theoretical underpinning of the concept of organisational culture seems to suggest, according to Brown anyway, that culture is something that can successfully be created by senior managers and then handed down to lower organisational echelons. Whether this can be borne out by fieldwork remains to be seen. Certainly, this specific example seems to illustrate some of the methodological thinking in the preceding chapter. It looks like a piece of 'common-sense' which is taken as a 'given' (or just taken-for-granted) without any real inspection of it. Furthermore, the level of oversimplification inherent in such a thought makes it unreliable as a generalisation and inaccurate as a comment on a single organisation - at least at the level of organisations with a national constituency and correspondingly large and diverse workforce.

Similarly, in discussing the organisational impact of the choice and style of venue for significant occasions within the organisation, Brown (1995, p.144) further asserts:

> ...moving a senior management board meeting from an isolated headquarters to the centre of operations might be employed to signal a genuine attempt by executives to really understand field problems.

It is at least as reasonable a contention that the people based in the 'centre of operations' will feel pique at having their space subsumed - albeit it temporarily - by senior managers. Surely the key point is that without careful testing via fieldwork Brown's assertions will remain simply that.

At this point, it is worth re-emphasising that both academics and practitioners each have a perspective which identifies the beguiling but simultaneously siren potential within the organisational culture notion that understanding the intricacies of the idea will enable organisational managers to increase efficiency and enhance organisational performance. Consequently, Bate (1994) makes an important series of assumptions about organisational change and development:

1. that organisational cultures will respond to well-directed attempts to alter them, as opposed, for example, to impassivity or the absence of discernible alterations as an outcome of such attempts;
2. only senior management will be able to initiate such changes as really make a difference, whether they choose to locate their attempts towards the bottom, middle or top of the organisational hierarchy;
3. that the alterations/changes that occur, if any, will be those intended to happen by senior managers;
4. and that all the outcomes will have been anticipated, rather than some (or none) were and others were not anticipated.

Whether these are reasonable and/or realistic in terms of the realities of organisational life as empirically examined in the institutions studied forms much of the thrust of what follows in subsequent chapters of the present work. These are devoted to the analysis of fieldwork data. For the present purposes, it will be sufficient to elaborate these assumptions, reflecting, as they seem to, the cutting edge of current thinking in the literature: they do seem to form a key part of the theoretical response to the functionalist orientation of writers in this area.

Bate (1994) has produced a significant contribution to the academic debate which is all of polymathic, idiosyncratic, engaging - and flawed. It is now appropriate to turn to his 'frameworks for thinking about cultural change'; in this part of the discussion because it illuminates much of the foregoing. It is a valuable account of how strategies for effecting organisational cultural change may be conceptualised and developed - as well as illustrative of a number of apparent theoretical weaknesses and contradictions in his exegesis. In the Peters and Waterman (1982) sense, Bate is both 'coach and cheerleader' for the notion that it is possible for managers actively to manage change within their organisations. However, as will subsequently be suggested, the highly charismatic 'coaching' style of the effective trainer (à la Bate) is an inadequate replacement for lapses from the rigorous logic of serious scholarship, in the quest to understand and explain organisational cultural processes. The Bate perspective on organisational culture proposes that it is a prerequisite of effective work on the part of an organisational analyst, whether internal or external to the organisation, to develop two methodological tools. These are firstly a particular 'language' (that is to say a 'script' shared between all organisation members) and secondly a particular 'grammar' (or shared method of thinking for organisation members). Organisation analysts must master these if they are to make the same sense of the processes they observe in the same way as members do. This is the 'repair of indexicality' to which Garfinkel (1967) makes reference, and it will allow the analyst best to understand organisation members' strategies. The argument is that where the analyst is either a member of the management or a consultant working on behalf of management this in turn will produce cultural development. Bate refers to 'conforming' behaviours here. Cultural 'transformations' - his second key tool in understanding culture - derive out of issues concerning 'grammar' and will be discussed subsequently.

> Organisation culture is not just another piece of the puzzle, *it is the puzzle*. From our point of view, a culture is not something an organisation has; *a culture is something an organisation is.* (Pacanowsky and O'Donnell-Trujillo, 1982, p.126) [Italic script for emphasis]

In an identical vein, Bate (1994) argues:

> We need to think about organisations being cultures rather that having cultures; the task for the cultural strategist is not to think *about* culture, but to *think culturally*. [italics added for emphasis]

All these writers produce a succinct account of the impact of the cultural orientation on organisational analysis. They share the Bate view that 'culture is organisation' and in so doing differentiate and distinguish themselves from the functionalist strand of theory most recently developed by Schein (1985, 1990), but which is traceable through some of the works identified earlier in this discussion, to Jacques (1951).

The functionalist approach (or perspective) on both the ideas of 'organisational culture' and of 'organisation' objectify them and therefore reify them. This produces theoretical distortions that render each construct an inaccurate and thus inadequate reflection of the reality it purports to reflect. So, there is an element of functionalist thought that finds merit in notions such as 'strong' cultures. For example, Deal and Kennedy (1982) are cited by Bate as proclaiming 'The impact of a strong culture on productivity is amazing!' Bate (1994, p.11) proposes that, with this logic:

> 'Changing culture' tends to be seen as a modular design-and-build activity, not dissimilar in conception from replacing a faulty component in a television set, or trading in an old cooker for a new one... [Supporters of this approach] talk about 'overhauling', 'renewing' or 'renovating' the corporate culture; or using it as a 'lever' to raise corporate performance.

Clearly, the limitations are apparent in such an approach. The relative crudity of the 'bolt-on' understanding permits little or no chance of analytical thought at the deep level of the fundamental beliefs and values of organisation members (whether they are high or low-placed in the organisation hierarchy). Furthermore, neither is it possible to locate anything of the picture of the nature of social reality organisational actors operate with, using this approach. So, methodologies that favour ethnography sit fairly uncomfortably in a 'design-and-build' theoretical structure.

The contribution of cultural anthropology to the debate is most helpful. By operating with the constructs 'organisation' and 'organisation culture' as synonyms, Bate (1994, p.14) draws attention to two 'key conclusions':

1. Given that organisations *are* cultures, there can be no theoretical
    or logical separation between strategies aimed at achieving
    cultural change and strategies designed to effect organisational
    change. 'Strategies aimed exclusively at changing the culture of
    an organisation are based on the false notion of culture as a
    'thing' and should be avoided on account of the fact that they
    are, in effect, strategies for something that does not actually exist
    - mythical strategies for a mythical entity'.
2. '...The important point, therefore, is not *what* we study but the
    different *way* we look at the organisation: the task for the culture
    strategist is not to think *about* culture, but to *think culturally*'.
    [author's emphases]

The discussion about methodology in the preceding chapter of this
study is designed to be in sympathy with this overall approach. It is
proposed that the most persuasive organisational analysis is the outcome of
an intellectual framework inspired by an anthropological and ethnographic
set of underpinnings, and these are more likely to locate and explain the
richness of members' lives in their organisational and institutional
contexts. This is what Bate (1994, p.17) calls 'the human, expressive,
symbolic texture of organisational life'.

The eighteenth century classical European theorist, Michels (1949)
proposed the 'iron law': 'Whosoever says organisation says oligarchy'. If
it is the case that 'culture is organisation' and 'organisation is oligarchy'
then culture must also be oligarchy - and indeed it is, but only from within
the narrow theoretical and methodological parameters Michels set for
himself. Whilst this is an interesting avenue of enquiry it is judged to be
outside the scope and purpose of the present debate, so, so much for the
relationships between culture and organisation.

The second key theme identified by Bate concerned
'transformations' and must be understood in the broader context of the
discussion about organisational 'grammar'. This concerns the shared
methods of thinking between organisation members arising out of their
common experiences which were referred to earlier in this chapter and
which now need to be considered. Bate (1994, p.81) cites Levy and Merry
(1986):

[Organisational] transformation [is the response to] the condition in which
an organisation cannot continue functioning as before. In order to continue
to exist it needs a drastic reshuffling in every dimension of its existence.

The impetus for such a transformational 'reshuffling' to take place will originate in behaviour on the part of organisation members. Bate (1994, p.83) provides three possible explanatory elaborations and the first of these is where organisation members but especially leaders no longer show interest in producing further organisational development. Secondly, bate identifies where opportunities to develop (through for example growth or diversification) are not taken up because the routines of 'business-as-usual' thinking are too deeply ingrained. Thirdly and relatedly, is where members' behaviours become so routinised that 'thinking processes become increasingly culture-bound'. This indicates that members operate with '...closed, self-sufficient and autonomous systems of thought that develop by making reference to themselves...' The import of all this is:

> The message is clear, cultures cannot survive by endlessly recreating their past, no matter how glorious this has been...even the winning team must be changed. (Bate, 1994, p.84)

Brown seems to miss more that he captures in his approach to culture, strategy and performance; and then the management of change. There is little room for doubt that in the real commercial world organisations sell products and services and attempt to turn a profit in so doing, and of course this is where this fieldwork was situated. In such a location, simplistic yet alluring notions such as Brown's typologies or Bate's 'both-and' formulae (which oppose the more usual 'either-or' options in the decision-making dyad) seem out of touch with the realities that the fieldwork will go to identify. There is little to support the proposition that other than at the most senior and hence well-informed organisational hierarchical levels, will there be anything other that a rudimentary understanding of such complex ideas, at best, of those espoused especially by Bate, but also a plethora of other management writers. It is at precisely these intermediary management levels that most benefit could be done with notions which 'free-up' thinking in this way. This may be particularly appropriate and even necessary, given the report of the fieldwork associated with this study. The intermediary management levels are the very locations where such cultural forms are made manifest, and it is to this matter that it will now be helpful for a consideration to be made. The term 'anti-culture' will subsequently be preferred to 'counter-culture' in an attempt to distinguish it from the now inaccurate interpretation of the term to mean the middle-class protest movements of the 1960s and 1970s that have been associated with it.

There is obvious overlap between the theories and methods of the discipline of Management Studies and that of the Sociology of Education. This is particularly clear in a review of such areas of mutual concern as organisational learning in its several meanings. However, common ground between the disciplines is most apparent in an analysis of the concept of culture in attempting to explain behaviours; whether in classrooms or staffrooms in schools on the one hand, or places of work including the decision-making arenas of senior managers, on the other hand. Hall and Jefferson's (1975) collection of essays broke new ground in the development of an alternative theoretical and methodological approach to the understanding of youth sub-cultures in the decades after the Second World War and until their date of publication. Hence, their work is in marked contrast to the functionalist analysis that preceded it. Even though this work is now rather dated in terms of its Marxian (and frequently Marxist) perspective, its methodological orientation is very much in sympathy with the ethnographic tradition set out above and further developed in Chapter Two of this study. No apology is made for citing a manifestly sociological reference, or indeed arguing that it is a key one from the theoretical and methodological perspective. The authors spent much time considering 'deviant' youth groups and a central thrust of the following section of this chapter is to recognise that the anti-cultural tendencies identified in the associated fieldwork are every bit as deviant as those processes examined by Hall and Jefferson (1975). Here, the definition of deviance in use is the classical social scientific understanding that focuses upon rule breaking rather that the more everyday understanding of the term with its emphasis on illegalities. The Clark *et al.* (in Hall and Jefferson, 1975) essay reflects on the nature of sub-cultures:

> ...Sub-cultures must be analysed in terms of their relation to the dominant culture... Sub-cultures must exhibit a distinctive enough shape and structure to make them identifiably different from their 'parent' culture. They must be focused around certain activities, values certain uses of material artefacts, territorial spaces etc. which significantly differentiate them from the wider culture. But, since they are sub-sets there must also be significant things which bind and articulate them with the 'parent' culture.

Alvesson (1993) provides a recent and stimulating perspective to the existing theorising. He links attempts by senior managers within organisations to produce culture change with attempts by the same managers to develop a compelling and persuasive management ideology.

This may be more effectively considered at a point where the fieldwork evidence has already been set out. Consequently, the theme is examined in chapter six of this study, rather than at the present point.

Sub-Cultural Theory

Sub-cultural theory has continued to expand. Some notable landmarks include North American theoretical founders such as Parsons (1951) who first coined the phrase 'social system' to emphasise the integrative ways that social institutions relate and interlock in urban and suburban society. Merton (1968) was interested also in fragmentation (and 'dysfunction', and in so doing developed and extended Parsons' thinking). In the context of this study, what would be valuable would be fieldwork evidence that might suggest that sub-cultures and anti-cultures are more likely to seem to form within organisations when problems of adapting to the onset of organisational change become apparent. Consequently, it may be the case *vis-à-vis* senior managers, that members will group together to manage or oppose or ignore, or produce any other response, commonly agreed amongst a group of them. Brake (1980) argues:

> Subcultures arise [then] as attempts to solve certain problems...which are created by contradictions...[in the wider organisation].

The classic study by Murdock (1949) is in sympathy with this explanation. His thinking in this area indicates his life interest in the whole filed of family and culture:

> Sub-cultures offer a collective solution to the problems posed by shared contradictions in the work situation, and provide a social and symbolic context for the development and reinforcement of collective identity and individual self esteem.

If sub-cultures are as powerful as Murdock suggests then it is difficult to understand how so many organisational analysts - both academics and practitioners - ignore the implications of this. It is suspected that an over-preoccupation with the individual as the unit of analysis, at the expense of the more macro and over-arching group focus, is part of the resolution of this difficulty. The whole idea of the possibility that, following Brake's thinking, sub-cultures may emerge when there are 'problems...created by contradictions...' is possibly significant, and certainly interesting enough to be worthy of research.

Within organisations (as well as outside them) membership of a sub-culture implies rather more than simply the existence of contradictions. Clark *et al.* (1998) refer to the clustering of sub-cultural group members around particular locations:

> ...they develop specific rhythms of interchange, structured relations between members, younger to older, experienced to novice... They explore focal concerns...things 'always done', or 'never done', set[s] of social rituals which underpin their collective identity and define them... .

In so doing, the writers convey a flavour of both the potential and the subtlety of the notion of sub-culture as a tool to enhance understanding of some organisational process.

Sub-cultures become anti-cultures when the underpinning norms and values and taken-for-granted assumptions about how the organisational world really works are oppositional, or perceived as oppositional (rather that merely different). This is when compared with the set of underpinnings promulgated by organisational managers on behalf of the organisation as a whole. In short, the *tabula rasa* of anti-cultures within organisations is to oppose mainstream cultures. However, fieldwork evidence indicates that organisational realities are rather more complex than simple dyadic models of culture-in-action, hence the foregoing is not meant to suggest that the organisations examined boasted merely two sub-cultures, a mainstream one and an oppositional one. Indeed if that were the case, it would be difficult for anti-cultures to exist at all - given how exposed they would be and therefore open to a sustained assault from the perspective of the 'official' and relatively handsomely resourced and ideologically sustained 'hegemonic' (Gramsci, 1971) culture offered by senior managers.

Sociology of Education as a Source For Theorising About Organisational Cultures

Hall and Jefferson (1975) locate 'counter-cultures' as the consequence of middle class protest movements in the now far-off days of the 1960s and 1970s. At the national level, they cite various pop festivals and 'happenings' such as 'sit-ins' and 'demos' as evidence of widespread radicalisation amongst the British and North American (and youthful) middle classes. The fieldwork associated with this study found no such exclusivity in the organisations studied and identifies people in a wide cross-section of ages and a similarly wide breadth of salary bands and of both genders exhibiting behaviours that may reasonably be defined as anti-cultural. This also explains the preference for the term 'anti-culture' with its connotations of modernity and its lack of association with one age group and one social class. One intriguing possibility (but one not examined in the fieldwork as it may reasonably be ruled into sociology but out of a management discipline research exercise) is that some - be that many or a few - of the members of the counter-cultural groups of the 1960s and 1970s, such as hippies, yippies, flower people and so on, have joined 'respectable' mainstream society. Such people are by now aged approximately fifty or older, and may have a greater propensity to seek out membership of anti-cultural groups in the organisations examined as a response to the impact of changed circumstances in their organisations.

This work, and work cited herein, makes reference to the different 'meanings' and sets of 'taken-for-granted' assumptions with which anti-cultural group members operate in their mainstream or parent culture and their anti-culture. In the light of the above discussion, this is an appropriate place to examine the literature in which these meanings may be contexted and hence understood, so that light may also be cast on the meanings offered and interpreted and understood in the fieldwork which is considered in detail in the last three chapters of this work.

A study of the minutiae of daily life in a secondary school classroom is, at first sight, not the most promising starting point for this task. However, Furlong's (1984) detailed account of the types of knowledge that pupils carry around in their heads and the ways that this may, and on other occasions may not, be instructive in interpreting communications of all kinds from school leaders, has obvious significance for the present study. She remarks:

> ...many researchers have tried to study the 'culture' of different groups by trying to identify both [members'] norms of behaviour and...underlying values. ...I have already argued that [these] action[s] cannot be understood in these terms.

Furlong set up a detailed observation based around the concept of 'interaction set' and was convinced that 'her' pupils were eloquent communicators at the non-verbal level with their classroom fellows. This was achieved through body language, eye contact and space management, and in this way they managed, in the rather elegant phrase of McRobbie (1978) and concerning another school class of adolescent females '...gently to undermine the *status quo...*'.

Hence they were able to assert the validity of their interpretation of the reality in which they participated over that of the teacher's version of reality in the classroom. Such overt opposition may be at its most observable in the situation of 'the blackboard jungle', whether the behaviour is from that of single sex or mixed classrooms. It may be the case that adults situated in work organisations also oppose the sets of values offered to them from senior managers, or, alternatively oppose parts of such value sets. When it does occur (if it does at all) their opposition is more likely to be discreet, and perhaps better organised in some settings, but less well organised in others, than when compared with children in their classrooms.

The Notion of Organisational Culture Set in a Critical Context

It is now appropriate to move closer to a view in the debate about the utility of the competing models of the meaning of the term organisational culture that have appeared throughout this chapter. At this stage, and prior to the consideration and analysis of the fieldwork evidence, the managerialist view may seem less persuasive than the critical perspective. What follows examines some aspects of more than a century of scholarly work that is situated squarely in a critical tradition, and it links with the chapter six revisit to the ideas of Alvesson (1993). The following discussion, then, is an examination of linkage between that scholarship and this study. It is necessary to take all of this recent thinking about organisation cultures and squarely set it in the progression of ideas in the twentieth century which have asserted the dominance of capital over labour.

Specifically, first reference is made to the emergence of Taylorist thinking around the time of the Great War; Fordism and the subsequent evolution of the human relations school of management in the inter-war years which remained influential until relatively recent times. In both the present and previous decade, a growing interest has emerged in the notion of corporate culture or organisational culture, and this has been substantially documented in earlier chapters of this study. The case will be argued that there has been control exerted by organisational seniors in each of these manifestations of managerial strategic thinking, and this has separately been by Hugh Willmott (1993), Williams *et al.* (1992) and Foucault (1977), each identified in their different academic traditions. There are interesting links in particular between Ackroyd and Proctor (1998) and the 'high surveillance firm' on the one hand and Foucault's concept of 'panopticism' on the other hand. An exploration of this linkage begins.

So, at one level of analysis an examination of the debate about power and control in organisations, which begins with a review of the impact of Taylorism in the early years of the twentieth century, may seem an arbitrary starting point. For example, classical Greek scholarship has much to say, directly and by inference, about people and their societies, and hence their membership of organisations. Similarly, during the Peasants Revolt in 1381, John Ball a collaborator of Wat Tyler, was reported to have observed on the Kent border, on Blackheath Common, whilst marching to London: 'When Adam delved and Eve span, who was then the gentleman?'

Both sets of thoughts would be adequate as a starting point. So, too, would the rich soil of eighteenth century social thought, on either side of the *La Manche* (or the English Channel, dependent upon the perspective adopted). Rousseau and Hobbes each offer valuable insight into the ideas presently under consideration. The nineteenth century may be considered as the century of industrialisation for much of what is now known as the West; as well as the age of revolutions; and as well as the early period of urbanisation - and also the century of the birth of Marx, Weber and Durkheim. Consequently the number of alternative possible starting points will approach legion.

The publication of *The Principles of Scientific Management* (1947 [3rd edn.]) by Frederick Winslow Taylor has, however, at least an equal claim to be the most valuable point of origin for this discussion. The publication is situated in the recognisably modern, capitalist-democratic, industrialised, and urbanised world of relatively rapid and relatively reliable transport and communication links. It is especially recognisable in the following quotation from that work, which captures something of what might today be called 'the industrial relations climate':

> As was usual, then, and in fact is still usual in most shops in this country, the shop was really run by the workman *(sic, et sec.)* and not the bosses. The workmen together had carefully planned just how fast each job should be done, and they had set a pace for each machine throughout the shop,

which was limited to about one third of a good day's work [that is, the maximum possible]. Every new workman who came into the shop was told at once by the other men exactly how much of each kind of work he was to do, and unless he obeyed these instructions he was sure before long to be driven out of the place by the men (1947, p.128).

Taylor's comfortable assertion that a 'good' level of production was precisely synonymous with the maximum possible level of production reveals a pitiless and compassionless *verstehen*. The quotation also sets a clear attitude to the position of the traditional craft controls as exercised by the workers; Taylor argued that it was indefensible that what he called 'systematic soldiering' should be regarded as a work norm. His 'solution' to the 'labour problem' was to develop and implement a number of fundamental principles of management:

1. A science should be developed for each piece or part of the manufacturing process in hand.
2. Workers should be trained in a scientific manner and also selected for their duties in a scientific way.
3. Management and workers should co-operate based on the science.
4. Each side of industry should do that for which it is best fitted.

Frederick Taylor set out to bureaucratise work through these principles. They underpin extensive elaboration in this work of the need of management to monopolise what ethnomethodologists might call 'work knowledge' by classifying it, tabulating it and generally breaking it down into as many formulae and *modus operandii* as was necessary to rob the workmen of their autonomy. Clearly, this furthers the consolidation of hegemony between those who own capital and those who labour for such owners. Taylor himself wrote of the need for what he termed 'a complete mental revolution' in the hearts and minds of the two sides of industry. Expressed as an insight from within a critical sociological tradition, such a thought is easily rendered as an illustration of the ideological climate that Taylor was attempting to create and sustain. One of the interesting gaps between myth and reality in respect of such an influential set of ideas and indeed the personality from whom they originated, is the way that Taylor himself warned against the prostitution of the use of his thinking. He observed:

...employers...should not [use Taylorian ideas] as [part of] an arsenal of devices designed to simplify and improve the management of labour.

Taylor advocated a kind of partnership between the two sides of industry. However, there was little danger of any assumption that such a partnership should be struck between parties of equal status or with an equally beneficial return to the parties. Taylor was simply sanguine about the prospect of massive productivity gains being exchanged by workers for a comparatively very modest increase in wages. For example, the well-known advocate of Taylorism, Henry Ford, introduced a substantial rise in income for his workers in 1913 with rhetoric concerning 'the $5 day' wage rate. It represented some 40% increase for those men whose work record and moral standing in their communities could be graded as 'A1 at Ford'. It was funded from overall productivity increases of many hundreds of percentage points - and the balance accrued to the equity holders of the business. There is no doubt, however, that Taylor's concern for high wages in return for high productivity was realised by the Ford pay arrangements for manual workers, and that this approach did mitigate the worst excesses of labour wastage. At its height in 1911, labour turnover reached 380% per year, per job at Henry Ford's Hyland's Park factory (see Taylor [1988] for an extended discussion). In this necessarily brief summary of some of Taylor's key thinking and some of the consequences that it generated, it is fair to context it as part of the range of managerial strategies available to exert dominance over labour. Taylorism itself was part of a broader movement towards the fragmentation of work, and all its related consequences, which comprised the move towards 'scientific management'. The labour process theorists beginning with Marx himself and also Braverman (1974) have subsequently developed and documented this debate.

The impact of Taylorism was highly significant and enduring. For example, the modern notion of 'multi-skilling' is directly related both to the Taylorian propositions about scientific training and selection and his 'one best way' approach. This emphasised the need to use resources of any kind (especially expensive items such as machine tools) to their maximum potential. Increasing the numbers of people competent to operate any such tool will militate in favour of its maximum employment in the period of time during which it could be pressed into service.

Indeed, the doing of a job that was 'Taylor-made' was a way of earning a living and living a life in an organisation that saw little fundamental difference between the machine and its operator. By the time the famous series of experiments conducted at the General Electric Company plant in Chicago in the United States of America was over, a more 'human' perspective on the position of the worker at work had evolved. Yet, the key question remained concerning the nature of the settlement between employer and employee: was it old wine in new bottles in respect of the way that employers still managed to control their people in work? The evidence seems to suggest that a vintage of coercion was still apparent, even though presented under a skin of human relations benevolence. Henry Ford famously observed in respect of the Model T vehicle that customers could choose any colour they wished - as long as it was black. One summary of the human relations perspective suggests that employees could make any number of empowered decisions (to use the modern jargon) they chose - as long as they were in accordance with the wishes and general objectives of the management of the day.

The 'Human Relations' Approach

What Mayo and his colleagues achieved in their extended study of initially the scientific and then the human dimensions of work organisation within the Hawthorne Works was significant enough to begin a dalliance of several decades by other academics in such matters. Its consequences upon large numbers of organisations in the USA and elsewhere was also substantial. The mechanistic approach of Taylor frequently gave way to more 'human' styles of people management - without ever totally fading out - and yet the debate about coercion and control by managers over their people was as significant as ever it had been. However, the most significant issues about process here concern the objectives of such 'humanised' approaches to working class work. If this new wine that emphasises the importance of human relations is put into the old skin of dominance and control by employers, then it will quickly look like Taylorian imperialism but simply in a different guise.

Mayo (1960) is an important source in attempting to make sense of these processes. He furnishes a highly detailed account of the procedures he and his colleagues adopted in the relay assembly test room of the Hawthorne Works of the Western Electric Company in Chicago, commencing in April, 1927. He wrote:

> The group was kept small - six operatives - because the company officers had become alert to the possible significance for the enquiry of *changes of*

mental attitude. (Mayo, 1960 [italics added] quoted in Clark *et al.*, 1994, p.238)

The italicised phrase refers to the possibility that, by separating out a small group of women into a separate test room and lavishing time and attention on them, this may impact upon how they perform their work duties. In that case, it was a sixty seconds per cycle assembly of four machine screws in a piece of telephone technology. The phrase is of interest as it points to early recognition of the proposition that one of the more effective forms of labour discipline was that which the worker imposed on herself. The research generated rigorously conceived and recorded production data and included variables such as humidity levels, working temperatures and rest period changes over thirteen separate iterations. It shows that output did increase from these six people, to around a total of three thousand assemblies per week, from a starting point of around two thousand five hundred per week. Mayo observed:

> The operators have no clear idea as to why they are able to produce more in the test room; but as shown in the replies to questionnaires...there is the feeling that better output is in some way related to the distinctly pleasanter, freer, and happier working conditions... . (Mayo, 1960, quoted in Clark *et al.*, 1994, p.243)

His account of the social relations of the test room is revealing. He examines the dealings between the man who was responsible for making the detailed observations of the women and the women themselves. In this, he makes it clear that the chief observer did not attempt to act out a role which allowed the group to perceive him as a surrogate foreman or supervisor hired by the company to raise production. Rather, the lead observer took a personal interest in the output achievements of each individual woman, and made clear his feelings of satisfaction as the group figures moved up to a faster rate. He also ensured that the data on output was rapidly and accurately recorded and then set out in a manner and in a place that was accessible to the women themselves. In the perceptual schema of these women, they had found some kind of 'freedom' that had been a constant source of conversation between them. What was this freedom? It seems that it was not access to training that would produce in some or all of them new skills and new understandings of the realities of the workplace. Neither was it a noticeable increase in pay, sufficient for a real increase in their standards of living. Rather, the individualised and group attention to their work needs seem to have generated the 'positive mental attitudes' discussed above. Mayo himself records this as follows:

> ...there was a period during which the individual workers and the group had to readapt themselves to a new industrial milieu in which their own self-determination and their social well-being ranked first and the work was incidental. (Mayo, 1960, quoted in Clark *et al.*, 1994, p.246)

However, the account so far has contributed nothing to the debate about worker resistance and the so-called Hawthorne Studies have also ploughed a rich furrow here. The classic account of this is Roethlisberger and Dickson's (1939) publication of work process events in the bank wiring room, where fourteen men worked on wiring, soldering and inspecting duties in the manufacture of banks of telephone switch gear.

Roethlisberger and Dickson were collaborators with Elton Mayo and wrote up a number of the most significant findings of their empiricism. After copious observation, they codified the rules of conduct generated by the bank wiring room workers as follows:

1. You should not turn out too much work. If you do, you are a 'rate-buster'.
2. You should not turn out too little work. If you do, you area 'chiseler'.
3. You should not tell a supervisor anything that will react to the detriment of an associate. If you do, you are a 'squealer'.
4. You should not attempt to maintain social distance or act officious. If you are an inspector, for example, you should not act like one. (Roethlisberger and Dickson, 1939, quoted in Clark *et al.*, 1994, p.248)

The fourteen men were subdivided in the research into 'Clique A' and 'Clique B'. The former were the higher status group and they observed all four rules; the latter were the lower status group and they kept three of the rules but ignored number two above. As their work output was low, this made them especially vulnerable to hostility from management, so they were fastidious keepers of rules three and four. Roethlisberger and Dickson describe the impact of the working relations they created thus:

> The social organisation of the bank wiremen performed a twofold function. To protect the group from internal indiscretions and to protect it from outside interference... It can be seen therefore that nearly all the activities of this group may be looked upon as methods of controlling the behaviour of

its members. (Roethlisberger and Dickson, 1939, quoted in Clark *et al.*, 1994, pp.256-257)

This classic study proceeds to examine and then find unsatisfactory a number of competing explanations of the work organisation of the fourteen men. For example, they dismiss as a misinterpretation that the employees were acting in their own economic best interests. They also argue that it was a fallacy to conclude that they were attempting to control the actions of management in one or more ways or that for malicious reasons the workers had positively set out to behave in a difficult way in their dealings with their management. Rather, the summary of this section of their book provides a succinct statement of the matter:

> In the studies…there existed informal employee organizations resulting in problems… The significant problem for investigation appeared to be that of specifying the factors which give rise to such informal organizations. In attempting to answer this question, the external function of one group, the bank wiremen was examined. This function could be characterised as that of resisting change. Following this lead the[ir] position…in relation to the total company structure was then examined…and its consequent relations with other groups within the company. (Roethlisberger and Dickson, 1939, quoted in Clark *et al.*, 1994, pp.259-260)

This work is so significant because, many decades ago, it pointed to the power of the insights that sociological analysis can deliver in the examination of culture and change. The net effect of the Hawthorne Studies was to cast a shadow over both the practise and academic study of work organisation from the inter-war years of economic depression through to the 1960s and perhaps beyond. In quite specific terms, Mayo and his colleagues delivered the view that the most effective inspector or supervisor or production-chaser of the worker is the worker her or himself. This contrasts relatively sharply with some of the thinking of Taylor considered above, but is interestingly sympathetic to the views about power and control promulgated in many other places within this study, but developed more fully in the next chapter. In respect of the empirical work associated with this study, it is clear that senior managements' attempts to change or influence the organisational cultures of their organisations are rooted in a rhetoric that originates in such thinking. Late twentieth century ideas in management studies and management practise (such as, for example, the 'empowerment' of workers) are also self-regulatory in the service of the chief aim of securing super-normal profits for equity shareholders. Patterns of acquiescence or resistance appear to be subtler now, based on the evidence generated by this study, but the echo they make is as substantial and as influential.

Willmott's (1993) seminal discussion elaborates this thinking. He establishes the notion of 'corporate culturism' as follows:

> The guiding aim and abiding concern of corporate culturism is to win the hearts and minds of employees...by managing what they think and feel.... . (Willmott, 1993)

The phrase was developed in response firstly to the triumphalist managerialism of Peters and Waterman (1982). One reading of that approach, one sympathetic to the orientation of this study, expresses anxiety when managerialists propose as serious analysis that culture change programmes to effect 'strong' cultures will 'secure unusual efforts on the part of apparently ordinary employees' (Peters and Waterman, 1982). Willmott (1991) proposes in a sardonic way that it is morally improper for employers or senior managers to overreach themselves in their attempts to produce successively greater and then greater levels of productivity from blue collar and/or white collar staff groups. He comments:

> ...the governance of the employee's soul becomes a more central element in corporate strategies for gaining competitive advantage.... .

So, an almost Faustian employer orientation is challenged in Willmott's notion of 'corporate culturism'. He proceeds to set the idea in a social but also an economic context:

> ...corporate culturism can be seen to form an important ideological element within the global restructuring of capital, labour and product markets that involve a movement away from the '$5.00 a day logic of Fordism' towards a contingent, fluid, organising philosophy of flexible accumulation. (Willmott, 1993)

A number of matters become clear from this remark. Firstly, we see Willmott's neo-Marxian orientation in his haste to set 'corporate culturism' within a specifically economic context, and one that emphasises the role of international capital. Secondly, he points to the manner in which global capital seems to be constantly restructuring. He argues that the development of worker autonomy is a further step away from Taylorist and

Fordist perspectives on power and control. The importance of '$5.00-a-day' was that it was designed to motivate workers (in a mechanical way similar to the way in which motor oil may lubricate the friction bearing parts of an engine or other assembly). That it is being abandoned in favour of a different motivator, and where this motivator is flexible rather than fixed and contingent rather than unchanging, is of some great significance in terms of its utility and its acceptability to organisation members at large. Finally, that the replacement for Taylorism/Fordism is fluid and also an 'organising philosophy' is both significant in the above terms and a route back to the slightly later thinking of Ackroyd and Proctor (1998) and the 'new flexible firm'. The fieldwork for this study has many examples of respondents speaking guardedly about their concerns. Willmott (1991, 1993) sets a context for such behaviour as follows:

> ...the fleeting, the ephemeral, the fugitive and the contingent in modern life...leads to a heightened emphasis on the authority of basic institutions...corporate culturism demands loyalty from employees as it excludes, silences or punishes those who question its creed... .

He eloquently identifies the mismatch between the needs of people in organisations for permanency and personal recognition - perhaps first identified by the women in the relay assembly test room in the Hawthorne Studies - and the returns that work brings in modern capitalist (or even post-capitalist) society. Specifically, Willmott sharply contrasts the disciplinary function of organisational membership with the needs of its members. Interview responses in this research that show real anger at the way that the organisational seniors behave where the interviewee has been a member for perhaps over twenty years are clear echoes of such a disciplinary context as that. Anger has indeed been one response, but even more chillingly, some organisation members affect a complete 'company man' response to the impact of unwelcomed developments at work. Peters and Waterman (1982) cite one respondent in a most approving manner. The person remarks:

> The company gives me great freedom to develop my own approach...there are certain elements that need to be in any party to make it successful, but if those elements are colored by you, a [names the franchise] dealer - purple pink and polka dot and I prefer lavender and lace - that's OK. That freedom allows you to be the best that you are capable of being.

Expressed in succinct terms, there seems to be a particular feeling in the heart and mind of one employee. The feeling says that if s/he can choose the order of the presentation of the colours of the plastic boxes then this will so liberate the person that all their potentialities will be fulfilled by that single, and very dubious 'freedom'. It is hard to give credibility to such a notion. So, it seems that one of the few remaining intelligent alternative readings available is that the speaker has been so comprehensively persuaded of the utility of such a set of life values that it is impossible for him/her to conceive of an alternative strategy.

Zuboff (1988) offers the neologism 'informate' as a verb to understand how the impact of technology:

> ...provides deeper level of transparency to activities that had been either partially or completely opaque... Activities events and objects are translated into and made visible by information when a technology *informates* as well as automates. (Zuboff, 1988, pp.9-10)

Part of the richness of the Zuboff contribution to the debate about power and organisations is that she demonstrates the complexity and subtlety of work relationships. She focuses upon those that prevail in the matter of the links between the supply of labour, the speed of technological change and the reality of employment in large organisations. She identifies the notion of 'intellective skills' to conceive the idea that:

> new technology signals not only deskilling [in the Braverman, 1974 sense but also]...abstraction, explicit inference and procedural reasoning...[this amounts to a] new reskilling process.... (Zuboff, 1988, pp.75-76)

No writing in this arena could conclude without acknowledgement of the seminal contribution of the French Marxist post-structuralist, Michel Foucault. This is especially so in view of the overlays between some of his earlier work and the outcomes of this study. As a result of this, chapter seven develops a little of the Foucauldian perspective (in particular, Foucault 1977).

The notion of sub-culture is an important idea in the overall context of the study and the next chapter reveals something of the richness of the respondents' thoughts along a number of cultural dimensions, including that of sub-culture. It attempts this by grouping them into response-sets based upon position in the organisational hierarchy, and by preserving their organisational memberships.

Summary and Chapter Conclusion

The chapter's opening objective is to set the wide context for the debate and structure the thinking that follows on from that point. A central element of that wide context is the possibility that the idea of organisational culture is ideological. However, there is no clear-cut agreement within the literature.

Usage of the term from the early 1950s through to today is subsequently presented, in an effort to demonstrate the variety of ways that the term has actually been used by authorities in the area. What seems to emerge is at least a pair of competing formulations. On the one hand is a perspective that appears strongly managerialist in character, while on the other hand is a critical perspective. One object of the empirical work outlined and analysed in the later chapters of this work will be to test this dichotomy and attempt to identify which, if either, of the two approaches has more utility based on that evidence. The brief discussion concerning sub-cultures is included to illustrate the anticipated complexity of the reality of organisational cultures, and also to underline the scale of the task identified in this summary.

At first sight, the sociology of education may seem strange territory in which to seek ideas helpful to theorising organisational cultures. Yet, thinking about the culture and sub-culture dyad, as well as the thinking about the culture and anti-culture dyad, is relatively well advanced in that literature. Consequently, it is potentially helpful in illuminating the analysis of the idea of organisation culture. The critical orientation to making sense of organisational cultures gains the ascendancy as, for example, the human relations paradigm is identified as part of the managerialist position. That is to say, sociological accounts of how organisations change, through processes emanating from senior managers, will inevitably start from an intellectual position that is not either explicitly or implicitly bound up with a managerial perspective on organisational events. One reading, for example, of the development of the human relations approach to management from the decade of the late 1920s and into the 1930s is that its purpose was to make happier, more contented wage workers, people more available for exploitation through expropriation. Such organisation members would be more likely to earn greater profits for their employers than would less content employees. The balance sheet of the Ford Motor Company in the period immediately following the introduction of the moving assembly line and so the first, integrated, mass production techniques of work organisation (in 1913) makes the point well. It indicates the origins of the process in recognisably modern, industrial society; in that year wages increased by 50% and profits increased by 400% (Taylor, 1988).

4 Penetrating Two Large-Scale Organisations

Introduction

The purpose of this part of the discussion is to begin to provide a clear account of the empirical investigation. The title of this chapter rather begs the question: how? What follows is presented as an approach to that question. This chapter elaborates the research methodology by firmly grounding it in the techniques of investigation actually implemented. Perhaps the central elaboration is the pragmatically cast discussion around the Graphics COPE package that will analyse the data from the research activity, the data from which forms the next chapter of this work. This element of the study is placed in this particular part of the document because it is wished to underline that the choice even of methods of analysis will itself tend towards influencing the data that are produced. Furthermore, this seems important especially in the light of the methodological sympathy towards ethnographic techniques shown in this work. However, before that issue may be addressed, the discussion examines the organisational contexts of British Telecommunications plc and British Gas (Eastern) plc. These related tasks are appropriate now that there has already been both a review of the general methodological approach used and also a summary of the academic literature judged relevant to the framing of the overall orientation of this work.

In this chapter, then, there follows an introduction that situates the investigations in the day-to-day management processes of each organisation. In the next chapter that evidence is set out. Each of the two organisations whose managements allowed participation in their work processes has already been identified above, and in an earlier chapter. There was no secrecy attached by the respective managements to the promulgation of either the investigation or the analysis of its data, but an immediate publication of material which could be recast into a potential embarrassment to either organisation would not have been welcomed by either of the managements. However, now that some time has passed since the bulk of the empiricism was completed, it is possible to proceed with confidence in a full account of the investigations and findings.

As identified elsewhere in this work, the action learning frame of reference was a key tool during the investigation of cultural processes within these companies. This term 'action learning', as has already been indicated, is used here to denote a set of methodological strategies which attempted to deliver the overall objectives of the study; making sense of the change processes working through the organisational cultures of the two businesses. Consequently, for most of the seventy-three respondents, the tools of investigation comprised:

    i.   a period of time between one and two days duration during which non-participant observation activity took place. This was a work observation activity using non-participant observation as the organising principle. The recording sheet for the observations forms a part of the appendices of this work.

Where managers were in posts that gave them responsibility for teams of other more junior managers then, frequently, an additional tool was used:

    ii.   a general, scene-setting interview which was unstructured to permit each respondent to develop his/her own set of perceptions about the organisational culture of their part of their business - or indeed of any organisational cultural perceptions they may have wished to share about the business as a whole. Typically, prompts were offered around the Deal and Kennedy (1982) framework (organisational culture is 'How things are done around here').

Schein (1985) provided the launch point for the development of this study's methodology, and this matter is further developed subsequently. Data from the unstructured interviewing approach is subsumed into the general report that follows, rather that articulated separately. In each case, all the data generated and relevant to each organisation were validated to some degree by the preparation and submission of a written report and subsequent personal presentation of the data contained. To BT management, this comprised a reporting to the whole Change Management Group whose role in the business and in this study is discussed shortly. In the context of the British Gas (Eastern) element of the research, where there was no separately identifiable change management group, it was the Board of Directors of the company, at one of their monthly Board meetings, where change planning was conducted. The result was that organisational validation for that element of the empirical work was transacted in their September 1994 meeting, after a one hour presentation with associated questions and answers.

> iii. This process of reporting to the senior managements of the two participating organisations was the final element of the research strategy; it is reminiscent of the Christopher Argyris' 'double loop learning' model (see for example Argyris, 1964 and 1991). Whilst such an approach to understanding patterns of organisational change is not within the spirit of this study, it is nevertheless interesting to note that there appears to be further validation for the fieldwork contained in that alternative perspective.

After the first contact with each organisation already discussed, an initial self-presentation was made to representatives of each management. This emphasised both the benefits that would accrue to the organisation through consultancy in organisation analysis/cultural audit and secondly that it would be at no direct financial cost. Consequently introductions were made possible by senior officials within each organisation and access was given to a range of their middle ranking colleagues. It is typical of a range of academic literature across management and the social sciences which are rooted in empirical investigation to make light of both the complexity of the negotiations and the concomitant high degree of anxiety, each of which surrounds these social and organisational processes (in particular, see Patrick, 1973 and Bott, 1971). Yet, the 'will they - won't they?' issue is all-pervasive at this moment and the degree of earnestness with which organisational penetration is sought is itself one of the variables, either positive or negative, in considering the likelihood of a successful outcome.

British Telecommunications plc

The General Post Office (GPO) was the British arm of state charged with responsibility for the delivery of postal and telecommunications services. In 1980, these two services were split into The Post Office and British

Telecommunications. By statutory instrument in 1983 shares in the equity of BT (as it later became known) were offered to institutional investors, employees and members of the public. The size of the payroll for the company declined from 220,000 people to 130,000 between the early 1980s and the middle to late 1990s. This was established through the carrot of a number of relatively persuasive redundancy packages coupled with the stick of changes in technology that required retraining for technical people. Reductions in the size of the payroll were not regarded as over at that time (and in 1998 the totals employed by BT are rather closer to 100,000). The whole purpose of Her Majesty's Government's actions in this respect was to encourage competition through the use of what economists refer to as 'the market mechanism'. Their rhetoric emphasised the need to produce efficiency and an approach to service provision that would put the needs of the customer in front of the perceived needs of the organisation.

Concerning this research, the initial approach to BT was made in the spring of 1993. It led to a number of contacts with managers who now form the major part of the company's 'Change Management Group' (CMG), located in the Saint Paul's area of the City of London. For ease of identification, and to reduce the risk of confusion, the current nomenclature of the group will be used; as a unified whole, it was not in existence at the time these early contacts began with this organisation (they shared 'head office' accommodation in a number of adjacent BT locations; the Newgate Street Tower, Lonrho House in Cheapside and thirdly in Paternoster Square). After responses which seemed to indicate some level of scepticism about the viability of an attempt by a single postgraduate student to make some sense of the organisational culture of a business as big as BT - it then had a payroll of 177,000 people - introductions continued so that more introductions could be effected with operational managers based in a number of London locations. The 'Country Club' management style (labelled and discussed by Blake and Mouton (1964) in their development of the 'managerial grid') was a first and instinctive approximation of how senior managers related to each other and their immediate personal reports. This was a judgement based upon observed evidence of the senior management's high level of concern for the well-being of the people in the business. It was apparent from conversations at both this stage of the research and subsequently (in the terminology of Blake and Mouton (1964)) that an immediate aim of the most senior organisational members was to attempt to 'shift', 'change' or 'develop' the organisation's culture to one embracing the 'Team Management' style with its focus on quality and achievement. A discussion of how far this was achieved in the period under consideration forms an important aspect of what follows.

From the perspective of the organisation the issue of personal credibility - specifically as they anticipated it would be perceived by such operational managers - was a chief focus of the early meetings with CMG people. There was a general awareness that little valuable data would become available if the perceived purpose of manager/researcher interaction was to develop an academic project, which could be perceived by those managers as arid. Consequently, it was proposed at 'Manager, Quality Programmes' level - a senior management post title that is no longer in existence - that the then-existing company 'Quality Network' of professionally trained people in management skills would be invited on a 'no obligation' basis to act as an introduction agency to produce live introductions to operational managers. Such workers had already developed their credibility in dealings with the operational managers and their teams as management development consultants and deliverers of professional training packages. Hence it was judged that the research role could accurately be presented to BT's operational people as an adjunct to this - and in so doing 'feed' from its higher status. Therefore researcher entry would comfortably be assimilated into the various sets of managers' everyday assumptions about how patterns of the way intra-organisational business such as training and managerial development were 'routinely' and 'normally' conducted.

From the perspective of the researcher, the priority in determining whom best to identify as subjects of research in an organisation then employing 177,000 people was the crucial early empirical priority. The middle management tier within any organisation is widely understood within the management literature to be of pivotal importance to the success or otherwise of senior management attempts to achieve the organisational objectives. The management literature starting with Fayol (1930) or even earlier supports such a contention. So, at the rational level, it was for this reason that middle managers were chosen as the focus for the study in each of the two organisations examined. However, rationality plays only a part of the complete justification for the middle management focus of the whole project; the professional experience of the researcher was in that tier and so it may be said that it afforded a certain amount of psychological comfort to be actively engaged in research with managers at the same hierarchical level. The crude definition of middle management that was used in the determination of which managers to meet and which not, was that middle managers do not ordinarily engage in the development of strategy/policy. This is usually the province of senior management; and middle managers ordinarily do have a number of colleagues who regard them as their line manager. This often distinguishes them from lower status grades in the organisation, such as junior managers. In both organisations, people were accorded the title of middle manager on the basis of technical expertise and qualifications in either gas or telecommunications engineering rather than because they controlled a number of subordinates, and of course this also reflects usage of the term in many other large enterprises.

Much could be said in support of these pair of criticisms of opposed and even competing methodological logics. They may lead to permanent empirical inertia. It is not the purpose of this work further to develop the work of Bendix and Lipset (1967) and other more recent scholars in squaring this methodological circle. However, in an unstructured interview with Quality Networkers (which do not themselves form part of this chapter), they were asked to identify operational teams and team leaders that would be 'interesting' and/or 'representative of the business' and/or 'amenable to co-operating' in such a study as the one in hand. Much of the balance of this chapter is devoted to the provision of highlights from these interviews. Occasionally, initial exploratory/viability interviewing was conducted by the researcher rather than the Quality Networker where the latter person judged this to be more appropriate. Furthermore, in the gathering together of those people both well placed enough and also willing to participate in the study, attention was given to the overall structure of the organisation in terms of its operating divisions and its geography. So, twenty eight people in middle management roles participated in the BT part of the study. They were drawn from the upper, middle and lower status and salary bands of the organisation (within the confines of the broadly understood and previously identified middle management tier) and they were spread across London, Southern, South Eastern, Midlands, North Western and Yorkshire English regions, as well as from Wales.

This is an appropriate place to make an observation or two about the process of entry to all the locations listed above where the study was conducted and some of the consequences (the methodological discussion in chapter two of this study refers to this matter, and a fuller account is available in Elsmore, 1994). It is clear that these points within the organisation which were empirically examined were initially identified through a process which contained an element of chance. In other words, in the first phase of the research (spring 1993 through the summer of that year), typically it fell to the Quality Network people to identify managers of their acquaintance as subjects of the study. This is judged to be both a strength and simultaneously a weakness of the research methodology. Certainly, as briefly considered above, any 'scientific' frame of methodological reference, which identified a sample through means other that randomly chosen ones, could be regarded as questionable. However, earlier framing of this study sets up a position outside that of conventional scientificity by expressing a preference for the validity and 'realness' of its data rather than the potential elegance of its quantitative and/or other analysis.

That the senior managers of the CMG within the company felt that it was necessary actively to seek the support and approval of their more junior colleagues before launching the project as 'live' may also be significant. Perhaps this also reflects something of the Blake and Mouton (1964) *motif* already mentioned above. It seems to permit the possibility that their own perceptions of the organisational culture within which they worked produced sets of working assumptions which emphasised managerial autonomy within work teams. A consequence of this may then have been that the role of senior managers was perceived by them as not to include 'interference' with the day-to-day work processes of operational teams. Furthermore, another apparently clear dimension of that organisation's culture was that it was then conceived of as possible to form a network of expensively trained and professionally remunerated managers, all of whom could be absolved of direct operational responsibilities. Their sole purpose, then, was to pursue the elusive goal of organisational quality as a full time activity, rather than as an element of their operational role.

No evidence is available as to how representative the opening assumptions of the Quality Networkers and CMG members were in relation to their organisation as a whole; a certain amount of speculative comment on this very issue was recorded in interview notes - to the effect that insights into one part of the business may not be of value to another part. However, the academic validity of these thoughts is questionable in the sense that each individual person saw only a very small fraction of the total number of operating divisions at any one time period - or at most two. As a result, the basis of their judgement is difficult to credit as wholly rooted in realistic and consistent observation rather that hearsay or in disconnected observation.

Though relatively easy to discredit from a positivist view, such opinions as these came sharply into focus when managers of teams presently in one operating division of the organisation began to contemplate the reality envisioned for them by their senior managers. The new vision would require such managers to transfer their teams and themselves from one operating division to another as part of a re-organisation. The other possibility seemed to cause a similar level of anxiety: the impending requirement to work closely beside colleagues transferred into their sphere of operation from another division in a different part of the organisation where those colleagues previously may have spent many years or even decades.

As will be indicated later, the reason for such anxiety is to be found in the managerial awareness of the impact of organisational culture clash or even culture dissonance on 'how things are done around here' (Deal and Kennedy, 1982). This awareness seemed to be heightened when there was a perception that not only were similar tasks completed differently in the incoming groups' former organisational locale or arrangements but that these processes were also inferior. Inferiority could have been judged in terms of time taken to complete tasks, or even the competence of the outcomes of the expenditure of individual and/or organisational effort.

Six organisations were approached in the first instance to assist with the research programme (further discussion of these organisations is to be found in chapter two of this study). First, some preliminary investigation ascertained the names and post titles of the Directors of Training (or their equivalent) in each organisation. Second, a letter was drafted which set out the (student) status of the researcher and the programme and also the potential benefits to the organisation of agreeing to co-operate. These included insights into cultural processes and this initial bid met with a number of different outcomes. In the public sector, in a large police service in the south of England, it generated a degree of interest with a number of senior officers, but was not to be proceeded with because of the (then unknown) academic and professional preferences of an incoming chief officer. One large government department replied immediately that they had recently undergone a cultural audit and that therefore they could not usefully participate. In the private sector, one paper mill management could not agree amongst themselves of the outcome of a cost-benefit calculation in relation to the proposed study and hence chose not to proceed further. Fourthly, one bank industry subsidiary wrote curtly by return that not only were they not able to participate but that they wished to apply a cloak of confidentiality even to the request for their co-operation. The managers of the two organisations that did see benefit in joining the study were in the two businesses identified in the chapter title.

Notions about abstracting a 'representative' and hence 'reliable' sample from some randomly drawn cross-sectional slice of that payroll were problematic for two reasons. Firstly, such an approach was judged to be very much out of keeping with the overall methodological orientation of this study. Secondly, this orientation was judged to be hopelessly romantic given the existence and pervasive influence of the complex social-psychological web of meanings and interpretations that form around the ways that actors in organisations construct and deconstruct their sets of working assumptions about how social reality is negotiated and then maintained. The discussion about methodology elsewhere in this study develops this logic; yet, there is also a widespread recognition in the academic community of the imperfections of all research strategies. That which is believed to be valid and so 'real' by the participants themselves is itself interpretable as inherently weak at the levels of replicability and representativeness from the positivist position.

The second phase of research within BT took place in the months of October, November and December 1995. It was made possible through the establishment of a pair of circumstances. Firstly, contact had become established with a management consultant with a thorough, first hand and recent knowledge of BT. The outcome was that a number of new introductions were effected and they centred on the newly established CMG referred to above. Secondly, that group was particularly receptive to the kinds of issues with which this study is interested, and members identified some of the benefits that qualitative data would afford them. The 'atmosphere' generated by this group of BT managers was qualitatively different from that perceived by the researcher to reflect the first group of managers and gatekeepers. The 'country club' seemed well to the rearground and this seemed to have been replaced or supplanted by a different set of working relationships between the colleagues. Whether this 'new' reality was also shared by the first set of gatekeepers is not possible to discuss as contact was made with them on a 'once only' basis. The emphasis of this study stood in sharp contrast to the entirely quantitative approach for accruing information about organisational culture that they had adopted thus far in their remit to understand the nature of their own organisation's culture. Their receptivity was due to an increasing awareness of the inadequacy of attempting to make sense of organisation's culture without the use of a set of extensive qualitative research methods. At the end of the empirical phase of the research in December 1995, a total of seventy-three managers from BT and British Gas (Eastern) had participated in the research programme, and it was this evidence which the CMG found of influence in assessing the future direction of their work.

At the level of the whole organisation, Höpfl (1992) sets out the issues in respect of BT; no similarly helpful study of Eastern Gas is available to cite; it is tentatively suggested that it may have come to similar conclusions to Höpfl (1992) anyway. She demonstrates the contradictions between espoused plans of senior managers and the organisational reality as experienced by middle and junior grade managers as 'Operation Sovereign', the senior management programme of organisational change, wound through its relatively tortuous path:

> This process [Operation Sovereign] created a great deal of uncertainty among the lower levels of management, many of whom were left uninformed and consequently insecure...many were...left with no job... . (Höpfl, 1992, p.25)

Clearly then, at the time of the empirical investigation associated with this study there was already a degree of turmoil in the feelings and perceptions of many organisation members, in their different grades within the employment hierarchy.

British Gas (Eastern) plc

This organisation was one of the twelve British regions into which gas service and supply was divided both for commercial and domestic customers. In 1996 the whole industry structure was replaced by another logic, and those alterations largely completed a shift of the gas industry within the British economy from the public sector to the private sector. That process began when shares in the equity of this business were offered for sale in 1985. The television and poster campaign which attempted to publicise this share offer made famous a potential investor named 'Sid'. This media creation is referred to by one interview respondent later in this chapter. There were also significant reductions in the size of this organisation; the national total of payrolls fell from 80,000 to around 55,000 in the period during which this study took place. As with the case of BT, the overt purpose of privatising and then reorganising this industry was to encourage the efficient use of resources through the working of the market mechanism via the breaking of the monopoly, which also this company had.

In contrast with the relatively extended timescale of the BT element of the study, the work with British Gas (Eastern) managers was conducted over a tightly compressed period of time, and came with the full support (and consequent authority which that afforded) of one Gas Region's Regional Management Team (RMT). Industry structure has since altered, but in the period 15th June to 23rd July 1995 thirty-eight managers (and eight staff in industrial grades) met the research tools already identified in order to participate in the study. First contact (face-to-face) with the organisation was on 16th April 1993 with the Training Manager, a post reporting directly to the RMT in the organisational structure. The meeting focused on the issue of the degree of similarity between the agenda of the researcher and that of the organisation. It must be recognised that these key markers or research parameters were common across both of the organisations investigated and so the subsequent research tools were also common to the two organisations. They were chosen because they occupied key elements in the Schein view (1985) of how best to make sense of an organisational culture. This underpinning by one of the leading authorities in the field afforded a degree of academic 'respectability' to this methodological cornerstone. However, if the research was to be repeated, then with the benefit of hindsight, it is unlikely that the research instruments would be replicated in an identical format. Nevertheless, the key markers were:

1   to examine what leaders pay most attention to;
2   to examine how leaders react to crises;
3   to observe the nature of any role modelling or coaching;
4   to examine the criteria for allocating rewards;
5   to examine the criteria for selection and promotion.

In the case of the then existing agenda of the RMT, they had two items for consideration. Firstly, they wished to obtain feedback from their employees concerning the recently concluded 'Succeeding With Organisational Change' (SWOC) exercise within the business. They preferred such internal data collection to be gathered by a person or persons not on the company payroll in order to emphasise the data's integrity and independence. Secondly, but more particularly, they wanted information on two related matters. These were on the success (or otherwise) of their *Charter for Change* document which had been promulgated recently and on the extent to which British Gas people were aware of the existence of the Charter and its potential impact on their working lives. After subsequent meetings with RMT members, it was agreed both that the degree of overlap/sympathy between the objectives was sufficient to proceed with a joint project and also that the research data generated would be of value and interest to the RMT. Consequently, it was agreed that the RMT would support the research by payment of hotel and travelling expenses to facilitate the visiting of each of the nine locations across the Region where significant numbers of employees were based. These nine locations comprised seven District Offices, each with engineering and clerical staff. Each was scattered strategically across the eastern counties as far north as Peterborough and Norwich. Next was the billing centre for the whole Region (known as Tower Point), and finally was the Region's Chief Office (known as Star House) with personnel, finance, training and other functions.

In return for the payment of expenses it was also agreed that a one hour verbal report would be made to an RMT Board meeting and this took place on 6th September 1995. This was subsequently supported by a written report which was circulated two weeks in advance of the meeting to Board members. The financial aspect was significant, not least because it rendered the programme akin to consultancy with the RMT as client. This conferred a relatively high degree of status as perceived by non- RMT managers in the organisation and probably provided a number of opportunities. These included the securing of introductions and visits to places and the opening up of lines of research questioning that otherwise would not have become available. However, moving around the organisation clearly identified in the role of 'consultant from Chief Office' may also have made impossible an equal number of such possibilities in other subsets of the organisation - perhaps the very counter-cultural subsets identified as of significance in chapter three, this study's literature overview. It may be reasonable to speculate here that only an indication of the extent of the degree of sympathy between the research outcomes in each organisation studied would help identify the effect of the impact of the role in which the research was conducted. This may apply especially where this role was relatively closely associated with the organisation's senior management.

Visits to each location comprised two working days, 8.00 am to 6.00 p.m., and in each of the seven Districts visits ordinarily began with an interview of approximately one hour with the District General Manager (DGM). Each of the seven was white and male, and all but one spoke in what would generally be regarded as middle class accents. As with the British Telecom element of the study, it was necessary to seek the assistance of operational managers as to whom best to interview. The same general specification was used: people in middle management grades (defined as above) that could be said to be 'interesting', 'representative of their fellows' and related. It is likely that each DGM was working with his own agenda - people chosen for interview seemed to be unfailingly efficient, speedy and courteous in their duties as defined by the variety of performance measurement devices in use at the time. The then-prevailing industry structure provided for a classically bureaucratic pyramidal distribution of management grades. In each District, a number of managers in each grade across the middle management tier were invited to participate in the programme, and by the end of the seventh visit to the District offices, at least one manager from each of the grades had been included. The structure of management posts in the two centralised centres (Star House and Tower Point) was similar. There, after Level One posts were allocated to their RMT holders, Tier Two posts were apportioned across the Region. These were known as R2 at the central functions or D3 in the District offices. Sub-DGM level was R3/D4 and then there were two more grades of management below that before the technical, clerical or administration levels were reached.

One important consequence for the assessment of such research is, then, how representative is the group studied of their colleagues as a whole? It is not the purpose of this study to produce positivist data which will therefore be testable by processes of replication; data which are validated by the data contributors and their senior managers does not need this kind of 'proof' of its internal logic and validity. As has been argued elsewhere in this study, there are fundamental problems with such positivist approaches anyway.

So, both in BT and in British Gas (Eastern), middle managers were first asked to respond to a Likert-style questionnaire, then proceeded to a semi-structured interview. Both schedules form part of the appendices for the study. It has already been made apparent that the purpose of the questionnaire was not to produce quantitative data for a detailed positivist analysis. Rather, it served the purpose of attuning each interviewee in a consistent way to the relatively subtle issues raised by the interview schedule.

In every case, the introductory questionnaire and subsequent interviewee questions were considered by interviewees in a location away from their usual place of work, frequently in the line managers' offices. On the one hand this may have reinforced any existing perception of the process as one undertaken at the request of the uppermost tiers of the managements of each organisation. Yet there was also a pragmatic benefit - it also served the purpose of providing a space where it was possible to converse and think without interruptions from the telephone or from personal visiting by other colleagues.

The subsequent chapter is a selection from the data that was gathered. A complete reportage of all the responses to each question would be both overwhelming and unnecessary. Rather, comments have been selected from each organisation's respondents on the basis of the frequency of their occurrence, or the degree of insight into the sets of rules, routines and taken for granted assumptions at the heart of each organisational culture that they suggest the respondent shows. The interview heads themselves are based on the framework of the key dimensions of organisational culture that were first developed by Schein (1985) for his North American empirical studies. In order to effect a successful crossing of the Atlantic, Schein's language and some of his meanings have been anglicised for this project wherever that seemed to afford the possibility of opening up organisational cultural insights rather than obfuscating them. Adopting his empirical approach also maintains the possibility of further cross-cultural work at a subsequent date by comparing data outcomes.

The final part of this chapter comprises the introduction to the Graphics COPE software package identified as significant at the outset of the chapter. The data analysis itself, contained in chapter six of this study, comprises two elements. These are sixteen Graphics COPE 'cognitive maps', which are exhibits within the Appendix. Each map has supporting text to highlight the Graphics COPE data analysis in terms of outcomes. This is followed by a discussion around the application to the data in the maps of the 'domain' analysis which is one of the Graphics COPE analytic tools, and the domain analysis is also in the Appendix (at Appendix 2).

The University of Strathclyde (in collaboration with the University of Bath) has published the Graphics COPE software package to contribute to the response of a felt need to systematise and generally render more rigorous the analysis of qualitative data. In a training session at the University of Strathclyde in November 1995, Professor Colin Eden of the School of Management spoke of the methodological problems associated with the analysis of large volumes of qualitative data. A central difficulty is how to distinguish key data from the welter of either less substantial or less significant material that typically surrounds it. The proposition advanced is that it is at this point that personal prejudice may unwittingly lead to the highlighting of aspects of the data which do not deserve such treatment and the concomitant possibility of the downgrading of outcomes which certainly would benefit from closer inspection. There is an extensive literature which outlines such methodological problems, and some of it has already been identified in earlier elements of this study. It is for this reason that the package has been used in this part of this research. The Graphics COPE documentation asserts:

> Graphics COPE provides help with structuring problems or situations whether…complex…[or not.] The software allows the user to work with a model of interlinked ideas using maps. …A Graphics COPE map is made up of short phrases (referred to as concepts) whose relationships are indicated by arrows drawn between them. The user enters concepts and arrows and the ideas can be moved, given styles, and, eventually analysed when a large enough picture of the issue in question has been drawn up. Graphics COPE is an ideas management tool. (*Graphics COPE User Guide*, February 1995, Banxia Software Ltd.)

For the purpose of clear exegesis, firstly, the Graphics COPE term **'style'** needs to be understood as 'a set of similar or the same elements, as part of the overall analysis' and secondly the use of the term **'concept'** is synonymous with the term 'interview response'. What makes the distinction between the two terms in the context of this research is that the latter are briefer summaries of the original remarks. Checks on the validity of this set of task outcomes are possible through comparison of the reportage in chapter four with the mapping in the following pages. All of the stages referred to above have been used in the data analysis phase, generating one map that identifies all the questions asked of the sample of respondents. Fourteen maps follow this; one for each of the sets of responses to each of the fourteen interview schedule questions.

Map sixteen, named 'supermodel', is a complex amalgam of all the proceeding map work. The map contains 590 entries and shows all the links between them. This level of detail accurately suggests that it will illegible if printed on a single A4 sheet. However, it is proposed that considerable value remains in the exhibit. It still clearly shows the links made between the questions and between the answers. Also, the judgement is made that this display, with the links, is of more interest than the alternative print-out possibility that the package offered. This is some 64 sheets of data that would require joining together before sense could be made of them and so before the origin and destination of each link could be comprehensible. An inevitable consequence of the employment of

Graphics COPE in this research project is a personal assessment of the degree of its robustness and utility; and an assessment of whether it delivers what it promises. This, also, is contemporaneously delivered.

Of particular interest is the way that links can be made between concepts so joining questions together, in quite significant and insightful ways. It may be the case that more credence and weighting can be given to some joins (or links) than others, in the overall task of hastening the development of a good understanding of the data. This may apply when respondents who occupy the more strategically important positions within each organisation develop the insights. Yet, such managerialism can also be superseded by recognising the power to explain and define phenomena that is given only those people who are permanently on the spot. This is so because they occupy lesser places in the organisational hierarchy and so remain in a location for longer than more senior colleagues whose duties may take them elsewhere more often. So, the issue of what level of credibility to place on what links is significant. The opportunity so to dwell on the matter is itself an advantage of the relatively rigorous approach a software-led approach to data analysis may bring. Perhaps the application of the common sense knowledge and understandings of the analyst is the most reliable means of deciding the issues. Similarly, if the non ICT-driven equivalent of the matter crosses the consciousness of the qualitative researcher using traditional techniques of analysis then it will be such common sense knowledge that determines outcomes. For example, the symbolic interactionist tradition of theory and research methodology that was developed in the first instance by Mead (1934) does this. Nearly a generation later, authorities such as Garfinkel (1967) and Berger and Luckmann (1966) pointed out the shortcomings inherent in ignoring all the rules, routines and taken-for-granted assumptions integral to social interaction in organisations. It is for this reason that one of the key sets developed within the data analysis of the following chapter is 'members of similar rank', recognising that such basic data was collected during each of the interviews conducted in this research. The data is displayed there separated into responses from each organisation. Of course, none of this thinking is designed to reduce the sharpness of the impact of service deliverers' thoughts on their organisation, or to reduce the validity of their perspective.

The use of the Graphics COPE links permits a number of other interesting possibilities. Firstly, the 'tail' of each link represents a potential cause or explanation of the 'head' to which the tail is joined via the link line. Where no arrowhead exists the link is a connotative one, i.e. it is designed to suggest a relationship between the concepts but causality is either unclear (usually), undesirable (rather less often) or unnecessary to identify. The fourteen interview questions are visible as the foci in the Graphics COPE model labelled 'supermodel', and are referred to as 'interview heads of discussion' in an attempt to capture the dynamic rather than static shape of interview dyads. This macro of the empirical work in the study permits the opportunity to make links across each of the questions; both from question to question and within each question. This also is insightful. Furthermore, it is possible to make links between the responses afforded to one question and responses to another. The heart of the analysis is reached where these fundamental links (and the others) and their points of origin and destination are examined by the Graphics COPE package's analytic capability. Not all of these analytical tools are appropriate for this kind of data, as will always be the case once a display layout is chosen. For example, in an inspection of the supermodel, a cluster analysis would merely identify the fourteen interview foci as clusters of data, and this is self-evidently unhelpful.

In terms of the links added in the supermodel, it is worth emphasising that each one that joins one map to another was the result simply of researcher interpretation. There is no wish to attempt to add a gloss of scientificity to the research outcomes. That would be entirely spurious. Some links, then, join maps together and others join individual responses together. The use of colour within the Graphics COPE framework permits the opportunity to make both an analytical means of separation between the styles and, secondarily, a visual impact with the 'styles' utilised to analyse data. The four styles developed for this analysis comprise:

1. Criticism of management   -   shown as red entries.
2. Support for management   -   shown as blue entries.
3. Interview heads of discussion -   shown as black (and upper case).
4. General issues   -   shown as green entries.

The basis of allocation to the first, second or fourth style was by common sense, aided by the experience of (brief) membership of the respondent's work group, as already described and discussed in chapter two of this work. It has also been mentioned in the preceding chapters as in the tradition of Garfinkel (1967). That there is some considerable degree of concern shown by organisation members towards the words and actions of their seniors is transparent through the colour coding of concepts. The consequences of the thinking about theories and methods and, in particular, the thinking about cultures and counter-cultures are available in the subsequent chapter of this study concerned with conclusions and recommendations.

The last two of the COPE 'styles' identify, respectively, the questions asked of the respondents and the destination of those responses deemed interesting enough for inclusion. However, in the context of the respondent's overall tone and attitudes revealed, they were not sufficiently identifiable with either of the first two categories for an adequate assignment of the response to be made. In combination, coloured styles with different types of links is another way of examining qualitative data and the detailed outcomes of both this and the 'domain' (and other) techniques of analysis will form chapter six of this work. We proceed now to the consideration of the evidence itself, after a brief summary and conclusion.

Summary and Chapter Conclusion

This chapter has provided the background details of how each of the two organisations was penetrated for research purposes. The conclusion, whilst obvious, is still important: joining the same organisations at a different time in each of their histories, or joining two other of the six organisations approached in total, would, in each case, have led to different outcomes. Social research is a dynamic and processual phenomenon.

5 Presentation and Analysis of the Evidence

Introduction

The format of this chapter comprises an extended review of the fourteen heads of discussion that comprised the semi-structured interviews with the BT and British Gas respondents. Then, further to increase the coherence of the study, each of the discussions of each interview question concludes with a summary account that analyses those responses. This analysis is itself achieved through the reconstruction of the responses into the format of a Graphics COPE map. The numbering scheme for the maps is that used for the interview questions themselves (as has already been indicated, the maps form part of the appendix of this study). The chapter concludes with a brief discussion of the domain analysis feature of the Graphics COPE package.

Responses to the Interview Schedules

All the direct quotations in this section of the study are numbered, in order to facilitate ease of reference in the subsequent chapters of the work. Square brackets are used *viz.* [ ] to assist in conveying the meaning intended by the respondent, based upon the verbatim remarks contemporaneously recorded in field work notes. Frequently, such remarks were clarified as to the meaning/s the respondent intended to convey, at the time the remarks were made, in the search for accuracy of recording. In each of the sets of responses there are a number of analytical remarks; these are intended to act as signposts for the analysis provided in this chapter. For the present purposes, the reported data is not complete. It amounts to approximately half the full set of responses. This editing is designed to convey the gist of the meanings that emerged from the interviews without overburdening the reader with unnecessary detail.

In the reconstruction of the responses to form the Graphics COPE map concepts, they were necessarily reduced in length in order to conform with the constraints that use of the software package imposed. Also, for the present purposes, a significant number of the responses have been reduced in length. This, typically, is where the respondent chose to elaborate a particular point with an example. Other responses are omitted altogether, where a degree of overlap with other responses is discernible. The *raison d'être* that governed the selection and formatting of each of the following items is the extent to which it indicates the 'flavour' of the interview response at the individual level or aggregate level. In the process overall, the priority was to maintain the integrity of the meanings that the respondent was perceived to have wished to share with the researcher, during the interview. Of course, the items first entered as verbatim responses below are themselves transcripted from raw notes taken contemporaneously with the conduct of each interview. Again, there, as in the present editing, the priority was to maintain the integrity of the meaning of each response - as well as to maintain a realistic insight into the data-set overall.

1.   **How do people in your organisation learn about the senior management's policy objectives for the organisation?**

In **BT**, the Total Quality Management initiative from the late 1980s identified poor internal communications as a significant barrier to improving the overall standing of the business, and the cascading of information via Team Brief began in response. There was a widespread awareness of the existence and general purpose of Team Brief. Virtually every interviewee mentioned it by name; each identified it by function. Several of the more junior managers in the sample emphasised how it was a useful tool also for upward communication, both in their managerial role as a Briefer and when they themselves met their line managers. In the November/December 1994 round of interviews, shortly after BT achieved national publicity as a result of the critical correspondence from a service engineer, no interviewee used the description 'BT Toadie' to refer to the similarly-named newspaper (i.e. *BT Today*). Not all managers were happy merely to list the various other organs of communication (including video presentations) within the business. They ranged over the theme of communications in more general terms:

1.1   'In the time since Sovereign, [this was a major reorganisation which took full effect after BT was privatised] I realise that we have become even more tribal; this tribalism has taken the ethos of the team too far and it's one of our worst facets.' [This interviewee felt that the restructuring and reorientation produced tighter teams of staff which had become too inward-looking.]

1.2   Another commented 'If Team Brief is so important, how much training in communications skills do Team Brief writers get...and the managers who give the major face-to-face briefs? In my team, we deride all their "management speak"!'

1.3   'Informal "networked" information was regarded as vital by another. Plugging in to "the rumour machine" helped one manager understand more of what staff felt and also more about "what was going on".'

Another addressed the political agenda by proposing:

1.4   'I read the BT papers to see whose star is rising.'

The political aspect of communications was in the mind of another interviewee who remarked:

1.5   'Team brief makes me wonder what isn't being cascaded; sensitive decisions about downsizing are one example...'

Two senior managers respectively commented:

1.6   'I am informed by Zone Board meetings and briefings direct to my home address. I also read Team Briefs and all the [professional] press...'

1.7   'I go to the General Managers' Meeting which is monthly and get the "Breakfast TV" video from the Board. My Director does a written briefing too. I am a member of the Group

Quality Council and we report directly to the top Board chaired by Iain Vallance.'

The next comments originated from heads of large departments:

1.8   'Team brief has been mandatory since 1991 and it's meant to be two way communication with our Directorate...in mid-February 400 managers doing my kind of job went to a "Common Event" in Birmingham where we looked at a position paper from the Director [which emphasised that] we are all customers of each other inside the business and competitors with all the other telecommunications companies now...'

1.9   'Our teams think tribally and in spite of Team Brief we suffer from 'mushroom management'. Our director says that we should listen to our people but we are still insular and reticent to contribute to the overall whole. My team works in an open-plan office...[so they are better integrated than many]. Tribalism has taken the team ethos too far and I am not too happy with the gung-ho'ness of some top management.'

1.10   'I think that the annual CARE survey is part of upward communication. My team reads thoroughly the Core Brief [i.e. the fixed part of Team Brief] and the half yearly results publication. The Core Brief is usually a single matter, e.g. treating our customers as individuals, not as "subs" [it is understood that this term was current within the organisation for several decades and is a contraction of "subscribers".'
[Reference to the annual CARE investigation concerns the organisational leaders' attempt, using a quantitative research methodology, to understand the changing attitudes of BT people to a variety of business matters].

Several managers of small groups of three or more clerical or manual employees said:

1.11 'We only get broad brush information from top management...what we need is more face to face meetings...'

1.12 'Our Team Briefs have taught us the Mission and Values of the company, through repetition we have them so often...'

1.13 'Upward communication begins locally through Quality Planning and another example is Investors in People. Top down information comes from Team Briefings.'

1.14 'In my little team we deride the "Management Speak" of the Team Brief document: why don't they say what they mean, downsizing is redundancy. Their language is not sensitive enough.'

1.15 'I feel in touch and effective because of all of the management information I receive. I get to join three monthly management forums chaired by my Tier Four boss. Also Team Brief and other cascaded information... I [this includes my team] am part of the Five Year Strategic Plan.'

1.16 'I am plugged into the unofficial rumour machine; my contacts in Group Personnel are helpful here. Official briefing comes through even the e-mail set up.'

1.17 'I think the most important document is the Annual Corporate Briefing with its strategy statement - it's a sort of Queen's Speech. "BT Toady" is just that.'

1.18 '...Some of the stuff is even faxed to us to get it onto the Team Brief at the last minute.'

1.19 'In BT Mobile we all go to the Annual General Meeting and hear presentations from senior management. My team don't read the notice boards where we have our values.'

1.20 'Team Brief is shouted at us as we leave, on Friday afternoons.'

In **British Gas (Eastern)**, the organisational structure was in a state of flux, and this impacted upon the choices of people to be included in the sample set of respondents. Nevertheless the respondents are divided into three groups based on their position in the organisational hierarchy. The group identified as the senior managers (from within the middle management band) are those people who were in District General Manager (DGM) posts or the central functions equivalent grade. Those identified as in the middle tiers were in department head roles, for example the Head of Engineering in a District Office, and the great bulk of the rest of the sample were deemed to be junior managers and controlled any number from three staff to approximately one dozen. Each of these breaks in the organisational hierarchy is intended to reflect differing levels of access to power and influence within the organisation as well as the more obvious and apparent differences in status and salary.

One methodological difficulty that needs to be identified at this point is that the people in DGM roles (or equivalent) did not have exposure to the same investigative tools as the rest of the sample. Rather, in recognition of their senior status in the Region - answerable only to Regional Board members - and on the advice of the research's patron, client and sponsor, within British gas (Eastern) these organisational members were given a semi-structured interview (of approximately one hour in each case) which afforded them the opportunity to develop what they themselves identified as matters of importance to the general themes of the research programme. Consequently, where they made remarks which illuminated areas identified in the main research tool's different foci, they have been included.

All of those sampled showed that there was a widespread awareness of the existence and purpose of Team Brief, in a fashion similar to that within BT; here, too, every respondent mentioned it either by its name or its purpose. It was appreciated as a means of keeping people in touch with changes in their workplace. However the quality with which Team Brief is completed is patchy and the variations between practices across the districts and in the two central functions are substantial. There was evidence both of thorough and genuinely two-way briefings as well as the opposite, in each of the nine geographical locations sampled. So, commencing with the most junior managers first:

1.01   'We have our Team Brief shouted at us on the way out of the door, usually at 4.40 p.m. on Fridays.'

Typical responses to this area pointed out that Team Brief was just one means amongst many of receiving up-to-date information about the Region and nationally in the gas industry. Many mentioned the newspapers *Gas News* and *The Easterner* in this respect. Senior management attempts to formalise organisational change and the place of employees in it, such as through *The Charter for Change,* met with only a limited awareness of such attempts. Employee responses on the Charter varied from a cautious:

1.02   'I think it's window dressing!'

1.03   '...I try and find out [what is going on]...Team Brief and word of mouth reports...'

A gas service officer (i.e. a junior manager as defined earlier in this chapter) observed:

1.04   'Team Brief is the main way, and it lasts 30 minutes to an hour.'

Other junior managers commented:

1.05   'The quality of Team Brief varies. Some are just boring read-outs; I pull out and select the main bits. We had a "first" this year - a business plan presentation to nearly everybody.'

1.06   '*The Easterner* and notice boards work - but in Team Briefs you don't get a chance to speak...'

1.07   '[We learn about policy objectives through] Rumours!'

1.08   'In my small department things are said when they need to be said [i.e. by me in my judgement.]...we get to know things quickly.'

Some quite contrasting remarks are cited in conclusion to this section:

1.09   'When Team Brief is linked to an open management style it leads to good insights into what's going on.'

1.010   'Uncertainty in the company has led people to ignore the *Charter for Change* [and other tools of communication]; enthusiasm has gone and people's careers have been blighted...'

1.011   'We may be too well informed [through Team Brief and other instruments] and therefore our costs go up... I support briefings even though we get a lot wrong.'

Turning to the middle band of managers in the organisation: two managers responsible for teams of manual and clerical groups respectively commented:

1.012   '[I communicate] Team Brief material from my line manager, but I also have informal chats [with my people] at about eight at a time...'

1.013   'Team Brief is the most important instrument of communication.'

1.014   'There are lots of things we find out first in the press, for example the details of the voluntary redundancy scheme...

1.015   'Team Brief in half an hour is not enough time for them to digest all the information.'

One very long-serving manager in a central function, and who professed to know the business and the Region well, commented:

1.016   'Team Briefing or special briefings, management and section meetings, boards, individual one-to-one chats...these are things which are generally welcomed by people.

1.017   'Not many people in my grade give a sympathetic Team Brief and allow questions...I've done this...'

1.018 '[My central office role permits me to observe that]...Team Brief seems to work pretty well...even if there is also some ritualism across the Region.'

Comments gleaned from the highest status organisational members on how policy objectives are communicated and discussed included:

1.019 '[Talking about policy objectives]...the RMT got sixty-four [separate] heads of discussion when they sought upwards inputs from the company...they were swamped [with this amount and this level of diversity of thinking].'

1.020 'I produce an information sheet for my staff [which focuses on matters local to us].'

1.021 'Each month I like to give all my staff a half hour update [on matters relevant to the business].'

1.022 'When the TQM thinking arrived [in my part of the company], I made sure that all of the Service Officers attended a two days workshop on it.'

Concerning *The Charter for Change* within British Gas (Eastern), it will be apparent that it appeared a dead letter in both the districts and for those in central functions. Only staff associated with RMT (or indeed its members) seemed to have any awareness of it. In two other cases where the Charter was mentioned in an unsolicited conversation, judgement was frequently suspended on the efficacy of the Charter until RMT would be able to demonstrate their commitment to 'the fine words' it contained.

Map One, Question One, Analytical Discussion One

This question was designed as a 'low threat' and conversational opening issue which simply sought information. The intention was to provide an opportunity for each respondent to 'clear his/her throat.' Yet, most respondents interpreted the question as an opportunity to comment in a supportive or critical way on how well they judged their senior managements to have done as effective communicators of policy. The choice of the map styles eventually used - to highlight the critical/ supportive dichotomy - emphasises respondent treatment of both this and other questions in the research exercise. The responses here reflect a noticeable level of anxiety from organisational members about the quality and quantity of those communications issuing from the highest echelons of their organisations in terms of spreading information throughout concerning policy objectives. Overall, the map records seventeen red (i.e. critical) entries; thirteen blue (i.e. supportive) entries and sixteen green (i.e. neutral) entries. Concerning the 'quality of information' aspect, particularly vehement condemnation came from the respondent who 'deride[d] the 'management speak' (1.14) of Team Brief documents. The respondent went on to complain about insensitive language. Another respondent acidly observed that *The Charter for Change* is simply 'window dressing' (1.02) and a third critic claimed that 'Team Brief was shouted as we leave, on Friday afternoons' (1.20). In contrast, other respondents reported that 'I feel in touch and effective because of all the management information I receive' (1.15). Also reported was that people used the 'rumour machine' to make sense of what was going on (1.16). 'The overall impact of the responses seems to be one which emphasises the anguish respondents felt at the organisational change they were experiencing, against a backdrop, for many, of what they saw as inadequate supply of news about the future direction of their organisation from its uppermost management layers.

2.   To what do the leaders of your organisation seem to pay most attention?

In **BT**, the interviewees were asked to make a general reply if they so chose, but then to go on to illustrate their comments with a recent example. Another wide range of responses resulted. Replies are subdivided into three broad categories that hierarchically split the middle managers. This is an attempt to illustrate the different concerns of the respondents based on their individual definitions of the situations in which they found themselves. Of course, these perceptions were inevitably informed by their personal and professional experiences within the organisation as well as the information to which their grade gave them access. So, the most junior group:

2.1   'Statistics on paper rather than how customers actually feel; how many calls my team answers, not the quality of what's said [i.e. 'clearing down' quickly on customer interaction appeared to be rated a higher priority by senior managers than taking the time to deal with the matter comprehensively and therefore just once. Managers now do 'call observations' to look at call quality. My team's responses are tape-downloaded and then subsequently used in a training session or a one-to-one counselling session.].'

2.2   'Performance! ...and meeting our targets. We're all customer-aware now. Also cost controls.'

2.3   'Quality of service, safety, costs and BS5750 are important. Using initiative is also a priority so that we can "win back" lost custom. My lads should be about wining business. The senior managers don't understand the customer's perception; they get sold the wrong thing and then they're unhappy and this is because our sales people aren't technically competent to diagnose needs. An engineering person used to go out and discuss needs. Now it's marketing people who sell and my engineers end up looking foolish if they turn up with kit which won't do what the customer wants it to do. For example, yesterday an engineer was asked to fit a wall supported box in a thin cavity wall!'

2.4   'Market place position, shareholders' perceptions of how well we're doing and etc; our messages are about combating costs and raising productivity. I perceive they have this thrust from the top but the message seems to disconnect lower down - we don't see the strategic ideas clearly; their "mission words" don't count with day-to-day life at the bottom.'

2.5   'Most people would say quality, performance, costs and people are the four equal priorities but attempting to deliver all four of these as equal objectives can be time consuming, counter-productive and frustrating.'

2.6   'Downsizing us! Personalities and personnel are coming a bad second...undermining of people is taking place...training people technically is down [in number].'

2.7   'At the top is Iain Vallance and he genuinely believes what he says...I believe him...at Zone Manager level, the priorities change...reducing costs through the Release Package...[is their priority].'

2.8   '[We have slogans like] "Right first time every time!"...but we [in this group] refer things up [when we judge this to be appropriate]...to cover our backs.'

2.9   '[Our leaders seem to pay most attention to] the competition; they're our drivers today as they take our markets from us.'

The middle group of the stratum responded to the question like this:

2.10   '[There is] a split [between our leaders]. Some are jobsworths and are proceduralists. There are also those who look at innovation and creativity and ignore red tape. The proportion is 2:1 [in favour of the latter group] in my experience...'

2.11   '[Our leaders seem to pay most attention to] our business priorities [emphasising] business improvement. We've moved from being procedurally orientated to a change culture to concentrate on the quality of the transaction. So, "time in answering" and "call handling time" need less emphasis and the quality of the response and the empowerment [of the employee to act effectively to, for example, solve the problem] is more important.'

2.12   '[Our leaders seem to pay most attention to] our competitive strategy; focussing on BT's markets and looking to core products not peripherals [for example] making the most of digital networks to add value in clever things...'

2.13   '[Our leaders seem to pay most attention to] profitability compared with the competition and going more global...'

2.14 '[Our leaders seem to pay most attention to] the customer focus, regarding complaints and failures not just our successes...our suppliers are to be of the highest quality... The team focus is necessary but it is slower in coming. For example, the Property Section shut down a yard and the manager was the last to know about it, on the day when the new company [as tenants of BT or as freeholders] moved in!'

2.15 '[Our leaders seem to pay most attention to] the quality option; putting customers first by extending hours [of many of our clerical and manual people] so that more 6.00 a.m. to 2.00 p.m. and 2.00 p.m. to 10.00 p.m. shifts are worked [at normal rather than premium rates of pay for the people concerned.] The procedural emphasis has altered, too. Job handbooks and manuals still exist - but the emphasis now is on [pleasing the] customers - to win them back [from the cable companies who had taken a 30% market share in the geographical location of this respondent].'

The most senior of the managers in the sample responded as follows:

2.16 'We don't have a grand scheme in our organisation, we're individuals and we act as such...I have a problem with the suggestion of choosing the quality option [as a potential answer to this question]; our quality can be awful! [For senior management] personal style in delivering difficult messages can be vital; [I don't like] the "rara" stuff - it's too bland...it doesn't bear fruit...'

2.17 '[Our leaders seem to pay most attention to three main matters.] Firstly, customer quality; we have a very heavy emphasis - 50% to 60% of the time...also improving processes: a process orientation is inevitable now but it could stultify initiative. We've tried to get leverage from the change to district levels of organisation from that of regions [in order to pursue customer satisfaction goals]. The second matter is that of financial rigour. The third matter is our focus on the market place and our competition. [To do this effectively] we ought to manage our people better. We're getting on with improving our processes but we only have CARE [the annual survey of staff attitudes] and this shows symptoms not causes. So where are our clear personnel strategies? At the mechanistic level we are involved in Investors in People and with National Vocational Qualifications, but our pilots are poorly structured and when we recently united two clerical functions to multi-skill the clerks concerned, we did it sub-optimally...also our careers counselling is too haphazard.'

2.18   'Customer care is a very strong focus...also the Regulator's role and the associated commercial realities regarding our costs [compared with the price increases to our customers that we will be permitted to make].'

In **British Gas (Eastern),** responses again varied across a wide range of answers, and the same thought applies in respect of the validity of the perceptions of the managers within each grade. Both professional engineers and service engineers emphasised procedural means of achieving high safety standards, and memories of the Royston incident were still fresh. Consequently, the events themselves and the subsequent Official Report were still influential in terms of their impact upon employees in these categories.

The events that passed quickly into organisation members' collective consciousness and became known as the Royston incident need amplification. They comprised a major failure of gas engineering procedures in laying new gas pipes and it could have led to many fatalities in the small Cambridgeshire town of Royston. In an accidental oversight in the work of a pipe-laying team of manual workers (and, significantly, their junior management grade supervisors) a high pressure industrial supply of gas was connected to domestic pipes which function at a much lower pressure. This caused gas at high pressure to be piped into many Royston homes and it consequently caused a number of explosions of gas cookers, gas fires, central heating boilers and other gas appliances. The subsequent investigation of the incident identified inadequate checking procedures during the laying of parallel high pressure and domestic pressure pipes in the same trench. The report proposed that a cross-over valve between the two pipes was fitted the wrong way round and hence it allowed high pressure gas into domestic pipe, rather than the domestic pressure level of gas into higher pressure pipe which was the original intention.

In response to the second interview question, non-engineers pointed to the need to control costs, improve standards of service and satisfy the demands of the Regulator concerning competition in the industry as a whole. Here, responses are divided into two simple categories; those from people who deal mainly with engineering and gas safety, and those people whose work is situated in the commercial sphere and whose duties are in all the other, non-engineering functions of the business. Statuses are consequently mixed within these pair of categories, and relevant thoughts from the District General Managers are incorporated as each discussed his/her professional background before occupancy of the present post.

As a direct result of the Royston incident, the engineers' focus seemed to be an uncomfortable one. They wanted to balance the proven and considerable need to provide a safe service of gas to their customers with the ever increasing need to deliver supply at a lower and successively lower unit cost. The engineers are reported first:

2.01　'On the operational side [leaders pay attention to]...Customer Care, quality and value-for-money...but the engineering side is procedurally orientated for safety and consistency...'

Several responses were delivered ironically:

2.02　'Presently it's "image to the customer", five years ago it was getting things technically correct; the Royston fiasco cost us millions!'

2.03　'[Leaders of the organisation seem to pay most attention to]...financial performance...and image.'

2.04　'[Our manual workers need to put into a position where]...Standards of Service and Customer Care are perceived to be [central to the business...]' [Standards of Service were synonymous with high safety standards and hence of considerable importance to professional engineers.]

The people in the organisation who actually deliver the services to the customers are the Service Engineers, and, in an attempt to validate findings rooted mainly in investigations with managers and supervisors, when opportunities to speak informally with Service Engineers arose, such opportunities were warmly embraced. One such conversation which began with the remark that comprises this question was responded to as follows:

2.05   '[Leaders of the organisation seem to pay most attention to]...well, that's got nothing to do with my job; my supervisor [name] looks after that side of things.'

It is, of course a potentially revealing remark as it appears to reject to any acceptance of what might be called a 'corporatist' view of work in that organisation. Turning to those people whose duties were not directly related to engineering matters:

2.06   'They attend to what they can measure...for example Standards of Service, Gold Flame [a competition between the District Offices to be the most efficient and effective]...financial and operational matters...'

2.07   '[Leaders of the organisation seem to pay most attention to]...cost-cutting and budgets!...[It's too] short term...'

2.08   'We're hot on procedures, and we even use scripts. For example, if a customer phones me up to report a heating fault, I have to ask 'Have you turned up the thermostat? and so on...'

2.09   '[Leaders of the organisation seem to pay most attention to]...cost consciousness and the financial side - but also quality consciousness and questioning all of our procedures.'

2.010   '[Leaders of the organisation seem to pay most attention to]...obeying the Regulator and serving the customer; profitability is less important that serving customer needs.'

2.011   'At District level, it's meeting our financial targets...'

2.012   '[Leaders of the organisation seem to pay most attention to]...debt collection, Standards of Service staying in budget...'

2.013 'Standards of Service has shot to the front but making [more] money by being more efficient is the real priority.'

2.014 '[Leaders of the organisation seem to pay most attention to]...the competition with the Regulator, manifested through ads. in the press [about] the global presence of British Gas in a country's economy...and in the UK, too...so therefore we should stay on as a large concern.'

2.015 '[Leaders of the organisation seem to pay most attention to]...their image [which] is most important. They want to be seen doing the right thing even including having a pretend commitment [...to the less privileged in the community]. They push [organisational] change without consulting us...'

2.016 '[Leaders of the organisation seem to pay most attention to the]...wishes of the shareholders; capital income and return on investment. [They talk about] Customer Care...but do they treat old ladies well when they close high street showrooms [compared with] industrial customers with their discounted rates...?'

2.017 'The largest influences are political and financial...our management haven't refocused us because of OFGAS and hence our profits are down and revenue down. So we need to reduce spending and therefore reduce staff..'

2.018 'They are constantly renegotiating downwards the time allowance to do this or that job. Economy is a god!'

It will be apparent that a considerable number of these responses show a clear awareness of the relatively new focus on business values in the organisation, as opposed to 'gas is a social service and I am a Civil Servant' rhetoric. This may have been prevalent before the business was repositioned by government into the private sector.

Map Two, Question Two, Analytical Discussion Two

After the more factual opening question, this was intended to set up an opportunity to offer opinion on the subject matter indicated. The question permits speculation about the existence of any gaps between the leadership level of interpretation of organisational priorities and that of the respondents. Their thoughts frequently indicated considerable cleavage in this respect. The overall responses were as follows: the map records twenty-two red (i.e. critical) entries; four blue (i.e. supportive) entries and six green (i.e. neutral) entries. There appeared to be a gap between what was surmised would happen as responses and how the questions were actually answered. Many of the selected respondents took the opportunity to share criticisms of their senior managements when this question was put to them. For a question that was not an obvious chance to be critical, it seemed that surprisingly many people took this opportunity to be so. Many of the responses seemed to offer subtle reinterpretations of the officially promulgated aims of the organisations. For example: 'Quality, performance, costs and people' is the official answer, but equal treatment between them is 'time consuming, counter-productive and frustrating [so we don't treat them equally]' (2.5). Standards seem important, but 'being more efficient is the real priority' (2.013). 'There are too many disconnections between mission set from the top and life at the bottom' (based on 2.016). [Their priorities are] what they can measure ... finance and operations [and so not less measurable factors such as the morale and sense of well-being or its absence, on the part of the people in the organisation]' (2.06). The more supportive insights into senior management recognised: 'leaders' priorities are about serving the end-customer in what is considered as a cost-effective and caring way. It is suggested, however, that the overall impact of these critical responses is loud and clear, and that it is again evidence of the anguish and pain felt by organisation members at the changed circumstances in which they were then required to work.

3.   When things go wrong in your organisation, what happens?

This question was included as a result of the thinking of Schein (1985). Schein appears to draw inspiration from the approach of Garfinkel (1967) with which it is also consistent. Garfinkel advocated a concentration on those features of social reality which are more, rather than less, likely to disrupt the *status quo*. This was in an attempt to see then make sense of the taken-for-granted (that is to say, usually hidden) layers of meanings which are integral to social intercourse in the context of work or indeed in any other social arena. It seems plausible to suggest that asking managers in an organisation about failure will always contain the potential for respondents to mislead the questioner - out of a sense of self protection, or a sense of loyalty to the organisation, or a number of other possible motives. It may also be that the misleading will not be conscious and intentional. Thus the comments recorded from members of both organisations may be inaccurate or inadequate. In contrast, it may also be argued that an effective means of determining the veracity of replies is to be present in the same room as the respondent when those replies are made, and make a judgement about that matter.

In **BT,** responses to this question are grouped hierarchically. The highest echelon of the middle managers considered the question as follows, and their sense of strategic involvement in the issue is apparent as several of them reflect upon the linkage between organisational structure and organisational development:

3.1   'I think when problems get spotted promptly by [very senior] managers they are a hindrance! Errors shouldn't get to senior management. When they have done sets of different directives arrive, messages get confused and all this is unhelpful.'

3.2   'Senior management handle problems with no finesse. For example, when a major part of the business was under performing through shortage of people they heaped in resources and the larger group produced an excellent performance. All the extra people were then immediately withdrawn; you can imagine the effect on the morale of the remaining ones.'

3.3   'We are quite good at managing hurricanes and IRA bombings, we're resilient to these catastrophes. But the stuff that goes wrong slowly we're not good at managing. For example we won't make our downsizing targets this year. This will cause a lot of frenzied activity [near the deadline date], but it will all be too late.'

3.4   'When we make mistakes we should try to analyse them coolly. If we kick butt this adds to the fear element and that paralyses us.'

3.5   'The top levels have information filtered away from them when it's bad news time.'

3.6   'A lot of what goes on here is hidden from senior managers, our ways of doing things aren't robust. When some senior managers came to talk to our people at an employees evening recently there was a stormy meeting because our people felt their jobs were insecure. My amazement is limited to the fact that our senior management were surprised to hear their fears.'

3.7   'When things go wrong we seem to praise people!' [There followed a detailed example which named a number of senior BT executives.]'

The more junior group of managers reported as follows, and the strategic sense seems to be replaced in many responses either with cynicism or with a sense of urgency surrounding the need to get the task completed:

3.8   'A lot of my work and problems aren't seen by the top brass [it's] only when process go wrong. When our statistics are down we get more overtime allowed; we do more work; and [our statistics] come up. Historically it's always been a mad panic. Managers may make unrealistic promises to their bosses...too much is expected of people in a month.'

3.9   'With downsizing we now have 51 people to do the work of 140 in the past. We have [an additional] 11 temporaries because our work practices can't change. The agency people [that is, the temporary staff] are all ex-BT and they cause friction just by being there because BT hire them and my people see their own jobs threatened.'

3.10   'At zone manager level they set up special 'hit squad' activities [when they have read and considered] failure reports.'

3.11   '[Senior management] tend to overreact and expect everything else is being dropped to deal with it.'

3.12   'Some years ago we got blamed when problems occurred. [More recently the] focus is on 'why?' not 'who?'. I think we may be going back to that. Team Briefings now have 'discuss action' notes if something is not done as specified in a previous Team Brief. For example [the wearing of] safety glasses in certain situations [is mandatory]; and the 'troops' feel that this is not helpful, even if it is a safety issue; the don't like the formal criticism.'

In **British Gas (Eastern)**, managers' responses are also arranged hierarchically, they typically made some general remark as an opening thought but were then encouraged to underpin their generalities with a specific and recent example of a 'thing going wrong'. The responses commence with the most junior grades of managers and, as with the BT junior managers, there is evidence of the same pair of oppositional values present. These are the need to understand organisational change in a cynical and perhaps ultimately frustrated way, in contrast to the need to deliver a job-task to organisational seniors within the stated time and financial budgets.

It may be significant that there are many direct uses of the phrase 'no blame culture,' and relatively few, if any, attempts to convey the generally accepted meaning of this notion using other, less succinct expressions. The phrase did not seem to have quite the same degree of usage at the date of the interviews as it has attracted in more recent times. It becomes possible to suggest, therefore, that its use is indicative of the mouthing of a variety of 'management speak', uttered by organisational seniors in the first instance, but then used by more junior organisational members. Their purpose was to use it as a verbal sign of their membership of a discrete grouping of organisational members who have - or appear to have - access to knowledge about the senior management's perceptions of, for example, the future direction of the organisation. In short, it may be reasonable to suggest that usage of such terms as this is one part of the processes in the micro-politics of work. There, and using the terms in the Becker (1963) sense, the organisational cultural vehicle of work-related language allocates organisation members into 'in-group' or 'out-group' status. In this line of analysis it remains open to dispute whether there are genuine feelings about the absence of 'blame' in the organisation, or not. What is apparent is that several organisation members are very clear about the presence of some managers who engage in blaming activities in their parts of the organisation.

3.01   'We don't witch-hunt anymore, our remaining workforce needs supporting to deliver what is required of them.'

3.02   'Complaints are passed down to the appropriate level to deal with them.'

3.03   'If we lash up in this office my line manager is supportive and I fall into line behind that view with my staff. His manager is different and doesn't understand what we do here...'

3.04   'They [that is, my organisational seniors] kick butt!'

3.05   'We are a "no-blame" culture.'

3.06   'We are immediately blamed.

3.07   'We tried to find out why the problem has happened so we can prevent it again.'

3.08   'My manager supports me whether he agrees with me or not; I've worked for him for 20 years. Sometimes we are insensitive. For example, we sent standard form letters and date them the same day as the complaint [this suggests to the customer that their complaint hasn't been investigated. I regret it when this happens.'

3.09   'We don't scapegoat now but acknowledge when training is needed.'

3.010   'We try to own our own problems and not pass them to more senior managers.'

3.011 'My manager responds quickly if our Standards of Service rate drops.'

3.012 'I generally think they don't notice and are slow to react.'

3.013 'I never ball out my people in public [but] people get told when they've made a mistake...'

3.014 'A major wrong rarely leads to an admission from senior management that they chose the wrong course of action.'

3.015 'Senior managers act promptly, usually.'

3.016 'I feel we now say "let's get together and put it right" with a slight admonishment. People do not like to accept individual blame so they cover up. We should be more open. We are trying to change to a "blame free" culture.'

3.017 'We are now closer to a "blame free" culture; most people try pretty hard; new circulars or lack of training can make problems for us.'

3.018 'One boss jumps to a conclusion even before he's asked the question and will go for a half day inquest and dissection. Another boss trusted us, I remember when he came he was a typhoon of fresh air.'

Comments which are contained in the introduction to the replies to this question point to the possibility that organisational members may not to be absolutely frank in their discussion of organisational failure. In the conversations with District General Managers (and their equivalently graded colleagues at Regional Headquarters and Regional Computer Centre) only one manager said anything at all on this matter. Here, there was a clear focus on what could be learnt from mistakes and errors by organisational members and the development of a thesis which challenged the very *raison d'être* of the then existing way of structuring the organisation, both within the Region and nationally.

In both organisations, then, there is ambivalence as to whether day-to-day organisational and social processes effectively manage situations 'when things go wrong'.

Map Three, Question Three, Analytical Discussion Three

This question was designed to be loose so that it could interpreted as widely as possible to elicit data that was as interesting and varied as possible. Given the precise subject matter of this question it is not a surprise that there were many critical responses here. Overall, the map records twenty four red (i.e. critical) entries; fourteen blue (i.e. supportive) entries and only one green (i.e. neutral) entry. Some of the critical responses were taciturn: for example, 'They kick butt!' (3.04). Other responses were ironic: 'When things go wrong we seem to praise people!' More irony: 'Major [problems] are ignored but minor ones are actioned quickly.' Other responses were straightforwardly critical. These included: 'Senior managers gave us a poor system because they didn't listen to us, they won't accept their mistakes.' Perhaps it was even more surprising to record so many loyal comments when the question was perceived by so many respondents to seek to attempt to locate 'dirt'. These included: 'We now ask, why the problem? Not, who caused it?' (based on 3.12). Other seemingly supportive comments included: 'We are a 'no-blame' culture' (3.05) and also 'My manager supports me whether he agrees with me or not' (3.08). This last response came from a relatively junior organisational member and so refers very much to local management rather than senior strategists at some distance from that particular place of work. Perhaps most interesting here is the number of supportive remarks when such support, based upon an interpretation of the whole of the evidence supplied, may be indicative of a wider organisation-supporting set of attitudes. This line of analysis may be sound because such responses required those respondents independently to frame oppositional replies in respect of the line of address of the question.

4.   When things go right in your organisation, what happens?

The logic of the inclusion of this question is in clear sympathy with that of the question that precedes it. It is also suggested that this question had the potential to repair any suspicion that may have been in the process of developing in the perceptual scheme of the respondent of any 'unfairness' in the intentions of the researcher or the schedule. It may be seen, then, as a 'balancing' question - but it is argued here that the question has value in its own right, both as a set of insights into organisational life and insights into the variety of ways that organisational procedures may be implemented.

In **BT** again, responses are considered hierarchically, and many of the responses seem to strike at the ritualism that surrounds what seem highly self-conscious attempts at praising effective work from organisational members. A significant number of the responses were certainly expressed in a self-conscious way; that is to say, they were accompanied by embarrassed looks and loss of eye contact as well as other behavioural indicators of such self-consciousness over praise. It is, of course acknowledged that such behaviour may be just as likely to emanate from the set 'Person domiciled in English culture' as from the set 'BT employee.' Along with the ritualism in some cases, is a relatively heavy sense of irony - such that it suggested that thanks for good work are never to be expected in the organisation, by those who expressed themselves in that manner. The remarks of the more junior managers are reviewed first:

4.1   'Anyone can nominate the "employee of the month" [in this zone]. High achievement may lead to an award...a Marks and Spencer's voucher...little engraved plaques...there is more recognition now than in the past...'

4.2   'I say thank you to my team but on the occasions when I'm thanked I often don't deserve it.'

4.3   'What on earth is the point of a letter of thanks from an Area Zone Board Chairman that doesn't have a genuine signature?'

4.4   'Praise wasn't allowed in our civil service days and still today many of us think 'praisees' (the people who are being praised) shouldn't really be congratulated.'

4.5   'When there's a lot of verbal acknowledgement around it becomes devalued. Sometimes such acknowledgements don't even seem to be sincere. What aspiring young managers want is promotion and pay rises.'

4.6   'If a T.O. [Technical Officer] gets a praise letter, I pass it up.'

4.7   'My team got thirty plus [new] customers in one week and this was record-breaking... I put the whole team in [for consideration for an award...] and they all got capital bonds to spend... When people get a thank you letter this is good, but it can cause a problem if people get left out. We never used to say thank you but we're getting better at it now. We can now [even] nominate our own people...and it used to [have to] be done by another [more senior person] at a distance.'

4.8   'We don't necessarily know... Recognition is occasional and surprising...a note added to something [else such as a document] is typical.'

4.9   [When things go right] we praise! At a recent management conference [for managers around about my grade] there was a presentation of Reward and Recognition [awards. This was] good because it was a visible thing. Managers don't say thanks to their teams...but I do... It [i.e. praising] seems more like a thing to do with blue-collar people...'

4.10   'There are two ways of being appreciated...oral from a tier two manager or written from a tier three manager - with a photo-copied signature.'

The middle status group of managers responded as follows:

4.11   'When we are 'overstroked' I believe our people accept this: our director is good at saying 'well done' and taking time with people; our culture of recognition is strong.'

4.12   'A formal mechanism [of rewarding people...perhaps weeks after the event that gave rise to it] isn't as effective as praise at the time [that a particular task is completed.]...we tend to look for things that didn't go perfectly rather that [praising people for what they have done].'

4.13 'Reward and Recognition...could be devalued by the average performance being recognised...and this would be wrong.'

4.14 'My manager is quick to praise.'

4.15 'I support the pride-raising stuff - what we want is for BT people to be proud of saying they work here, even though we may shortly ask them to accept redundancy.'

4.16 'Our [thank you] letters [from our senior managers] often don't have proper signatures on them. What's their point?'

Interestingly, there was little sense of the strategic value in giving praise to organisation members, from the perspectives of the following most senior managers. There was no focus on praise as a motivator of people in a time of inability/unwillingness to reward through salary rises. These senior managers said:

4.17 'Recognition and Quality awards are perhaps uncoordinated and there are too many of them. Our praising is too bureaucratised: we are bloody good at emergencies...the Bishopsgate bomb, the 1987 hurricane...and senior managers recognise this - but they overlook our reports of everyday good work from our people...'

4.18 'We try to celebrate success. 'Recognition of good work has been very poor...'

Within **British Gas (Eastern)**, responses are also grouped in a hierarchical way, starting with the more junior managers' replies. The first respondent [as well as a number of others] points to a perceived shortage of confidence in the emotional baggage belonging to most organisation members known to her. This may be significant in terms of the way that this organisation can best manage processes of internal change and organisational renewal.

4.01 'In the past, a whole section got recognition. Now, we need more one-to-one personal recognition.'

4.02   'Some managers appear to take the credit themselves.'

4.03   'When we've done well with SoS [Standards of Service] I usually leap up and down and yell "We've done it kids!"'

4.04   'The letter of praise gets seen by a couple of top managers and then the service engineer gets a few bob - twenty pounds - at a team meeting.'

4.05   'When a customer thanks us for being professional when they panic when they get their bills...I like this.'

4.06   '[When things go right]...we never hear anything about it! We don't praise enough...we're not quick enough to praise...'

4.07   '[When things go right]...nothing happens...at either normal right or spectacular levels of right!'

4.08   '[My immediate] manager responds quickly here...[her] notes, sweets, cakes go a long way...'

4.09   'We're driven today by political forces. Managers broadcast up their successes when they are big. People emphasise the positive to try to secure their future with the company... Things may be a little ritualised regarding praise and recognition.'

4.010   '[When things go right]...nothing!'

4.011   'They praise you for ace work and thank you for normal work.'

4.012   'Locally [in the Districts] they praise quickly but at senior Regional level and at the national centre nothing in the way of praise comes out from them...'

4.013   'There is not much encouragement...I'd like someone to debrief me when I come back...'

4.014　'We communicate well on paper, but not verbally, especially with the grass roots...'

4.015　'Excellent work is acknowledged by a letter from the District General Manager, and Marks and Spencer's vouchers - and people value these.'

4.016　'Managers should sandwich a telling-off in between two praising comments.'

As with BT, the more senior managers commented in a relatively non-strategic manner, and indeed this may be a significant feature of the then-existing set of management perceptions and processes. The issue is explored in the next chapter of this study.

4.017　'We are trying to get away from our old operating methods - we now write letters of thanks but I now feel sceptical.'

4.018　'We work quietly without blowing our own trumpet.'

4.019　'[When things go right]...we give verbal thanks, and make customer care recommendations.'

4.020　'We're better at praising people now and saying thank you - does it come from the right level though?'

4.021　'My Director hasn't got a report about it [how and when to praise people] yet.'

The sense of irony in the last reported remark is sustained by the absence of any thinking shared by the most senior people about the strategic benefits of non-pecuniary rewards. None of them addressed this theme. It seems then that a valid cultural insight may be that the non-pecuniary aspect of organisational life is not valued. In functionalist terms, this might be plotted nearer to the 'feminine' end of the Hofstede (1984) 'masculinity/femininity' continuum in that part of that organisation. It may also be equally possible that there was no significance at all attached to that remark.

Map Four, Question Four, Analytical Discussion Four

This question was designed to be 'the balancing question' in respect of its predecessor, although each respondent could not possibly have deduced that until each person heard this question. The map records twenty red (i.e. critical) entries; thirteen blue (i.e. supportive) entries and three green (i.e. neutral) entries. The question was designed to be one where respondents could almost celebrate their loyalty towards, and their membership of, the organisation that had employed them in many cases for a number of decades. Yet, over half the responses were critical. Interestingly perhaps, even key comments included: 'we don't know [what happens when things go right] ... nothing happens ...' (4.07). 'Our [thank you] letters [from our senior managers] often don't have proper signatures on them, what's their point?' (4.17, also see 4.10 and 4.3). 'Some managers appear to take the credit themselves [rather than say thanks to their people]' (4.02). The supportive comments included one manager who remarked: 'When we've done well ... I usually leap up and down and yell "we've done it, kids!"' (4.03). Other comments included 'If a Technical Officer gets a letter of praise [from a member of the public], I pass it up' (4.6). Other supportive responses had a certain poignancy: 'I support the pride raising stuff ... even though we may shortly ask them to accept redundancy!' (4.15). In response to this question, some 'neutral' replies each had a lesson for senior managers rather than outright praise or criticism. Included was: 'Managers should sandwich a telling off in between two praising comments' (4.016). The overall impact of these responses seems very clear indeed; surprise at the extent of unhappiness expressed when respondents had a chance to enjoy their organisational memberships.

5.   **Who are the really influential opinion formers who work around you and who are senior to you in the organisation?**

The *raison d'être* of the question is found in Schein (1985) but not exclusively so. Hofstede (1984) and a number of other authorities point to the importance of 'organisational heroes' in the formation, development and maintenance of each organisation's culture. So, the question composites the Peters and Waterman (1982) focus on the proposition that 'strong cultures' have effective 'hands-on' leaders with Schein's view of the importance of charismatic figures in an organisation.

In **BT**, responses are listed with the most junior managers' comments first:

5.1 '[Really influential opinion formers for me are...gleaned] very much from a working day's insights - so, the customers tell us [all about how we're doing with them...] ...also colleagues' insights too...Management have little impact. "BT Toady" is appropriately named...and I think I'm typical for my grade here.'

5.2 '[Really influential opinion formers for me]...are from a long list - management information and discussion, my pay group, my team, and my mentor in the BT Management Programme of which I'm part...'

5.3 '[Really influential opinion formers for me are]...my colleagues and senior management ideas expressed through *BT Today*. They consulted us over the introduction of WorkManager [a software package which overturned existing work practices in the allocation of manual jobs from managers to the service engineers by individualising and rationalising the allocation of tasks]. We saved heartache - a bit - by it [the consultation]. The feedback from the people [involved] since the introduction of WorkManager has been that...I don't see people anymore' and 'The camaraderie has gone'... As jobs are allocated [now] one at a time, T.O.s [Technical Officers] must ask for work, and they don't know what's coming so they feel a loss of control and helplessness at being machine-guided...'

5.4 'External [influencers] include legislation which help us to develop policy for the company...and social influences too. For example, in respect of smoking and drinking on company premises bans did not come from Industrial Tribunals...I think that *BT Today* is too chatty for me and I favour the press cuttings file - but now cash prevents [managers on my grade] from seeing them now...'

5.5 'My sources include my Tier Four because I am a Chartership student and he is my mentor... As a graduate in the Zone -

there are four or five of us - we get pigeon-holed. My opinion-formers are the people that I trust - and there are fewer of them now...'

5.6   '...There are three or four more verbal people...they have experience and personality...'

5.7   '[Really influential opinion formers for me are...] my line manager and other people outside my team...'

5.8   '[Really influential opinion formers for me are...] my peers...'

5.9   '[Really influential opinion formers for me are...] my boss and his boss - just them...'

5.10   'Articulate and able people in the teams are the opinion-formers [during Team Briefs]. Other people separate their views from 'the company line' which they peddle only in company time...'

5.11   'When senior managers have it in mind to start a new initiative - for example the procedural changes caused by Network deterioration leading to new types of covers and joints for shrouds - they go to a few people first. These are the opinion formers in the business...'

5.12   '[Really influential opinion formers for me are...] my boss [who is a general manager] and other general managers...along with my mentor [a Director] and [the magazine called] *The Manager*.'

5.13   'I'm alarmed at the people who appear to be the opinion formers in the business today. There are not so many people on the main board who have a technical training background...'

5.14   '[Really influential opinion formers for me are...] my boss. He's a really good communicator and we chat about business issues. I respect his opinions - he's very intelligent... This [influence] is stronger than anything I've read. My customers

- the line managers - also influence me [but] they do sing different songs [dependent upon whether] they are from...[names department] or...[names department].'

5.15   '[Really influential opinion formers for me are...] my boss, the top influence, colleagues, customers, the [more intelligent parts of the] press, my professional body and the Change Management Group of specialists within it.'

5.16   '[Really influential opinion formers for me are...] in three groups. The most important influencers are press cuttings, colleagues/peers and senior people in my department [names department]. The second group of people are the service deliverers themselves in my department, and my circle of family and friends. Least important is company originated material from management, [such as] management information.'

5.17   'Customers influence me, managers have little impact.'

The highest echelons of managers observed in answer to this question:

5.18   '[Really influential opinion formers for me are...] the General Managers - they control huge numbers of people and are very influential - because they mix with all the layers [of people in the organisational hierarchy].'

5.19   'Starting at the centre I would say my last boss - he is charismatic, a chaos-maker and a mad bugger. Next my Zone Board, then the employees themselves [I try to get to their Team Briefings, Focus Groups and Care Visits]. Fourthly, my Personal Contract Group peers are significant.'

5.20   'One difficulty for us is to separate the industry from the people in it; we have no industry-wide body such as the Society of Motor Manufacturers and Traders [in the automotive industry]. My views and knowledge come from within BT because that's where most of it is...I [do] read the press cuttings, *The Economist* and other things...'

Within **British Gas (Eastern)**, responses are offered first from the more junior managers:

5.01   'As [also] a [names union] shop steward, trade union sources help straighten the bias in management views.'

5.02   'The trades union branch [locally] and at national level through the Gas Committee and the District Gas Committee. The general workforce isn't organised to change easily - our culture blocks us.'

5.03   'My sources are a mix - current affairs stuff from the management magazines, market pressures and/or regulatory pressures; I like to look for the links between them.'

5.04   '...my friends, I understand the whingers, but they won't - and can't - make suggestions for improvements. My boss's enthusiasm rubs off on me, but usually the pessimists form opinion up here - we're a long way from Regional Headquarters.'

5.05   'Initially, media comment and Team Brief comments, plus informal contacts with peers and seniors. There's quite a lot of communication...everyone's kept informed...even if it's slow in coming...'

5.06   'My major influence is my departmental head, [names head]; he's my role model.'

5.07   'My team influence my views. We communicate well for example during Team Brief - we're always talking...'

5.08   'The management team here [on the district] inform me, also, walking about helps, plus there is union involvement in the nuts and bolts of other departments - their strengths and weaknesses...'

5.09   'My Christianity informs my views [at work].'

5.010   'The national press [such as] *The Financial Times* and *The Times*. We [i.e. peers] all share articles as they come...'

5.011   '[There are none...]. Over the years too much knowledge and experience has been lost...there's too much secondment to other jobs.'

5.012   'I ignore the press. The union and management mail us.'

5.013   '...My line manager and a recent work scheduling officer [on this district]. He was enthusiastic and young...and was my mentor...'

Middle managers expressed these views:

5.014   '[Really influential opinion-formers for me] are a mix: current affairs organs for [an understanding of] business and market pressures and/or regulatory pressures to see the links. [In my position I don't always know whether to be truthful: should I say that twenty people are to go, or that I don't know what's going to happen?].'

5.015   'The Board...'

5.016   'My DGM brings us back the news and fires us all up.'

5.017   '[Really influential opinion-formers for me] are magazines, press summaries, newspapers and my boss and other bosses and other staff, too. I sit out in the open office and join in on the banter so they can see I'm in on the team.'

Map Five, Question Five, Analytical Discussion Five

This question, aimed at directing responses towards leaders, had made an impact upon the respondent to the extent that the respondent's own thinking had been influenced. It sought to address some of the most positive achievements of senior managers in their roles as 'cheerleaders and coaches' (Peters and Waterman, 1982). It would have been a great surprise to have recorded a majority of views that were critical of senior managers in response to this order of question and this was borne out by the summary data of responses, as follows. Supportive comments included: '... my last boss - he is charismatic, a chaos-maker, and a mad bugger' (5.19), 'The District General Manager brings us back the news and fires us all up' (5.016), 'My boss and his boss, just them' (5.9). Critical responses included: 'Customers influence me, managers have little impact' (5.17) and 'Trades union sources help straighten the bias in management views' (5.01). The last comment seemed to rest on a significant edifice of attitudes and opinion which was inimical to management interest. Overall, it is judged as significant that over one third of the responses were critical ones, given the relatively high degree of tacit management support that could be said to be vested in the framing of this question.

6.   **Looking at the people who work around you, who would you identify as likely to be promoted at some future stage; what would be the promotable characteristics?**

In **BT**, these are responses from the most junior managers:

6.1   '[They would need to be] flexible and able to work well under pressure; [They would need to be]...knowledgeable about BT and be able to manage customer criticisms without taking it personally...'

6.2   '[They would need to be] motivated, doers, and respecters of their colleagues; successful team-builders who can maintain loyalty.'

6.3   'In reality, people are stifled by downsizing and so want to stay in their present job [where they are known by their boss and so where they feel safe...]'

6.4   '[They would need to show]...a grasp of the area they were in: technical skills, managerial skills and etcetera. The responsibilities of the new post will involve personal and leadership skills. Balancing 'task' and 'process' [such people will] be able to organise, prioritise and be realistic. They will be good networkers...professional qualifications are not always necessary to do a job...'

6.5 '[They would need to be] team players, with good interpersonal skills and willingness to act as a substitute and use the management tools provided... They will be professional e.g. they'll type not write and long hours will be looked for; 8.00 a.m. to 6.00 p.m.'

6.6 'They should look for awareness of the whole business, not just their patch. They should be energetic and capable and not a 9.00 to 5.00 person. [They will need] a degree of technical knowledge and product knowledge, formal education is quite important, too, so you can talk to people at their level...'

6.7 'There's so little promotion around today that I can't answer the question. It's not open, but sponsored through an "old boys" network.'

6.8 'Senior managers identify potential and encourage it by allowing them to substitute for us when we're away. Motivation is maintained with great difficulty given the ring fencing [of promoted posts] that exists.'

6.9 'They will need to accept and be comfortable with change and also be responsible for their own development as well as for others.'

The middle management band respondents added:

6.10 'High professionalism, leading to kept promises and someone who can anticipate customer needs; people who really do understand that "quality is a journey".'

6.11 'Such people have good interpersonal skills and are really good at inspiring respect at all levels; they are competent in their own area of expertise and also able to accept new challenges.'

6.12   'There is very little promotion anyway.'

6.13   '[They would need to be] really good at inspiring respect at all levels through high interpersonal skills.'

6.14   'It has been refreshing and helpful to have very senior managers imported into the organisation from outside.'

6.15   '[They would need to] have the right attitudes: people who will challenge the *status quo* objectively for example "Could we do that this way/better?" '

The most senior managers responded as follows:

6.16   'Key characteristics are in the area of creativity and innovation: making things happen. [This is the task of senior managers.]'

6.17   ' "If I don't agree with the policy I won't do it" used to be a part of our culture.'

6.18   'The key things are a natural desire to promote harmony among direct reports - harnessing the energies of those with opposing views. Promotable people need charismatic qualities of leadership.'

Within **British Gas (Eastern)**, the most junior group of managers commented:

6.01   '[They will need to be] capable of dealing with people, people who could benefit from training because they had potential.'

6.02   '[They will need to be] people oriented not task oriented, and good on paper [i.e. literate].'

6.03 '[They will need to be] someone not frightened to take responsibility and who has potential for further promotion.'

6.04 '[They will need to have] good product knowledge, be good communicators, show the potential for leadership skills [to be developed], and show good motivation.'

6.05 '[They will need to be] flexible - not a 9.00 a.m. to 5.00 p.m. person. They've got to stay 'til 7.00 p.m. or be in at 7.30 a.m. as needed. They will be a change-embracer. There is a place for product knowledge and technical expertise and experience, as well as academic qualifications.'

6.06 'Before the "old pals" were promoted, now, it is achievers of targets with drive and enthusiasm. [People who will] accept challenges, be flexible, and be a self-seller.'

6.07 'People will need to be good communicators. That is interactors with their colleagues. They won't need great technical knowledge and experience.

6.08 '[They will need to be people with] positive attitudes, a doer and customer focussed. But [a promotable person] also considers staff too. They are a team leader and team member.'

6.09 'Age is one characteristic, they will be younger people with academic qualifications and probably the ability to think sympathetically in the current culture of the business orientation. The present culture protects the weaker parts of the business.'

6.010 '[They are people who show a] willingness to learn, further education, etc. They are presently smiling and working hard and are technically competent.'

6.011 '[They will be people who are] not necessarily dedicated company people but they will show enthusiasm, open-mindedness, job related qualifications and experience [this view might be a little out of date now].'

6.012   'People who get promoted are not necessarily ones who know their job fully. It's who you know and not what you know. It should be people with people skills and who are clever.'

6.013   'I don't know, they see different things in people. At one time in Marketing they got graduates who obviously had high qualifications but who had little experience...'

6.014   'Education background [is important]...HNC...good people skills...flexibility, adaptability for different posts in your level - total commitment.'

6.015   '...graduates are respected, as with managers who have proven track records...'

6.016   '...good workers - they know the system, they work hard, they help others - by doing their work if they are slack. [They are] ambitious people who have "supervisory qualities" and who speak fearlessly...'

6.017   '...but people want to stay safe in their present job [rather than risk a new boss...]'

The middle status group of middle managers said:

6.018   'Business awareness, problem spotting and solving, people management skills and the ability to treat others with respect; these I'd reward with promotion *in today's market* [appeared to refer to changed values]. They would understand the customers' needs and know enough about me to decide quickly whether or not they could develop a rapport with me.'

6.019   'They'd need drive and hard work, and be "hard men" [*sic*].'

6.020   '[People who get promoted are] seen as being good at their pre-promoted job; they reflect the same - the culture - of their interviewer, and therefore their new boss.'

Map Six, Question Six, Analytical Discussion Six

This question was designed to open up feelings and attitudes and indeed values that may have indicated the extent to which the respondent was aware of the 'new agenda' for promotion in his/her organisation. Of course, this 'new agenda' emphasising for example, selling skills in front of engineering skills, could be said to be a part of the new organisational constructs erected by those senior managers who wanted culture change as a 'top down' activity. Overwhelmingly the responses seemed to understand the agenda and spoke supportively of it. There were relatively few critical responses. This seems to indicate that the new agenda is understood, but it retains a wistful quality of regret that the 'old days' have receded into the past and that less desirable personal qualities have now become more prominent in those organisation members who are deemed likely to succeed in the immediate future. The ability to 'work long hours' and to 'work hard for nearly 100% of the time' is also indicative of such wistfulness, in the wider contexts of both all the responses and then the set of responses emanating from each individual respondent. Critical comments seemed to be thoughts which were forthright in their condemnation: '[the] little promotion around today [is] 'sponsored through an "old boys" network' (6.7, see also 6.8), '... people want to stay safe in their present job [rather than risk a new boss arising from a promotion who may think less well of them, then expose them for a redundancy]' (6.017).

7. **Could you say anything about the day-to-day working relationships between the people you regard as promotable and their colleagues?**

Across both organisations, a number of respondents felt a degree of difficulty in answering this question; it suggests a line of analysis that seemed to have been previously unexplored with several respondents - as is evident from their replies. Those of the most junior **BT** managers are recorded first:

7.1   '[The relation between the two groups are]...hit and miss. With six or seven in a team [of customer service clerks] you see very quickly who is able; the teams change managers

[here] quite regularly...the leadership qualities are the something extra that I look for...'

7.2   'Be leaderless and do-it-yourself if you want to get promoted...[That is my experience...].'

7.3   'Keeping people motivated in an age of retrenchment [is difficult].'

7.4   'The non-promotables may well be the ones who feel more threatened of being worn down by the Release Scheme...'

7.5   '[Regarding] the promotable group - there's a development workshop on and one of my Technical Officers is very good but he tells everyone he's very good and this winds up people and he doesn't realise this...'

7.6   'Mentoring would help, but it's not followed: we're all too busy but perhaps we all should do this. Trial and error decision-making is more normal. Networking takes time! You need to know who to ask, and that's difficult when we continuously reorganise...'

7.7   'Enthusiasm does rub off if you put people together. I mix my mini-teams; skill mixes are required. For example, a fifty-seven year old "redeployee" is very enthusiastic and this influences younger workers - they ask [to work] with him.'

7.8   'Some people are negative and they influence colleagues, they're in the wrong job.'

Middle band managers commented:

7.9   '[The people who are promotable] act as sparks and play critical roles, as I see it. But across the business as a whole they are mavericks.'

7.10   '[The working relationships] depend upon the relative size of each group, broadly speaking, critical mass is a key and so we are dependent on numbers.'

The most senior managers in the organisation said:

7.11   '[The people who are promotable] are indistinguishable from their ordinary peers. We use groups of people as "heroes" - sales teams [who produce extra-ordinarily good sales figures] and boffins [who invent or streamline technology that we need to use].'

7.12   'We have these two breeds of managers; those with the baggage of the Civil Service past and those who believe that if they treat their customers well and work hard they will get their promotion. However, those projects which will attract acclaim and fame will have the former type of manager appointed to lead it, while the latter sort of manager gets the job of trying, for example, to shift the work patterns of manual grades without being able to offer premium pay rates for such flexible working. It's a shit.'

In **British Gas (Eastern)**, there were very few responses reported:

7.01   'After my promotion, I had no training and I was shortly on my own! But by being nice to the clerks on the bureau in my first week we were top district office and beat the [names district] District even though they had new telephones [and so should reasonably have been expected to be most productive with the new resource].'

There were thirty-four of the junior managers in the sample who made no response to this question at all. Ignorance of this whole issue was consistently reported. One middle manager observed:

7.02   'People are supported in their new role by their previous experience in the post before their new position was

> confirmed. We don't have a formalised mentor system; informal can also mean a multi-mentor system [as well as a system where no mentor is in place].'

None of the District General Manager grade (or equivalent) staff addressed this matter.

Map Seven, Question Seven, Analytical Discussion Seven

The purpose of raising this issue was to seek information about the quality of working relationships observed between the two identified constituencies, and more responses wanted to shed light on the matter in a neutral way than either chose to support or criticise senior management in respect of this question. Perhaps the most striking response was that of silence on the matter altogether. This may be best explained by the relative absence of promotion opportunities in each of the two organisations for some considerable period of time both before and after the questions were asked. The result seemed to be a reluctance to treat an issue that seemed therefore to have become a hypothetical one beyond the working lives of most of the respondents. Response 7.12 is particularly heartfelt in tone. 'Mentoring would help, but it's not followed' (7.6). Amongst the supportive comments was: 'Enthusiasm does rub off if you put people together' (7.7). Overall here, there was only a modest response to this question, possibly for the reason identified above.

It is difficult accurately to interpret the fact that none of the District General Manager grade of British Gas respondents chose to respond to this interview head. Speculation, of course, may range across a number of possibilities. These include the lack of a simple understanding of the meaning of the question in the overall context of the research instrument. Also possible is that there was a continuum here. At one end was a concerted concealment, conspiracy and suppression of insight and at the other end was a relatively simple lack of comprehension concerning the importance of the impact of the question area on the organisational lives of their people.

8.   How are people chosen for promotion?

This third question surrounding promotion was designed to provide a further opportunity for respondents to reflect on these matters and to help illuminate the attitude picture within each organisation at a time when, as has already been suggested, each organisation actually had very little promotion to offer its respective people. This applied whether the people were in managerial grades or not.

In **BT**, the most junior managers are reported first in response to this question. Whilst the level of awareness of the procedures appeared both uniform and relatively high, there was rather little in the responses that suggested a thorough going and robust insight into the more subtle layers of selection for promotion, amongst the more junior managers. They said:

8.1   '[People are chosen for promotion]…by open advertisement.'

8.2   '…annual appraisement is the official route.'

8.3   '[This is] changing dramatically … [What the person has done in the] last two years in the job is less important and the "right person for the job" is the criterion now - to the detriment of product knowledge.'

8.4   'Boards work on the last appraisement. These ask about promotion and whether the person is interested. The only people that I know that have been promoted are [those indicated on the appraisement form to be] "qualified for promotion".'

Middle managers responded as follows:

8.5   'We now have new procedures for promoting our people and I was involved in developing them. We aim to produce "Team Managers". We analyse each job and produce behavioural norms and frequencies of tasks. We emphasises clear communication skills, leadership skills and motivation skills.'

8.6   '[People are chosen for promotion on the basis of] appraisement backed up by The Performance Measurement

System. This examines his [*sic*] academic qualifications, sick record, and professional experience inside the company. In the interview, can he [*sic*] solve the problems? Has he [*sic*] the brain and heart to carry out his [*sic*] solution?'

8.7   '...advertisement, interview board, [maybe] assessment centre...now it's informal chats after being "noticed", [now that we are] bureaucratised into rapidity and responsiveness...'

The most senior managers said:

8.8   '...appraisement marks, job adverts and boards [all] are the last vestiges of [our decades in the] Civil Service. And we do it still! We are slow and ponderous.'

It seems that the senior managers in BT are the least sanguine about the efficacy of the then existing set of processes for choosing managers for promotion, and their most junior colleagues appear to show what, in contrast, looks like rather touching faith in the same processes and procedures

In **British Gas (Eastern)**, the responses of the most junior managers are reported first, and in contrast with their opposite numbers in BT, these British Gas junior managers appear to operate with a more subtle understanding of promotion process and procedure:

8.01   'The informal side is very important.'

8.02   '[People are chosen] mainly on their track record, that is, what we know about them. Have they moved the business on?'

8.03   'We've tried to formalise panels; Personnel is represented and [names colleague] and I are the rest of our panel.'

8.04   '[Here we promote through interview, and] I decide on the criteria beforehand and devise questions based on them and grade the answers.'

8.05 'Both my personal experiences [of promotion] were based on my work experience.'

8.06 'We use a systematic approach - but we don't always follow what the numbers tell us...'

8.07 '[I don't think that we do this as well as we could, because] Operations Managers appoint people - but Service Officers are their bosses...so they don't get invited on to the selection procedures!'

8.08 'I've promoted people from what I know of them. I've promoted someone from general clerk to progress clerk...'

It is also recognised that not all of the junior management group sampled operated in the sophisticated manner suggested above Paragraph 8.01. Middle managers said:

8.09 'The personnel forms [allow us to] give a score [to each candidate's application]. They can be loaded in favour of a charismatic personality, but we won't [do that]. I've never been on a panel which didn't appoint the top scorer...'

8.010 'District offices are parochial and lenient, head office is systematic and objective [in selecting people for promotion].'

8.011 'I use a systematic approach; but I also go by "feeling". Have they got the right personality for the job?'

8.012 'In the past [when we sought to promote people] we were task- oriented, based on whether they could do the job well. It was a little hit and miss. Now, the potential for future promotion is a criterion and [so] it's a more systematic.'

8.013 [From what I know of the] Personnel Department, it tried to, and achieved, systematic and objective processes. It often tried to hold them [i.e. operational managers] back from their old prejudices...'

8.014   'I ask juniors to shadow seniors, to see how they do.'

It will now be apparent that these middle managers are similarly sophisticated vis-à-vis their more junior colleagues.

Map Eight, Question Eight, Analytical Discussion Eight

The purpose of this question was to attempt to seek factual information after two preceding questions that sought opinion. The matter itself also, of course, has substantive importance as it seemed to be significant enough quickly to impact upon members' understandings of culture and change within their organisations. Applying the three styles to the responses given was a particularly difficult task here. Responses included: 'We've tried to formalise panels [and agree questions beforehand]' (8.03). This 'neutral' fact-giving response is interesting because it shares a fact about more 'professional' selection procedures and leaves the organisational outsider wondering about parallel procedures before this arrangement was instituted. One senior manager observed: '[People are chosen for promotion by] Appraisement [which] is the official route' (see also 8.2). 'I ask juniors to shadow seniors to see how they do' (8.014). This is also interesting insofar as it seems to imply that there may also be unofficial routes, and that there is now a reliance upon job performance to select members capable of achieving in promoted posts. Other comments included: 'District offices are parochial and lenient, head office is systematic and objective [in selecting people for promotion]' (8.010). 'It keeps on changing, now the system is bent to get the person we want' (based on 8.3). Overall, the general tenor of the responses was information giving to an outsider who seemed interested in company policy on the matter. In terms of criticism, it was subdued in this respect, and so was wholehearted praise for presently existing promotion procedures, too.

9.   **When a new job arises, what criteria do selectors use to make new appointments if they want to attract new people into the organisation?**

The *motif* of conscious organisation change continues as promotion issues are rested in favour of a consideration of the issues around hiring new people into the organisation.

In **BT**, some of these junior managers appear to show an awareness of the unwritten rules which can inform interview agenda. It may be that they were more comfortable in addressing themes when the head of conversation was about how new members ('Outsiders' in the classic Becker [1963] sense) are recruited. Earlier responses to questions surrounding entirely intra-organisational processes that may be interpreted as guardedness may be better understood in this light.

9.1   '[We use past work experience, academic qualifications and our overall judgement of each candidate's ability to fit in with the existing arrangements]...it's a covert system though...'

9.2   '...ability to fit in with the management...'

9.3   'I've seen job descriptions altered to limit the field [of potential applications]. Who you know and where you are [are also important considerations].'

9.4   'I have no [direct] experience here...but I was hired by a psychometric test and interview by the Personnel Department...'

9.5   '...academic qualifications [are important] - for example graduates aren't available inside the company - so we'd hire in.'

Some of the middle managers used this question as an opportunity to rail against what they appeared to see as injustice in the way that the organisation had reinvented itself/been reinvented after its statutory change of ownership. They said:

9.6   'One third of our recently hired [names BT manual role] are agency people [i.e. temporary workers]. They aren't even employed by BT. More recently we have had an increase in tension between BT people and agency people; in some centres there's a definite divide; they share canteens but [have a number of conditions of service which are not shared.] Also, agency people come and go and have different disciplinary procedures.'

9.7   '[I would want to look at each candidate's] knowledge and experience from the past in general, then their knowledge and experience in technical specialisms...[considering] the persons themselves [is important, as is the question:] can they manage new circumstances and work flexibly?'

The most senior managers said:

9.8   'We hold a Board to find the right skills but I like to get a man [*sic*] with the right attitudes and then we'll teach him [*sic*] the business...'

In **British Gas (Eastern)**, the most junior managers' comments are as follows:

9.01   'If I was appointing a clerk to have supervisory responsibilities, I'd look for a supervisory qualification and good experience. If I needed a "redeployable" [that is, a person employed in the organisation and seeking a post, because their present post had disappeared, typically through reorganisation] I'd look for a happy personality on the day, but not be prepared to meet someone [in the context of an interview] until I'd had a reference from their present boss...[I'd treat other internal applicants differently, because you have to treat carefully these redeployables.]'

9.02   'We used to look for qualifications, but now it's ability to do the job.'

9.03 'I've tried to appoint people with adaptability and flexibility and appropriate skills.'

9.04 'Do we ever get the right person given that the interview is so poor an instrument? Fifty per cent of the candidates I interviewed last could hardly answer our questions at all. I try to look for a good track record, reliability, independence and a good degree of self-motivation.'

9.05 'We use very systematic procedures in short-listing...if they are nervous at interview then we reason that they will also be nervous in [any legal proceedings for which we are the responsible officials in prosecuting the cause of the company.]'

9.06 'We use systematic criteria: qualifications and experience are important...[and] appearance...[and] slotting in comfortably.'

9.07 '[When interviewing candidates for appointment it is] making them talk, to see what they can offer and what responsibilities they've had [that I think is important].'

9.08 'We appointed twelve clerks recently, after a highly scientific programme led by [names colleague] who has a Grad IPM qualification.'

9.09 'When appointing school-leavers, their school record...have they researched the job?'

9.010 'We sometimes get very few male applicants for some jobs [and we like] to get a spread of age and sex in a [large general clerical] office. It's usually at clerk level where outsiders start [when they first join the company].'

The middle managers said:

9.011 'I go by a mix of qualifications and experience...and a set of appropriate attitudes. This makes for a system that seems covert to some of our people.'

9.012   'They must know the company and know what their skills are...I look for their work experience and academic qualifications...'

It will be noted that a number of the respondents at both junior and middle management level were satisfied with an examination of the processes surrounding the appointment of external applicants. Nevertheless the covert agenda ('of the importance of choosing the right s rt of chap') is visible in several of their responses.

Further developing the theoretical schema of Howa Becker (1963) it is possible to deduce an 'out-group' in the mind-set of certain respondents - the 'redeployables.' These people seemed to be dehumanised to some extent in the nomenclature they received, their names and individual professional and personal profiles were lost as they were amorphously joined together into a lumpen group. In such a role the redeployables are relatively easy to demonise, that is, they may be blamed for their own misfortunes. This would be convenient and relatively comfortable, as it would simultaneously absolve, in such circumstances, senior management and central government facing hard questions about the morality and ethics of setting on the road to dismissal such large numbers of people. These are themes that are explored subsequently in a fuller way than at present.

Map Nine, Question Nine, Analytical Discussion Nine

The purpose of this question was to give respondents an opportunity to reflect on the interface between their organisation and people outside who wanted to join, possibly with a view to judging about where the individual organisation would feel better placed - inside or employed outside their organisation. The tenor of the responses was rather like the predecessor question. There was a heavy emphasis on information giving (neutral) responses here, too. However, the numbers of respondents who were supportive of their senior managements was very evenly balanced by their colleagues who found the opportunity to be critical. Comments included: 'We like to get a spread of ages and both sexes [in this large office]' (based on 9.010). 'It's a covert system, past work experience and qualifications' (based on 9.011).

In contrast, the all male dimension of the perceptions of the BT managers in each of the three grades is noteworthy. It was judged that the pursuit of that theme may preclude subsequent themes, so it was, reluctantly, not further developed in the interviews.

One Personnel official who was involved in hiring staff for junior clerical positions remarked: 'Interviews are a poor instrument; 50% of the candidates...last week could hardly answer our questions' (based on 9.04). Overall, comparisons between map eight and map seven are substantial. However, it is interesting to note the relative ambivalence of those members who may have felt disadvantaged by a comparison between their roles and similar ones with other organisations.

10. In the history of your organisation, are there any really significant people whose contribution to the place is still remembered?

A significant slice of the presently published academic literature in the organisation field emphasises the role of the individual in the 'making' (in the E.P. Thompson (1994) sense) of the present realities of organisations.

Consequently, this question was included in the schedule in order to provide an insight into the accuracy of such a view. It is suggested that the responses are particularly interesting and possibly also significant, indicating, as they appear to, that even charismatic individuals seem to make little difference to the organisations' shared history once they leave that organisation, for whatever reason. In **BT**, the responses of the junior managers are first:

10.1 '[I'm thinking of my last boss.] He used to like to drink late into the evening with his team at the social club, and then insist on their presence at work very early the following morning. He was a lively man, but...'

10.2 'What I can remember is their personalities and the human side, the things that happened at the Christmas parties and the more unusual work incidents. I think recalling myths and legends is helpful, they can be good for morale.'

10.3   'It's frightening how quickly these people disappear from memory.'

10.4   'My first boss [in this town], ten years ago, was an enormous man. Today, I have a negative experience of my boss...these big figures seem all to have gone.'

10.5   'People [understood as an attack on the basis of this question] shouldn't take the folk-lore of a company seriously.'

10.6   '[Names senior manager] who was on Level Four turned a technical backwater into a very interesting place to work. [the productivity of his group has increased substantially] and he is a hero/role-model.'

10.7   'One unusual senior manager - I remember he became a Labour candidate - he emphasised caring relations between staff...he gave guidance well...[There's nobody around like him now, that I know].'

The middle managers reported:

10.8   'In the mid-1980s my boss left because of a value clash. She took me from a civil service view of management, a policing and controlling role, and she made me look at my own development and how I operated as a person as well as a BT manager.'

10.9   '[Name], who reported to the General Manager, drove the region. You couldn't contradict him because he was abrupt and persuasive and clear-headed.

10.10   'The rapid turnover of managers here means no-one comes to mind...'

10.11   'One manager hid behind hedges to spy on engineers... He wasn't respected...'

The most senior managers reported:

10.12 'It's frightening how these people disappear from memory.'

10.13 'Since 1986, this place has never recovered from the retirement of [name].'

Both the middle and more senior BT people seem to share the perception of their junior colleagues about the relative anonymity of life in the organisation at the time of research compared with a previous time period.

In **British Gas (Eastern)**, the replies of the most junior managers are reported first. They appear to show little consensus. Some flatly observe that the 'new' organisation bears no relationship to the *ancien regime* they joined perhaps many years previously, while others are quite happy to concede that there are considerable continuities between organisational life past and present. The junior managers said:

10.01 'The past has gone here. Last year was a 'Year Nought' [in the Kampuchean, Pol Pot règime, sense]. The cultural changes put in place by the DGM will last as long as the office is here.'

10.02 'My first boss...he promoted me...and left me alone a lot. He was always fair... Another boss was two-faced.'

10.03 '[Referring to a previous manager for whom the respondent worked:] Mr [name] is now an industry national figure. He was...horrendous, he tried to belittle and frighten people. He was a procedural freak who stifled initiative.'

10.04 'Our last manager ruled by fear and brooked no opposite opinions to his own. We cheered when he moved to another job!'

10.05 'No one's indispensable...'

10.06 '[Name] was the General Manager here, he was known as 'the Guv'nor.'

10.07   '[Name] was moved to [help develop] another area, because of his technical expertise.'

10.08   '[Name] was thought of as a bit of a bastard, but he was loyal to his staff.'

10.09   '[Name] was a very forceful personality, an authoritarian person who didn't encourage initiative. People were frightened of him...'

10.010 'In twenty six years, I can recall no-one as above [i.e. as identified in the question.] Racism has prevented me from getting promoted. I applied for [a large number of] jobs and got no interviews [because my name is obviously a black person's one...'

10.011 'My former, former boss used to wake up on the bed in the occupational health surgery - [after consuming too much alcohol]. Characters developed because they'd been in their jobs a long time, but people don't have the time to develop characters today!'

10.012 'I remember an ex-Area Manager, Mr [name]. At a [formal] interview he asked me what car I drove - and this was class snobbery I think. He was always [to be known as] Mr [name]...'

10.013 '[Name] used to send women home for wearing trousers, ten years ago...'

10.014 'An ex-colleague, [name]. He stood up for accuracy to the penny. He took retirement as the company changed and moved away from people and towards objectives he couldn't relate to. We lunched every day for fifteen years and I miss him as a friend and as a colleague...'

10.015 'Our ex-Area [names professional role] was a good politician. He spoke and listened to his men [*sic*], and visited us monthly.

10.016 'In [my] twenty seven years [of service] all the past managers influence is gone because of the speed of change.'

The middle management group reported as follows, and they reveal, it is suggested, the same ambivalences as their more junior colleagues:

10.017 'My influencers still work for the company. [Name] was [known as] an autocrat! [Next, the respondent appears to draw an unfavourable comparison between the former head of engineering in his area and his own less successful attempts in the role. He argues tacitly that the company is no longer driven by an engineering logic but rather it is chiefly influenced by accounting and commercial pressures.]'

10.018 'Nobody leaps into mind - I look forwards anyway and not backwards...'

10.019 '[Name] was a [names professional role]. He showed charisma when we had a [major] cock-up. He had to see the Chairman but he was open and honest that there had been a cock-up. We worked together to achieve a solution and it took six weeks before our department could resume its service to the rest of the organisation.'

Map Ten, Question Ten, Analytical Discussion Ten

This was regarded, in advance of execution, as one of the interview schedule's most crucial and potentially most revealing areas of enquiry. It sought to identify cleavage between 'official' accounts of the recent history of each organisation, and the histories that organisation members carried around in their heads. Such stories/myths can be revealing and, when they are relatively solid constructs, also influential means to reject more officially promulgated accounts of organisational life. The question also attempts to validate the insistence by a number of authorities that the role of cultural heroes is crucial in the process of organisational change. See, for example Peters and Waterman (1982) or Schein (1985, 1990). The data recorded here points to the complexity of the relationships between individual and organisation, rather than some obviously causal juxtaposition.

It is interesting to note that there were relatively few responses which were neutral; respondents reported here were largely clear about the past in each organisation, whether their reading of that contributed to a supportive or critical presently held perspective. Replies included: 'Our last manager ruled by fear and brooked no opposite opinions to his own' (10.04). 'One manager hid behind hedges to spy on engineers [and] he wasn't respected' (10.11). 'My first boss, ten years ago [won enormous affection when he faced off a media figure, but] today I have a negative experience of my [present] boss' (10.4). 'Mr [name] is now an industry national figure, [but when he worked here] he was a procedural freak who stifled initiative' (10.03). Amongst the supportive remarks was: 'My first boss was ace, kind, firm and a tight organiser.' 'Mr [name] turned a backwater into an interesting place to work...he is a hero and role model [for young managers]' (10.6) 'In the mid-1980s, my boss took me from a policing view of management to a professional one.'

One person commented (but not recorded above) that a significant personal influence on him had been: 'Sid! Of the telly ads.' Overall, here, as one respondent to this question expressed it, the numbers of characters in the industry was waning now because people did not have the time to be characters! (10.011). The initial expectation of the sharing of deep insights based on this question was not borne out in the responses. A provisional conclusion may be either that the question was poor or that the simple causalities identified in the significant contributions to the literature identified earlier in this paragraph may be more complex than was first thought. An alternative conclusion points to the enigmatic role of the leader in attempting to make sense of the organisational cultures of large organisations. However, at the pragmatic level, respondents certainly seemed to enjoy the question and this may have benefited other areas in the sense that they may subsequently have felt enabled to respond in a more forthright manner than they otherwise would have done.

11.   **Have you always worked for your organisation from this particular building?**

The purpose of this question was to attempt to gain an insight into the rate of professional or other geographical occupational mobility prevailing at the time of conducting the study. For the management groups, and as a dimension of organisational culture, the question may suggest the following. That managers have a greater or lesser raft of experiences upon which to draw in the context of the group and individual dynamics surrounding the spatial relationships choices that are inherent in the decisions about where/how to deploy their teams. It may be that where the managers have had wide experience of different building lay-outs they will be able to take advantage of their own experience of living with the consequences. This may leave them best placed to select what they conceive to be optimum team lay-out in the premises where they presently reside.

In **BT**, the replies of the most junior managers appear first:

11.1   'These premises are one of the best I've ever worked in.'

11.2   'I've worked in six grotty buildings [in my years with this company] - poor heating and ventilation... But the whole team developed good team spirit.'

11.3   'Previously, we had more space per person...now, we have a lack of privacy...and old, disgusting toilets...parking is a problem here, too...'

The middle managers said:

11.4   'In my last office it was open plan, and I was near the restaurant - it was frustrating being looked at all the time. Here it's much easier in a small office where team building is easier...'

One senior manager remarked:

11.5   'My office isn't too extravagant, I know how space speaks...'

In **British Gas (Eastern)**, junior managers first:

11.01   'These premises have changed to support the cultural changes; named car-parking spaces went first, the partitions next and then the individual offices for the top managers just recently.'

11.02   'I like the smoke-free environment of a large, open plan office, most of the other district offices are dumps.'

11.03   'There's so much light, modern, airy space here that it makes me feel quite lethargic! When you're packed in, it's easier to get a buzz going and get staff more involved and committed.'

11.04   '...here we have the "big" office and the senior managers on show.'

11.05   'In here [a large open-plan office] it's an open, happy and friendly atmosphere. There's no back-stabbing.'

11.06   'In the [names] District General Office, it was very noisy; spitefulness was evident and people looked at their enemies in an unpleasant way. You had to suffer it.'

11.07   'I am a keen supporter of open-plan - they advocate breaking down [such] barriers - but they insist on their suits and they should dress casual. They advocate cross-departmental co-operation, but they don't do it themselves.'

Few of the middle managers chose to contribute to this topic, *viz.* at the most senior level in the organisation:

11.08   'No DGM expressed regret - to me - about the loss of his named parking space or the loss of privacy in surrendering his own office.'

Map Eleven, Question Eleven, Analytical Discussion Eleven

The purpose of this question was partly to glean an insight into rates of geographical mobility within each organisation and partly to try to understand the extent to which organisation members themselves saw space as a cultural issue. High rates of mobility may have made the development of a 'settled' set of cultures more difficult. An additional objective of the question was to attempt to understand something of the prevailing feelings and attitudes about either being asked to move place of work regularly or, for those who stayed in one location, to have their style of working changed for them.

Specifically for many organisation members at the time of the research, this meant moving from relatively small offices, just large enough to accommodate one team, to large, open plan offices where many teams of people worked. Numbers could have altered from a score or so people in one office up to two hundred and fifty in the largest district office visited. The managerial objective was to facilitate 'multi-skilling'. This meant, for example, asking telephone clerks also to deal with written contacts. The rationale was that they knew the answers so they should be able readily to communicate them to their customers. However, a significant number of the people involved did not have the written English skills adequately to convey meanings and this caused initial difficulties. This may have been indicative of low geographical mobility.

There seemed to be a relatively high degree of understanding of many of the subtleties of organisational interactions between members at different hierarchical levels within their organisations. For example: 'I know how space speaks' (11.5). Also of interest here is that, again, a majority of those reported here were critical of their seniors. Such responses included: 'We're too open here [in a new open plan design of office]; there [in our last, much smaller set of offices] you could get a buzz going [within each team group]' (based on 11.03). 'Previously we had more space [per person]. Now we have disgusting toilets, lack of privacy and poor parking, too' (based on 11.3). 'I'm a keen supporter of open plan offices and breaking down barriers, but the managers insist on their suits - they should address these matters' (based on 11.07). Amongst the positive comments was this double-edged contribution: 'In a grotty building...the whole team developed good team spirit' (11.2).

12. Has Information Technology changed your job recently?

At the theoretical level, questions about IT permit the generation of thinking in the tradition of Foucault (1977) about the impact of 'panopticism.' Such questions also may tend to open up much of the literature about techniques of management control, Fordism and post-Fordism. Some of this analysis is first referred to above, in chapter three. However, the subsequent chapters of this study develop this set of themes in rather more detail, relying initially on some of the following perceptions about the matter. At the pragmatic and practitioner level, this question was also designed to elicit members' responses and provide insight both to the speed of intra-organisational communications and also the degree of spread of IT training programmes, within each of the two organisations.

In **BT**, the most junior managers respond first:

12.1   'Customer Service Systems was big news since 1985. BOAT is our electronic mail system.

12.2   'I think that the PC environment is now in real decline...after seven months the IT changes have left me confused - who's responsible for what?'

12.3   'The big change was four years ago, when we moved to word processor applications and spreadsheets. Since then, very little has happened.'

12.4   'WorkManager, lap-tops, Excel, Windows [environment] word processor facilities all require us to train - and not just with a box of manuals. [All this is to support] multi-skilling.'

12.5   'Some people don't get into the technology...[but]...in-house software makes me more productive...'

12.6   'I don't know how I did it before.'

12.7   'Use of PCs means that I can do lots of stuff. I've done the courses and its enhanced my skills and I can [now] see trends from the spread sheet stuff. My present skills are now increased...'

12.8   'Most of our kit is worn out and slow and therefore breaking down; and it's frustrating and costs a lot in maintenance.'

The middle managers reported:

12.9   'I hate information technology even though I used to work closely with computers. I have 'technical dyslexia' and will only use a machine for word processing.'

12.10   'There's a rail strike tomorrow so I'll work at home on my PC.'

12.11   'There's [still] not enough [IT kit]. When I came here from [names last employer] there was just one PC here, and that was just four years ago.

12.12   'The IT help desk has people on a different planet to us, they should come over to see our problems.'

The most senior managers commented:

12.13   '[One manager described BT's internal IT policy as a] shambles and a disgrace. We have a history of failed initiatives, so people invent their own systems. We use both PCs and Apple Macintoshes and in this building alone there are 47 local networks many of which cannot intercommunicate. This is a prime example of our inability to use internal IT effectively.'

12.14   'I've got rid of my terminal - because it's not my job I decided! I don't e-mail either; I use the telephone...I won't second guess my Tier Three managers [i.e. some of my personal reports] by using a terminal to do their job...'

12.15   'IT hasn't changed us much here - we can't get our new system to work, even moderately.'

In British Gas (Eastern), regarding the Central Office System, an IT vehicle that provided e-mail and word processing, one (rather enthusiastic) junior manager commented:

12.01   'With COS, I go everywhere, man; never pay my fare, man!'
[The remark appears to be a personal celebration of the very
modest cost of such transmissions.]'

Acronyms were widely used, perhaps firstly to describe the variety
of IT packages at the disposal of different groups of workers (but at the
more subtle level of organisational discourse, understanding of these
acronyms and the implied ownership of the skills to run the software may
also have been used as boundaries to mark out where one territory within
the organisation ends and another begins).

12.02   'CRISP, TBSS, BOSS, Quantom, Itron and WIZ were
industry-specific, then industry standard packages such as
Lotus 123, dBase4, Excel and Freelance were mentioned.'

There was an increasing awareness on the part of several of the
managers who participated in the study that IT solutions also themselves
create new problems:

12.03   'We used to be uninformed, but now people copy everything -
so now we need training in what to copy and in what not to
copy.'

The same thought is echoed a little more subtly here, where one
manager reflected:

12.04   'I now have less scope to exercise and develop my managerial
skills because I have less contact face-to-face with people
than I used to have.'

12.05   'Cell phones permit Same Day Service systems to work well,
also the boilers that we work on get more and more complex
each year, so the regular technical bulletins we get are vital
for fault finding. Our training has improved no end to what it
was, on hi-technology stuff.'

12.06   'COS has helped put information at our desk that we used to have to run over to the main building for...'

This interesting piece of analysis reflects one middle manager's view of the (lack of) interface between human systems and IT systems:

12.07   'The new IT Help Desk [for staff use] has been great, but the people who run it are on a different planet to us, they have no sense of urgency or people contacts. They should be intermingled with us...'

12.08   'COS reduces phone use and for the untrained typist it takes longer to type a complicated question that it does to ask it on the phone...'

12.09   'FOX comes here next year...'

12.010 'The new TBSS system will allow us more flexibility and closer monitoring of staff...'

12.011 'IT has changed my job dramatically. I used to head up a paper-based system with the clerks reporting to me. Now we are computerised I am responsible for ensuring good data but I feel less effective because my skills aren't being developed because I'm dealing with fewer people [as opposed to data-entries, each day].'

12.012 'Using IT allows us to get a critical path done and see if we are over-using resources...or so we're told...'

12.013 'I use COS to write my own letters now, but there's so much rubbish flying around...'

12.014 'Digital mapping in the drawing office will...'

12.015 'I have piloted a 'calls-per-person' information sheet for management...'

The middle managers' responses tend to confirm some of the theoretical insights which had begun to be opened up at the head of the recording of these responses (i.e. above Paragraph 12.1):

> 12.016 'The firm's productivity is higher, because the minimum level of [IT] competence is lower, given the user friendliness of the new software packages...'

Map Twelve, Question Twelve, Analytical Discussion Twelve

The purpose of the question was to ascertain how respondents felt about the impact of information technology led changes to working practices. It was assumed that there would have been considerable investment here and IT is, after all, a significant causer of change across organisations. So, an answer in the affirmative was taken-for-granted. Contributions included '[With IT] I can now do lots of stuff [and be more productive]' (12.7). 'COS puts data on my desk that I used to have to walk over [to the next building] for' (based on 12.06). 'I can work faster now with e-mail and WP packages. I sometimes [use IT to] work at home' (based on 12.10). Some of the criticisms were substantial: 'Our IT policy is a shambles and a disgrace. In this building we have 47 separate and non-communicating networks, with PCs and Macintoshes' (based on 12.12). 'IT has changed my job dramatically, I now have to ensure good data but my management skills aren't being developed as I see fewer of my people each day' (based on 12.04). 'The IT help desk has people on a different planet to us, they should come over to see our problems.' Overall, it is judged as very difficult to draw firm conclusions from these responses. At the time the questions were asked, there were so many newly installed IT initiatives that were not bedded down in organisational procedures that drawing firm IT conclusions about them seems implausible.

13.   **When did your part of the organisation last restructure? With what benefits...?...problems...? In the case of the latter, were they anticipated?**

Conventional knowledge is what Garfinkel (1967) calls 'thinking-as-usual'. Within the management literature there is hence great importance placed on the impact of structure and its effects upon the working lives of people in organisations, whether as managers or in other roles. This question was included as a result of Schein's (1985) thinking which emphasised such an approach. Of course, the focus on the impact of structures is as old as organisations themselves; it has passed into general circulation that in Ancient Greece the *arbiter elegantiae* observed:

> We trained hard, but as soon as we reached a level of competence they reorganised us...

In **BT**, the most junior managers are reported first, and they reveal quite contrasting attitudes in this matter. There is no agreement within the following responses about the extent of the benefits or problems as a result of restructures:

13.1   'Some restructures have hindered. For example, we had a call centre and a correspondence office and they were merged [on grounds of efficiency].'

13.2   'This is a plus, because our roles were very confused...'

13.3   'Sovereign built brick walls [in the organisation structure sense] which are now being dismantled: reorganisations should be about more than just reducing staff numbers.'

13.4   'Moving to functional roles helped...'

13.5   'There have been two main benefits since Sovereign: it clarified our roles and helped us to be more objective. Secondly, it brought together previously separate areas into one close knit one.'

13.6   Reorganisations keep us on our toes!'

13.7   '[There have been] no benefits. Policy decisions are not acted upon when problems appear.'

13.8   'Lack of familiarity with managing people has caused teething problems...'

13.9   'We have some reservations, a big worry is relations between Business Communications and Personal Communications.'

13.10   'Restructuring has meant double and triple skilling for many of my people; this is probably good for the business but has put the remaining ones under considerable pressure.'

13.11   'We now focus on the residential customer and this is very important because of competition with cable TV: our fight back is better organised because of our restructuring. Also, with no regional headquarters we can respond more flexibly. For example, in 1988 BT was heavily criticised over the way we handled obscene phone calls to our customers. So we quickly set up a Nuisance Calls Bureau and this was immediately effective.'

13.12   'I don't know what the goals were in detail, of Sovereign.'

The group of middle managers said:

13.13   'In my specialist discipline we moved away from a specific role towards a generic role. This challenged us to become highly competent generalist managers and therefore easier on the customer...'

13.14   'My role is to improve the relations between senior line managers and their people problems in relation to [my specialist discipline.] I don't think that we can do this well, and that we will be recruiting in two years time...'

13.15   'Sovereign touched me hard - it gave me more staff and responsibilities - and my job is now more interesting, and so as my boss' role grew he had to delegate more to me, so I've grown too.'

13.16   'In Sovereign, I doubled my geographical area but lost some of my responsibilities...'

Within **British Gas (Eastern)**, respondents had experienced a number of minor and partial reorganisations - particularly in the central functions located at Regional Headquarters and Regional Computer Centre (these were colloquially known as 'desk shuffles'). However, it was the Regional Organisation Review (Ro[a]R) that occupied respondents concerning this area and this was unsurprising given that it was both recent in relation to the date of the study, and major in its scope and reach.

Career opportunities became available for those junior managers who were judged able, by their seniors, to measure up to the new and more demanding person specifications regarding suitability for promotion:

13.01   'In Ro[a]R I was fortunate. Just before it, I was made a Service Supervisor then I was made a Service Officer...'

Not all of the experiences of each District or central location were the same, in respect of the impact of reorganisations on working practices or attitudes to the business. In one of one of the British Gas (Eastern) locations:

13.02   'Ro[a]R meant a lot of blood here with early retirements galore and this was even though they didn't want to go!'

Perhaps more typical of the generality were these responses, from a junior manager and a middle manager respectively:

13.03   'Ro[a]R didn't go far enough! Regional management haven't addressed how to win over clerks. There seems to be no consequences when the dinosaurs refuse to change their ways.'

13.04   'As an Engineer, I became more customer-aware through Ro[a]R.

Responses revert at this point to the hierarchical format used throughout this chapter, with the most junior responses set out first:

13.05   'As a result of the last mini [re-organisation] we're [i.e. my team members and I] now all together again, from three separate islands of tables.'

13.06   '[The last reorganisation] was a cock-up!'

13.07   'Ro[a]R brought me into [names new department]. It was a new opportunity for me.'

13.08   'Last year's reorganisation caused me problems. I went to [names new department] and they put me on renewable contracts, even though I'd received assurances. It took me eighteen months before I got my tenure back.'

13.09   'During Ro[a]R I was in [names location]. People were hurt and fed up by lack of information and proper counselling. All this happened because there was no forethought [on the part of senior managers] about informing people...'

13.10   'Problems weren't anticipated as a result of the last reorganisation, it caused just more uncertainty. I like working here and dealing with the other departments [and] I want to be able to achieve the objectives...'

13.011   'I got the job I wanted...'

13.012   'Ro[a]R brought no benefit to me at all. I now seem more like a first line supervisor [than a manager] and this seems retrograde for me...'

13.013   'Ro[a]R upset many. I did OK and maintained my job. Some people were asked to do a lower grade job although their pay and conditions were protected. I can't identify any benefits that I got...'

13.014   'The length of time that Ro[a]R took [was the chief problem.] It took from May 1990 to November 1992.'

13.015   '[I like] the job variety [that I now get as a result of the last reorganisation]. I do telephone, cashiering and bureau work.'

13.016 'I was in [names department] before Ro[a]R, then I got a brand new department to lead out of it.'

13.017 '...Ro[a]R still seemed racist...'

13.018 'Change overkill and the physical movements have been exhausting.'

13.019 'Ro[a]R was very prolonged, and the uncertainty went on for years. It wasn't handled well; [the senior] managers are amateurs.'

Several of the middle managers have been included in the earliest of the responses to this question. Of those that remain, the following is of interest:

13.020 'I was demoted one whole grade... But I was put on protected pay and conditions...'

A retrospective thought that attempts to summarise the respondents' feelings about the impact of the Ro[a]R would be that it was a timely industry initiative given the context of the industry's relations with the government of that day. This seems to be so even if that was not each person's first response to this matter. The above replies indicate that such first responses identified assessments of each respondent's changed personal positions as a result of Ro[a]R. This appears to apply, as is clear from their remarks, even when there were as many losers as winners in the Ro[a]R process overall.

Map Thirteen, Question Thirteen, Analytical Discussion Thirteen

This multi-layered question was designed to be one of the key insights into the organisations. The plan was to move through the three layers as seemed appropriate in each interview with each respondent. The subject of reorganisation was a 'hot' one at the time of the research and the responses reveal a great deal of pain and anguish at both the manner in which the reorganisations were carried out and then their continuing subsequent impact upon members concerned. Response 13.03 seems particularly interesting, as it draws, tacitly, on the management literature (see, for example, Kouter, 1984, 1989). The critical responses were sometimes, in the common-sense judgement of the researcher, 'a cry for help, bordering on despair.' For example: 'The last reorganisation was a cock up!' (13.06). Other critical responses were much more analytical: 'Double and triple skilling people is good for the business but it has put the remaining people [after large-scale redundancies took effect] under great pressure' (based on 13.10). 'The thirty months RoR took was the chief problem.' 'Sovereign built "brick walls" which are now being dismantled; reorganisations should be about more than just reducing staff numbers' (13.3). 'We've had more "people problems" with functional rather than territorial organisation.' The more positive comments included: 'Reorganisations keep us on our toes!' (13.6). Also '[As a result of Sovereign] my boss' role grew, he had to delegate more to me so I've grown too' (13.15). The clearest overall impression of the responses is that they show the difficulties, often unnecessary ones, under which organisation members were asked to labour during the times when their senior managers felt there was no alternative but to change the previously accepted ways of completing tasks and delivering business objectives.

14.   What do your competitors say about your organisation?

This perceptually rooted question was included at the end of the schedule in the hope that the respondents may by then have been in a position to attempt a summary view of their response to the changing state of their own organisation. It was intended that this question would provide a suitable vehicle from which such a summary could be encapsulated.

The actual responses are, of course, what follow and it was interesting that in the BT managers' replies, this area provoked perhaps the widest range of responses of all the areas of the foregoing interview schedule. A small minority of them were certainly summary thoughts as was anticipated, but other approaches opened up a number of significant themes. These are examined, to some extent at least, in the next chapter of this work. Amongst these alternative readings of the question, from both junior and middle managers, are those which reflect differing levels of what the BT senior management might be pleased to describe as complacency:

14.1   'They think our service quality is fantastic.'

14.2   'I think they're frightened of BT, many of their staff are our ex-ones.'

14.3   'They'd like to [be able to] respond as quickly as we can...'

14.4   '[People in Competitor {X} say]...BT are a hard act to follow...'

14.5   'We can exploit the bad publicity about [names competitor]...'

14.6   'They fear our financial muscle and are envious of our experience in the field and the quality of our service as perceived by general publicity...'

Others, from a mixed group of middle and junior managers, have less sanguine perceptions:

14.7   'They see us as a lumbering dinosaur. We still rely on phones; I need a modem and I haven't got one yet. Competition is good for us; I'm [also] a customer for [names competitor].'

14.8   'They see us as big, slow and complacent and because we work on the averages they know they can dent us.'

14.9   'I am amazed we've still got the market share we have: we are shackled in our old organisation culture.'

14.10   'They take us as seriously as we take them.'

14.11   'We're too big and need to be reduced in size...'

14.12   'I've seen what the opposition can do...they're cheaper [than we are].'

14.13   'Our [direct and immediate] competition say we are too dear and that we think we are still a monopoly service provider.'

14.14   'They see us a large bureaucratic monopoly, resistant to change - a dinosaur!'

14.15   'They like our size as they are niche [orientated in their mission formation and hence also their marketing] and we are everything.'

The most senior managers in BT had the following perceptions in response to this question:

14.16   '[They see us as a] big, fearless opponent, and as a professional company which will stretch its opposition. [But] they play on our weaknesses though. We are [also] expensive and not small and local...'

14.17   'BT is expensive, slow and behind in the technology race.'

14.18   'They can't flatten us, but because we work the percentages they can dent us. [On the other hand]...[names competitor] would now see us as a serious company...'

In **British Gas (Eastern)**, there was a similarly wide range of responses indicating a wide range of levels of understanding of the processes through which the organisation was passing.

This Service Engineer is referring to the experience of not winning a contract for which the company tendered, against competition from a much smaller and more local gas and plumbing business:

14.01   'The mob who took over the council servicing contract from us were envious of our working conditions. I don't think we're expensive, my brother works for a firm that charges more than us. Our servicing costs are very competitive.'

Other junior managers, in contributing the following remarks, reveal a degree of difference, as sharp as the BT managers, in their perceptions of how efficient/inefficient the business really is. They said:

14.02 'They probably say that we're over priced and over-staffed.

14.03 'Our competitors cheer the Regulator! They say we've had it too good for too long. I think we've been very protected as an industry.'

14.04 'We're experts and global and successful. [Then, after a prompt from the interviewer]...I've not ever given any thought to the possibility that our costs are too high.'

14.05 'The competition are money-grabbing thieves who cream off the best customers...these undercutters are leeches in the industry.'

14.06 'We're large, unfocussed and overly bureaucratic; we pay to advertise the appliances but the customers buy on price from the John Lewis Partnership.'

14.07 'We're dear, impersonal and inflexible...and bureaucratic.'

14.08 'They laugh at us as we do their breakdowns and escapes.'

14.09 'We're too pricey - but they can't knock us for much else because we're so well geared up for kit and stuff.'

14.010 'Some [competitors] that don't know us think that we are a good organisation; those that know us a bit see us as an easy touch; our large customers will soon go to them.'

14.011 'They know deep down that we're a good company.'

14.012 'In [names a large department store], a popular model of gas cooker was £550 last year, here [in my showroom] it was £699.'

14.013 'Our safety responsibilities cost us; if there's a leak at 2.00 a.m. our competitors call us out to deal with it.'

14.014 'The government is wiping out a great British industry. Our customers say our prices are too high, but I don't believe them though...'

14.015 'My college colleagues from BT and Calor Gas say we are useless.'

14.016 'They pump up their image and [pump] down our image. They only win on price because the Regulator rigs the market [in their favour].'

14.017 'British Gas has come a long way since privatisation to improve its standards of service to its customers. We're still not cost conscious enough though, and we're a little lost and meandering...'

14.018 'We are difficult to compete with because we're cutting costs and going global...'

14.019 'Some [competitors] will love us because they will be great at undercutting us!'

14.020 'I guess a lot of effort moves us an inch, [but] they're faster to respond...and they don't have our overheads...'

14.021 '...we're expensive, and our competitors laugh at us for not chasing business. We're doing silly things like losing industrial and commercial sales representatives when we should be drumming up business.'

14.022 'I don't know what our competitors say about us! They may say we're a big, slow powerless organisation, not snappy and fast responding...'

14.023 'We're big and lumbering; and I hope that they're wrong!'

Map Fourteen, Question Fourteen, Analytical Discussion Fourteen

The purpose of this question was to seek general responses that may have been framed in the context of perceptions from an outsider looking inwards to each of the organisations. There were no shortage of opinions in this matter and the selection contained in map fourteen has more entries than any other map, reflecting the status of the question as the most popular one addressed by the total number of respondents. Whether all the opinions are equally as well informed as each other may be less important than the general 'mood' that their totality indicates, in terms, at least, of making deductions about the impact of change on organisational members. The less well informed comments may be explained, perhaps, by a combination of poor senior management communication of information and reluctance to read and understand that which has been communicated. Amongst the responses is 14.9. This was one of the very rare usages of the term 'organisational culture' that was unprompted by the interviewer. It showed, it is suggested, a key insight into the organisation by the context in which the phrase was used. 'They see us as a large bureaucratic monopoly having difficulty meeting new market challenges, a dinosaur.' 'We're dear, impersonal, inflexible and bureaucratic' (14.07). 'We are seen as more efficient than we actually are ...' 'I guess a lot of effort moves us one inch, they are faster to respond and they don't have our overheads' (14.020). The more positive comments included: '...customers say our prices are too high, but I don't believe them though...' (14.014). 'They think our service quality is fantastic' (14.1). 'They fear our financial muscle.' 'They say we are experts, and global and successful. I've never thought [until this interview that] our costs are too high' (14.04). Overall, the responses to this interview head of discussion showed a great deal of loyalty to the organisation, whether the tenor of the remarks was critical or supportive. Also of significance here is the way that understanding of the new market conditions in each organisation seemed either to be fully understood - or not understood at all. The conclusions to this study address this point.

Domain Analysis

This final section of the united exegesis and analysis chapter considers the application of the Graphics COPE tool of 'domain' analysis. The 'domain' analytic command permits an examination of all the 590 concepts that are entered into the 'supermodel'. It then lists the numbers of concepts that link inwards and the numbers that link outwards (or onwards) and the number of connotative links for each, and then gives a total for each concept. This is useful as an accurate means of identification (using the principle that busy nodes in the complex of links that comprises the 'map' will be more helpful in identifying potentially crucial links and distinguishing those that may be considered more marginal). In this complex and quite substantial data-set, this is an opportunity which has value that is difficult to overestimate. The domain analysis which was one of the available set of analyses within the COPE toolkit identifies the responses that are the most linked, and the logic is that these are in some way central (both literally and so also analytically). In the 'domain' analysis a cursory inspection of the supermodel indicates that there will always be recorded a majority of links around the interview heads of discussion. This is an inevitable outcome of the choices about initial structure of the mapping activity when the decision was made to employ the Graphics COPE approach. However, and interestingly, the 'domain' analysis seems to produce a striking insight into the data-set when the first fourteen highest sets of links are discarded (as each points merely to the fourteen interview heads of discussion). The next fifteen concepts in descending order of value are all in red, and it will be remembered that this colour code denotes remarks that are critical of management. Here, value refers to the richness of the quantity of inter-linkage between each concept. There is, then, a consecutive string of fifteen 'red comments'. They are located at the apex of the domain analysis. This seems to be a proof of the level of concern shown by the respondents in respect of the actions and words (or lack of either or both of these as the case may be) of their senior managements, during the time-period over which the questions were asked.

It is clear that the maps reveal many responses that indicate deep unhappiness at not only the *pace and direction* of organisational change, but also the *efficiency and efficacy* of the way change information was communicated to organisation members. A closer inspection of this evidence is possible through an examination of the 'domain' analysis data immediately behind the supermodel. The highest number of links, seven, are revealed around the comments:

> 'Ro[a]R didn't go far enough! Regional management haven't addressed how to win over clerks. There seems to be no consequences when the dinosaurs refuse to change their ways' (13.03).

'I'm amazed we've still got the market share we have: we are shackled in our old organisation culture' (14.9).

The first response was in answer to the question: 'When did your part of the organisation last restructure? What benefits/problems resulted, and were they anticipated?' The second response was in answer to the question: 'What do your competitors say about your organisation?' The first was from a member of the regional energy company and the second from the telecommunications company. Of itself, it is interesting to note that each organisation produced an equally rich insight into its own culture. This may be indicative of the need for a further investigation of the same themes in order to attempt to measure and/or assess the rate of change in organisation members' attitudes as they continue to experience processes of organisational change.

The 'domain' analysis found no concepts with six links but another pair with five links:

> '[One manager described BT's internal IT policy as a] shambles and a disgrace. We have a history of failed initiatives, so people invent their own systems. We use both PCs and Apple Macintoshes and in this building alone there are 47 local networks many of which cannot intercommunicate. This is a prime example of our inability to use internal IT effectively' (12.13).

> 'Ro[a]R was very prolonged, and the uncertainty went on for years. It wasn't handled well; [the senior] managers are amateurs' (13.019).

Again the remarks originated within each company studied, and in the case of the first of these pair, the originator was a senior organisational member, commenting on the question in the schedule about the impact of information technology upon his job. The second response appears to be a considered and outspoken personal insight into one person's reality in the midst of experiencing processes of organisational change. It was a thought in reply to the analysis concerning organisational restructuring quoted in full in this section, above.

All four of these remarks may be read as respondents actively seeking an arena in which their critical and unprompted thoughts could be aired and then considered. Perhaps the same could be said about some of the responses, which had four links around. Of the four responses so recorded, two are:

> 'The last reorganisation was a cock-up!' (13.06).

> 'Change overkill and the physical movements have been exhausting' (13.018).

Both of these remarks are responses to the question about organisational restructuring. This question, situated near the end of the list of heads of discussion seems to have been well placed (judging by outcome) to afford an opportunity for respondents at many organisational levels to speak unambiguously about their concerns.

Seven responses had three links around them. They were replies to the significant question about restructuring, the identification of problems surrounding the use and implementation of information technology, and also insights into the last question asked: 'What do your competitors say about your organisation?' In reply, one response from each organisation's respondents is worth featuring here:

> 'Some [competitors] that don't know us think that we are a good organisation; those that know us a bit see us as an easy touch; our large customers will soon go to them' (14.010).

> 'Some [competitors] will love us because they will be great at undercutting us!' (14.019).

Originators here are, respectively, British Gas (Eastern) and BT. Concerning the IT issue, two responses commented that 'the IT help desk has people on a different planet to us,' and 'Now we need to get back in touch with our own people [as a result of IT Changes]. Concerning the restructuring issue, two further remarks from people in the energy company were 'RoR upset many' (quoted from 13.013) and 'During RoR people were hurt and fed up by lack of information and proper counselling.' (quoted from 13.09). Based upon an assessment of the facial expressions, posture and associated gestures of these respondents it is safe to conclude that these are heart-felt thoughts.

It is proposed that the use of a software programme to assist in the analysis of relatively 'soft' data is helpful. In a Graphics COPE training session in the University of Strathclyde in November 1995, Professor Colin Eden of the School of Management spoke of the methodological problems associated with the analysis of large volumes of qualitative data. A central difficulty is how to distinguish key data from the welter of either less substantial or less significant material that typically surrounds it. The proposition advanced is that it is at this point that personal prejudice may unwittingly lead to the highlighting of aspects of the data which do not deserve such treatment and the concomitant possibility of the downgrading of outcomes which certainly would benefit from closer inspection. One apparent irony is that 'sins of omission and commission' are more likely to be overlooked in the assessment of the validity and quality of conventional methodologies than in more novel ones. There is an extensive literature which outlines such methodological problems, and some of it has already been identified in earlier elements of this study.

It is for this reason that the package has been used in this part of this research. The Graphics COPE documentation itself asserts:

> Graphics COPE provides help with structuring problems or situations whether...complex...[or not.] The software allows the user to work with a model of interlinked ideas using maps. ...A Graphics COPE map is made up of short phrases (referred to as concepts) whose relationships are indicated by arrows drawn between them. The user enters concepts and arrows and the ideas can be moved, given styles, and, eventually analysed when a large enough picture of the issue in question has been drawn up. Graphics COPE is an ideas management tool. (*Graphics COPE User Guide*, February 1995, Banxia Software Ltd.)

6 Empirical and Theoretical Conclusions and Management Recommendations

Introduction - an Overall View

This chapter draws together the conclusions that have emerged in the immediately preceding discussion which itself is the result of the empirical work elaborated earlier in this study. This chapter also attempts to resolve what, from a narrow and positivist perspective, may be irresolvable. That is to say, the chapter also briefly considers the development of a synthesis, in the context of this largely interpretative study. One way of achieving that objective may be through the manner in which the task is defined. If a synthesis is framed in the sense of fitting together ideas into a composite whole, rather than its more usual sense of developing 'thesis - anti-thesis - synthesis', this would be helpful. In that case, the notion of synthesis is simply abandoned as a piece of positivist architecture. It imposes meaning upon social behaviour that it seeks, in reality, to understand.

Some current examples of managerialist literature are examined earlier, in chapter three. For example, this includes significant elements of Schein (1985, 1990, 1992, 1994) and also Bate (1994). One thread that unites such thinking into a threnody is the imposing of structures of meaning onto participants in a research exercise. It can never be entirely the case that the meanings and motives, for example, of questionnaire authors, will always precisely overlap the interpretations of those people who are asked the questions. The extent to which there is not an exact overlap is argued to be the amount of misunderstanding in the data. It is contended in chapter two of this work that only when respondents are given an opportunity to show through their behaviours (including what they choose to say) can we reasonably expect to be able to begin the complex task of making sense of such behaviours. Hence, it has already been proposed that either or both of theorising and methodology development that fails to take this into account seems irredeemably flawed.

So, the literature discussion that forms chapter three of this study makes a key point. It is made clear in that chapter's summary and conclusions that the idea of organisational cultural change may be used as a mechanism simply to extort more work from middle and junior grade managers (possibly amongst a larger group of employees). It will have been noted from the data set out in chapter five of this study that there are marked differences in the stories and views of those who participated in the study. This practice of extorting more work seems to be occurring against an economic background that has a labour market where alternative and viable employment elsewhere is scarce. The notion of culture change could be said to amount to little more than one form of collective bargaining where the uppermost tiers of management have the balance of bargaining power tipped decisively towards them. The process of 'tipping' incorporates what Willmott (1993) has already been quoted as identifying as significant: 'the abandonment of the '$5 a day' logic of Fordism in favour of a more contingent, and fluid organising philosophy of flexible accumulation' on the part of organisational managers and owners of substantial equity in the organisation. Willmott goes on to argue that such organisational membership 'demands loyalty' on the part of the more junior people in the hierarchy, 'whilst it simultaneously excludes, silences and punishes' the same people.

It has not been possible to include in this study an account of the complete and ceaselessly changing economic and social relations that prevail in the national economy in which the two organisations studied are situated. This context is rapidly becoming more global than regional. A significant part of the explanation for this at the economic level has been through the rise of competition from the Pacific Rim economies (and elsewhere) as well as other factors. The consequence of all this that was promulgated to organisation members of both organisations studied was that far reaching change was demanded by the new trading conditions. These new conditions included national factors already identified in quoted responses to the interview prompts, earlier in this work. However, there are also other factors, not previously referred to in a direct way, such as the continued emergence in Britain of a 'twenty-four hours a day' society. In such a set of arrangements, in which providers of basic services such as gas and the telephone system may more reasonably be expected to work in time frames outside 8.00 a.m. to 6.00 p.m., new and larger demands on organisational members seem inevitable. There are also the economic and social international factors mentioned above. What is highly relevant to this study are the consequences of these. These consequences made a powerful argument with which senior managers were able to demand more output, then reward that with lower job security and generally diminished conditions of employment, as demonstrated in chapter five of this study, in the words of organisation members themselves.

For many organisation members, the award of a relatively generous severance package was inadequate compensation for a decade or more of income to which they could have aspired, had they been able to remain with the organisation. For some of those people made redundant or asked to accept retirement earlier than expected, they may have already served approaching thirty years. This long- service *motif* applied equally across the profile of each of the two organisations. One of the themes that emerged from the informal conversations within the non-participant observation element of this study concerned severance policy from the organisations. It quickly became clear that it was the widely understood objective of each senior management team first to 'shed' or to 'downsize' (or even to 'rightsize' according to some British Gas people!) from the fifty years and older age groups. The apparently euphemistic language used to express the thought is interesting. Through the illustrations provided, the language gently distances the users from the relatively uncomfortable social and economic consequences of the action of dismissal through redundancy or early retirement. Equally interesting is the proposition that the same words were chosen to label and consider the process, irrespective of which level within the work hierarchy of power and influence at which the speaker was situated. The language, then, which is a cultural artefact *par excellence,* seemed to sanitise the activity. The introduction to the empirical work identifies the extent of fall in the size of the payrolls of each organisation since each organisation had its statutory basis overturned.

Further conclusions about items of language are possible, also from the evidence in chapter five. It shows something of the impact of how use of language does seem to sanitise meaning by disguising the 'real' meaning, as perceived from, say, a more neutral academic perspective when compared with that of an organisational participant. Here are some illustrations. In British Gas (Eastern), at the time the research was conducted, styles of speech concerning how to address collectively (both in speech and in written communication) indicated two groups of employees. These were 'staff' and 'industrial staff'. Whilst this itself represents an advance over the nomenclature of earlier decades ('staff' and 'men' (*sic*) or 'staff' and 'manual workers') it nevertheless perpetuated the divisions between the two groups. These were real divisions. Interview evidence includes comments about the relative justice of newly appointed office staff having superior sick pay and annual leave arrangements over service engineers with twenty five or more years of service in the organisation. In BT this issue of how to conceive of all organisation members had been addressed. All officially promulgated statements referred to 'our people' or 'BT people'. There is a clear inclusiveness here. However, it was understood in an ironic way whenever the experience of organisational reality seemed to contradict this inclusive ethos. Within BT some technical and manual people, nevertheless, continued to perceive unfairness in their organisation. In general conversation that was not written up for formal inclusion in the research evidence, BT manual workers pointed to differences in sick pay and annual leave arrangements. Their position was worse than that of a newly appointed clerical employee even though they may have had twenty years or more of service.

Language, whilst probably the chief dimension, is not the only dimension in which the symbolic world of organisational members is acted out. The way in which members account for space and handle space is significant in this cultural world. One senior organisation member who participated in the empirical investigation but not as an interview respondent achieved much respect - even admiration. Part of the way s/he did this was by visiting the most distant offices and places of work of his/her people, and by improving lines of communication to his/her office backwards from the whole business. The actions were important for the clarity of the symbolic message about how that senior manager saw his/her relationships with his/her people; space speaks.

Key themes along the theoretical dimension of this study have been in terms of discipline and control, accommodation and resistance. Each theme is rooted in the central idea of the impact of industrial, bureaucratic society upon the individual and the work group. These ideas have become institutionalised within the large organisations studied, and so in the hearts and minds of many organisation members. Notions of Taylorian approaches to work are shot through the empirical evidence set out in previous elements of this study. Supporting these notions, frequently, are deeply ingrained attitudes concerning the work ethic. So in this chapter for conclusions, there is an attempt simply to unify these themes with the main concerns of the study - the experience of organisational culture and the experience of organisational change, in relatively large organisations.

Synthesis of Data Outcomes

Having paid attention to some of the linguistic context in which each of the interviews was situated, at this point, a focus on explicit identification of the gaps between the perceptions of uppermost tiers of managements and their more junior colleagues seems appropriate. Such 'gaps' are especially visible in the following synthesis. In it, little or no attempt is made to distinguish British Telecom from British Gas (Eastern) people. It is argued that the evidence shows that from the perspective of each individual organisation member who was interviewed, no matter where that person fits into the hierarchy, 'lived' organisational membership amounts to a similar, bureaucratised set of organisational relationships. The perceptual differences seem most marked in relation to some of the questions asked. Here is a selection of comments around the question and response couplets.

Turning to question one responses, the differences of perception are most marked at the level of what material was selected by each respondent to answer the prompt that is described as a 'low threat, throat-clearer' of a question in chapter five of this work. So, heads of the large departments who responded had sharply differing interpretations of what the question (concerning the learning of senior management's policy objectives) was about. One response simply outlined a perceived contradiction between what was perceived to happen and what was alleged to have happened in this respect. Two other responses from similarly senior people identified the issue as a procedural one and outlined matters of recent historical fact. This is to say, their responses saw the question as one about the mechanics of organisational communication rather than about the opportunity to inspire through explicit leadership activity. The emphasis on procedural matters (also understood in this way) is visible in the British Gas (Eastern) responses from their most senior people. However, in another response for example, a different and rather more critical focus is visible. This interview suggested that the most senior tiers interviewed within that organisation were out of touch with the feelings of all organisation members as a whole. This was because they did not successfully anticipate both the volume and volubility of the inputs from their more junior colleagues, when they asked for such contributions. The 'proceduralist' emphasis of the most senior people is a rather different perspective compared with a number of responses from people in the lower status groups in each of the two organisational hierarchies. Responses ask in a relatively anxious manner about the team brief activity; identify more of the context in which team brief is situated and point out that rumour also briefs people.

The respondents were asked about organisational priorities and, specifically, what their perceptions were about the main priorities, at the time each of the interviews were conducted (Question two), sometimes the most junior groups of managers accurately paraphrased the official agenda. So, some responses reflect this. Another response suggests that the 'real' priority is about reducing the size of the organisation's pay roll; a further one even identifies what may be called the sub-text of the official agenda. One of the most senior managers interviewed in the study, however, seems to suggest that there is no formal set of arrangements in place (to determine priorities). No other respondent from that organisation shared that perception with that senior manager. Similarly, in British Gas, there was a difference between what many recognised as the official agenda for making priorities and actual priorities.

When the respondents were faced with the enquiry about situations when matters in the organisation 'went wrong', some of the respondents chose to define this term at the outset (Question three). Junior managers responded critically to interventions at too early a stage from their very senior colleagues. The 'critical path' orientation of responses is an interesting perception, one mentions the possibility of bad news (self-defined) as being 'filtered away' from the 'top levels'. Another response supports that perception and points to the most visible of gaps concerning the differences in perceptual set between uppermost levels and more junior ones. The response shows that the senior management 'were surprised to hear...fears [of their juniors about job security]'. This was at the time when the issue of job security was a 'live' one in the organisation as a whole. Similarly, in British Gas, there was a gap in perceptions. Other responses identify a difference between the 'official' policy and the perceived reality for that respondent. Yet another response is deeply critical of senior managers and details some of their perceived professional shortcomings.

The question that sought to 'balance' its predecessor was focused on the consequences of 'getting it right' as self-perceived, in terms of organisational practise on an everyday basis (Question four). There was, again, a sharp difference between perceptual sets based on level in the organisational hierarchies. So, a number of responses from people in junior grades were critical of ritualised attempts to 'do the right thing' by employees whose work standards had impressed their seniors. Many other responses spoke warmly of an improved approach to recognition of achievements by employees. The political dimension of organisational life was not neglected, and overall the junior managers perceived inconsistencies in the ways that praise was handled by their seniors. These more senior people perceived the issue as a non-strategic matter, and that, of itself, is an interesting observation because 'selecting in' the process of praise (in the Schattschneider, 1960 sense) may put the whole matter of relations between senior and junior grades of people on a different footing. From the management perspective, the non-pecuniary rewards policy in an organisation does seem to be strategically important. This is one point of difference between the two organisations examined; the BT managers who were respondents seemed more clear about the potential in praising their people than did the British Gas part of the sample of respondents.

Another question, concerning opinion formers, confirmed that many junior managers used their immediate superior (or his/her superior) as a role model in terms of sources of opinions about the organisation that were deemed worthy of attention (Question five). However, peers, the press both technical and the daily and Sunday papers, and also 'national figures' were all cited by numbers of people as influencers. Few respondents mentioned the trades unions as sources of valuable insights regarding their organisation. This may be explained by the way that the question was worded, i.e. towards individual people and hence away from institutions.

The emphasis on individuals (rather than a larger unit of analysis) continued, by enquiring about respondents' immediate colleagues and what 'promotable characteristics' they could be perceived to possess (Question six). Some respondents immediately rejected the grounds upon which the question was based. Many others addressed themselves to relatively full accounts of qualities that they perceived as valuable. It is possible to suggest that the qualities for promotion have become inflated with the relative paucity in the numbers of promoted posts available within each organisation. Consequently, the very high levels of personal and professional qualities that were deemed either essential or highly desirable could act as 'a self-fulfilling prophecy' (Rosenthal and Jacobson, 1968) in the explanation of why so few people actually achieved promotion around the time the interviews were conducted. These qualities are comprehensively spelt out in the responses from the more senior managers and then articulated in even more detail by their more junior colleagues. Here are some of the responses from that level: 'flexible'; 'motivated', 'adapt[able]', 'commit[ed]'. The responses from the most senior people emphasised similar aspects of behaviour. The pattern in responses from British Gas people is again a similar one, with the more junior people 'talking up' the requirements, also possibly to explain their lack of receipt of promotion.

Question seven seemed to be interpreted by those who responded to it as a further continuation of the theme of self-evaluation in the guise of thoughts about colleagues. Again, relatively high standards were set in the discussion about the qualities of promotable colleagues and the relations that prevailed between this group and the other members of their teams. The more junior respondents seemed to perceive that there were many ways of describing these social relations; their more senior colleagues who were respondents were similarly unfocused in that respect. However, a large number of respondents had nothing to say about this question and this may indicate that understandings of the question were different to those anticipated.

The next question overtly explored the social relations of the workplace (Question eight). It asked about the methods that were used by senior managers when people were to be chosen for promotion. The responses from the more junior people ranged across clear procedural statements. Occasionally, the responses reveal an awareness of, and a willingness to discuss, an approach to the question area that is more complex than the procedural layer. One response begins to examine the subtler, cultural layers in the interview prompt area. It refers to 'informal chats after being "noticed" [by senior management.]'. Another response explains what was perceived as 'the reality' of promotion. A second focus of interest in these responses is the gender dimension. All of this becomes quite apparent when no reply mentioned a woman colleague as someone who might be considered as promotable, and comments that were made all had personal pronouns invariably in the male gender. One response from the total of over seventy respondents even reflects the suitability of women for promotion in a negative way.

The subsequent question asked about criteria used by appointment panels when they met to appoint people outside the organisations into them (Question nine). The orientation of the question was around the potential that may exist for the origination of 'in-groups' (in the Becker, 1963 sense). It was also intended to provide an opportunity for discussion of potentially sensitive material in a context outside of the organisation and so, it was anticipated, in a safer context. Responses identified both the procedural and the subtler layers of possibilities in the question. There were several examples of responses where respondent perceptions were rooted in the procedural realm (when distinguished from charismatic or inspirational possibilities). Each comes from the more junior end of the respondents' list. Other responses addressed the tacit agenda of the organisation undergoing cultural change, and they also are from the more junior respondents. The more senior managers in the sample showed the same level of awareness of the importance of appointing 'the right sort of chap' across both organisations. There seemed a clearer and less proceduralist orientation to this process from that group.

Question ten sought responses about organisational heroes (chapter three above, mentions 'the Bill and Dave way' - also known as 'the HP way' - as a celebration of the workplace 'achievements' of William Hewlett and David Packard). Idiosyncrasies, unsurprisingly, figured in many answers provided especially by the more junior respondents. However, what, perhaps, could be termed 'the cult of personality' was certainly not recognised by the middle ranked and more senior BT people who participated in the study. Concerning the more senior British Gas people, they seemed to reflect the same approaches to this matter as do their more junior colleagues.

Another question opened up the matter of geographical occupational mobility (Question eleven). The question was conceived as an attempt to consider the impact of physical structure on the organisation, and many responses from people in different grades do this. However, one senior manager responded very subtly; he proposed that he knew how 'space speaks'. Another response points to the linkage between structure and management control in both the disciplinary and more broad senses. A further response from a senior manager tacitly acknowledges the way that his reports will be likely to censor their comments that are critical of a new approach when they discuss such matters with him. Nothing was offered in response when a supplementary question sought such extra insights, based on speculation around that theme.

Question twelve sought insights about the impact of information and communications technology on organisational process. Some of the responses were nothing short of ecstatic; others were rather more pessimistic. In terms of perceptions, presumably the greater strategic knowledge of the more senior managers in the sample led to their wide perspective in this question area. So one response is a swingeing condemnation of hitherto existing buying policy. A senior person made it. Either no junior manager amongst the respondents had a sufficiently wide view of the business to participate in such a discussion, or such a topic was too uncomfortable for a junior manager to discuss with an outsider.

Question thirteen asked about the impact of restructuring on organisational life, and for the benefits or otherwise to be assessed.

Operation Sovereign was the name BT gave to large-scale change; many responses from junior or more senior BT people directly addressed its impact upon them. They were well placed to do that, some two to three years after the event happened. Similarly in British Gas, the big re-structure was named there as the Regional Re-organisation Review. Its acronym is culturally interesting: RO[a]R. It seems to imply that there is a potential for a fierce bite to be taken from people so affected! At the perceptual level, there were people who felt they had 'won' in restructuring activities in each organisation, just as there were people who felt as if they had 'lost'. It is not clear what else can be made of the responses to this matter.

The final question examined attitudes and perceptions about industry competition (Question fourteen). In each organisation, there were some people who felt that their organisation was perilously placed. However, other responses show a great deal of pride in respondent organisational memberships, even if some of it could be said to be misplaced. The more senior BT managers had even-handed responses that pointed both to a perceived strength and a perceived weakness within their organisation. In respect of the responses from British Gas people, the same remarks seem to apply.

Conclusions and Recommendations

Overall, in this work, a number of features are now apparent. Attempts to manage the changes to organisational cultures by the uppermost tiers in an organisation have brought about perceptions about change held by middle and lower tier members that emphasise that it is both a 'top-down' process and one in which everyone must participate. Many of the responses highlighted in the previous paragraphs that quote evidence from chapter five of this study emphasises that central point. These perceptions, then, seem sharply divergent in the context of understandings about the change process held by the uppermost tiers. According to the evidence gathered in this study, their more junior colleagues face a regular and sustained set of contradictions. This was between the perceptions of their seniors about the ways that change initiatives are said to be managed, and the evidence of their everyday experience as organisation members. This suggests that what may be intended by organisational managers is not what actually happens as a result of initiatives set in motion to achieve various outcomes. It is of profound sociological significance that it is the uppermost of these two groups in their respective hierarchies that is best able to impose its own definitions of each situation. The definitions developed and utilised by that high status group will be presented as the most accurate and somehow the 'best' interpretation of realities, to other groups in the organisation. It does not negate the significance of the versions of reality about the nature and impact of organisational change that are related by the more junior hierarchical layers; it merely outmanoeuvres them in the often tacit but occasionally quite explicit 'power plays' between these two groups of organisational members.

In summary thus far, when senior managers instigate organisational change processes, there are unintended consequences to their actions.

The second feature of the study is also now clear; the achievement of organisational cultural change cannot sensibly be set up as a short-term or perhaps even medium-term goal. If organisation culture is about the deeply held values and beliefs of organisation members that they seem to cling to, almost no matter what their senior managements direct, then the slow speed of change that is attested to here is inevitable. In the light of the empirical evidence associated with this study, it seems that the only other reading of it that has integrity is that organisational culture change is so slow that it is almost imperceptible. Consequently, it seems a non-effective area of senior management interest and activity, in the sense that the effort (and perhaps costs) of achieving change through such mechanisms may be uneconomic.

Thirdly, and looking at the whole of the evidence furnished by this study, organisational cultural change is seen by a significant minority number of organisation members interviewed to be both managerialist and exploitative. In the social process of interviewing, sometimes that which is intimated by facial expression, and by silence and by tone of voice, is at least as significant as the words used. All three of these ideas are considered in the conclusion and recommendation lists at the end of this chapter. The notion of organisational culture cannot be viewed as a monolithic notion, certainly in the context of the two organisations examined. There is far too much evidence cited in this study to permit that. Yet, there is also evidence of senior managements continuing to make strategic claims and statements that the organisation is 'one company'. This cites the words of the corporate statement of values that was current among BT people during the time of research (see, for example Höpfl's (1990) emphasis upon the BT 'new value', that we are all, now, 'one company'). The evidence at anything other than a relatively superficial level for this proposition is quite slight. This is the case in spite of the degree of loyalty to the organisation shown by a number of respondents that, judged from the perspective the interested outsider, sometimes bordered on the irrational. Both of the organisations had changed in respect of members, equity owners and consumers of the services, but at what cost?

An organisational culture, then, cannot be seen as a 'sacred cow', where workers are asked to accept and internalise beliefs based on what they understand their senior management's vision is of how things should really be. Alvesson (1993, p.23) provides a helpful means of making sense of this. He understands 'organisational culture as world closure'. By that phrase he identifies the apparent ability of organisation managers to filter the experience of the industrial (and perhaps even wider) world of organisation members so that the perspective they hold will increasingly become a joint one. At this point, it will be no surprise that the notion of 'Total Control Management' is preferred to the widely used term 'Total Quality Management' as a means of conceptualising the attempts by some senior managements to filter the world view of organisation members. Indeed, this is borne out in the fieldwork evidence in a number of places. For example, talk of a senior local manager setting the calendar to 'Year Nought' seems as transparent an example of such an idea as it is possible to find. The 'folksy' ideals of 'value for money' and 'customer service' may contribute to an agenda of Total Control while masquerading behind a notion of Total Quality; Alvesson (1993, pp.28-29) comments about the 'confusion of culture with management ideology'. His thought addresses attempts to legitimise the actions and values of senior managers when they may call into play the so-called 'changed' cultural norms of the organisation. Of course, the leaders have frequently themselves imposed these new rules as part of a new agenda, in the first place. It may be that they will be quickly seen through and hence all such change will, in the long run and perhaps also in the medium term, be doomed to failure.

Plainly also, the experience of individual organisational members has been placed in the wider context of the group and whole organisation in this study. Consequently, there has been much tacit argument that has derived from propositions about the experience of labour discipline and labour control by those people who formed the sample for the study. It is proposed that an intelligent reading of the evidence suggests that labour discipline must now be understood in at least two ways, in terms of its impact upon the individual organisational member, who is, it must be added, typically a white collar worker. Firstly, there is the obvious and highly visible set of work rules that determine the place, hours of work, annual leave and remuneration. These are some of the ways that others organise work for members.

The subtler dimension of control has been a chief concern of this study. Not only did senior managements attempt to exercise control over more junior colleagues, but they also seemed to have begun the process of attempting to control customers. This was observable in the nascent stages during the time of the empirical work, but has become especially more observable since. In short, processes of 'customer-care' seem to have become another arm of the marketing activities of BT.

'Control' from the perspective of the middle and more junior employees frequently has meant the internalisation of strict rules about labour discipline. This seems to have led to all the evidence that indicates how comprehensively individual organisation members have bought into an ideology of self-regulation and self-censorship; a form of 'self-policing'. Over the time-period of a long career within the same organisation, this process of strict self-regulation will most certainly be likely to mould individual identity and personality. As a result, a Marxian perspective would see little overall difference between, say, the 'classical' approach of Frederick Taylor and the 'human relations' school of Mayo in terms of outcome. Both approaches would be said to indicate both exploitation of organisational members and commodification of each person's work duties and each person's 'self' in the Meadian (Mead, 1934) sense. Within the Marxian view, a Foucauldian approach emphasises the idea of a disciplinary set of technologies and these will assist the second understanding of the term develop from the rather cruder first meaning.

An examination of this thinking at this late stage is helpful because it provides one interesting and potentially valuable means of understanding the structural realities with which this study is engaged. Foucault (1977) utilises the notion of 'panopticism', first shaped (very much earlier) by Jeremy Bentham. This dealt with the ways that people in their places of work could be understood as 'prisoners' supervised through the all-seeing eye. Foucault's direction here is that change processes impact upon the body, and that 'body' is a metaphor both for the individual and the corporate entity. It permits Foucault the notion of 'political anatomy'. As a result of such close and hence oppressive observation, we arrive at an understanding of the domination and control that comprised people's experience of work. This, naturally, renders the panopticon, the place of imprisonment, as the workplace itself, and it also renders the people 'docile'. Foucault himself observed:

A body is docile that [it] may be subjected, used, transformed and improved. (Foucault, 1977, p.136)

The remark is in the context of a discussion of eighteenth century mechanisms of control, particularly associated with the French republic, but not necessarily confined to one geographical (or indeed historical) location. In the England of that day, the emergence of the First Republic and the strength of Napoleon Bonaparte was greeted with widespread anxiety in London society, commerce and Parliament about the possibility of a revolution that would parallel the events in France.

In the newly emerging industrial society, Foucault emphasised the extent of the control that disciplined the body:

...in every society, the body was in the grip of very strict powers, which imposed on it constraints, prohibitions or obligations... . (Foucault, 1977, p.137)

It is clear, then, that at even this preliminary stage, there is considerable scope for the development of an application of the Foucauldian perspective to the field- work generated from this study. However, such an application is the substance of another and separate piece of work.

So, the concluding discussion for this study as a whole needs to be the drawing together of the conclusions reached, coupled with the management recommendations that seem to derive from them.

1.   Perhaps the clearest finding from the fieldwork as a whole is that attempts to change corporate cultures on a massive scale are nearly impossible to achieve, certainly in the short, and probably also in the medium term. Time periods of over a decade may be necessary for older organisation members to leave through retirement whether this is voluntary or forced, early or at the normal age of around sixty to sixty five years. A decade may also be the minimum reasonable time for organisation members who are not yet at or near retirement age to learn and then personally imbibe new sets of deeply held attitudes, values and beliefs appropriate to new institutional ways of 'doing things round here' (Deal and Kennedy, 1982). In spite of all this, each of the two organisations attempted to establish a new culture. Since the measures of privatisation referred to at the beginning of chapter four of this study were enacted, over a decade *has*

passed. It is not in the terms of reference of this study to detail each structural alteration that has taken place. Suffice it to note that each organisation would seem to be unrecognisable to any person who left it at the first opportunity in the early and middle of the 1980s but who rejoined it now. Numbers are many fewer, the impact of technology on job duties has grown and many other ways of working have changed, too. Cultural change appears to be possible over such long periods, but whether what is in each person's heart and mind really changes or whether each simply learns expediency, is rather harder to determine. This is very difficult to establish in an employment market that has offered few alternative employment opportunities to dissenting organisational voices. It remains a suspicion that, at the level of generalisation, people will do and/or say whatever is expected of them, in order to cling onto employment when the local and national labour markets are both tight.

2. It is clear that the idea of organisational culture as experienced in real organisations seems to be different compared with the ideas expressed in management studies texts. It is not, then, something which it is possible for the highest echelons within an organisation to create and sustain. Rather, it is the unique set of organisational and behavioural outcomes of an established work group. It is about all the members' deeply held attitudes, values and beliefs, rather than some of them. It will therefore tend to include rather than exclude whole sets of sub-cultures and whole sets of anti-cultures. These will tend to endure whatever the extent of organisational change applied to them, short of demolition of the whole work group. For example, line managers within each organisation are reported as implying that they will happily pay lip service to the wishes of their seniors, in the hope of supporting the people who are their personal reports, until a particular rictus of change is over. Again, it is worth emphasising the question about whether this is evidence of a real change in all organisation members' hearts and minds or simply evidence of expedient behaviour. As with the first conclusion, this is also very difficult to establish in a British or regional labour market that continues to offer few alternative employment opportunities - especially to organisational members who are professed dissenting organisational voices. Members of both

organisations seem to have responded personally to their senior managers' attempts to lead culture change initiatives. The field-work evidence in the study identifies in very many places that their responses to the 'Sovereign' initiative in BT and the RO(a)R initiative within the gas company were deeply personalised. This may imply much about the way that subsequent managerial offences in this area should be shaped. It is clear that senior managements ignore such personalisation at their peril.

3.   Top down attempts to change an organisation's culture can be exploitative both in terms of the extra effort required by an individual to stay in charge of work duties and also emotionally in response to work conditions that have been changed by senior managements in an attempt to effect cultural change. With exploitation has come the anguish and pain recorded in chapter five and illuminated by the cognitive maps discussed in chapter six and contained in the appendices to this study. It has not been part of the remit of this study to examine the consequences of culture change strategies developed by senior managers in a really detailed way. Again, such a notion would form part of another, but closely related study. What is clear is that the rates of sickness absenteeism through stress has increased in both organisations (no statistical information is available in support of this assertion. Evidence for it is apocryphal). It is clear, however, that the national data shows that sickness absenteeism through stress-related illness has increased substantially over the period during which this study has been conducted and over the last whole decade and more.

4.   Sub-cultures and anti-cultures can be at least as powerful in their locales as the officially promulgated culture with its associated agenda for organisational change, or even simply the pre-existing 'official', that is to say, formal structural way of proceeding with work tasks and activities. Again, the field-work reveals many deeply jaundiced accounts of official behaviours which are indicative of the existence of organisational sub-cultures and anti-cultures. It is unlikely that people who are members of such oppositional groups within the organisations studied will ever be 'won over' by the new *status quo* developed

by a grouping of their organisational leaders in combination with their immediate seniors. It is suggested that such people will always be more likely to disagree with changes to working practices, but with varying degrees of volume, dependent upon who comprises the audience at a particular time. For example, in one small team office in one geographical location, within one of the two organisations, there was a document jointly updated by team members which recorded infelicitous remarks heard from or written by senior managers. The document was an object of ridicule and was used by its creators as 'evidence' of the 'conspiracy' perpetrated by senior managers on more junior grades, to extract more work from them for less reward than they were fairly entitled to receive.

5.   It remains a clear insight from the field work that so many of the managers and others who participated in the study remained loyal to the organisation that employed them, almost in spite of everything. Their perceptions of their organisational realities were uncomplaining and accepting of the substantial difficulties they found, each of which hampered them in producing the quality of work output that they frequently made it clear that they wished to provide.

6.   The matter of non-pecuniary rewards - part of what may be called the 'psychological contract' between employer and employee - seemed to be underplayed in at least the case of British Gas. The business of motivating large numbers of people at a time when monetary reward may not be either possible or appropriate is a serious matter judged from the management perspective. There is evidence that the matter has been neglected from the empirical work in this study.

7.   Issues around the degree of success in communications emanating from the highest echelons in each organisation come to the foreground in the discussion about promotion and motivation at a time when little or no promotion is possible. The message that a number of respondents in junior grades within each of the organisations studied wished to share was a pessimistic message. It seemed to say, sometimes tacitly and other times more explicitly, that the absence of promotion

accruing to them was because of their inability to measure up to work norms that sometimes appeared to be unattainable anyway. At other times, they were merely extremely professional levels that they set themselves. The result appeared to be that they were explaining the delicate position of their organisation in terms of their own inability consistently to achieve the highest levels of work performance and then maintain that indefinitely into the future. In short, a number of the more junior respondents seemed to blame themselves for organisational challenges that were not being met. Hence, they explained their own 'failure' to be promoted in those terms. A more rational perspective may not share that conclusion.

This research has four principal recommendations. These are:

1.   That middle and senior managers who have significant numbers of personal reports should receive training in the area of culture change. That will allow them to understand both the degree of complexity of the notion and the extent of the potentially harmful effects of ignoring the possibility of confused or even mischievous interpretations of their strategic directioning. This may be helpful in eliminating some of the worst excesses of management zeal that tried to change working practises in ways that were always likely to end in failure for the task objectives and personal pain for its team members. The research evidence in the cognitive maps reveals a number of example of clumsy management planning - or its lack - which unnecessarily inflicted losses of one kind or another on more junior organisation members. Exploitative relations will always be inimical to the best long term arrangements within organisations and the opportunity of the strong to exploit the weak always seems greater during times of rapid change.

2.   Culture change seems most efficacious when it becomes a strategy that organisation members seek to introduce through representations made by middle and junior managers and their personal reports, directed towards their most senior managers. This would require considerable investment to develop in each such person a macro- or meta-organisational perspective that

would give them sufficient personal, professional and emotional distance from their everyday duties to envisage such ideas. Culture change seems more 'real' and is more likely really to establish itself in the hearts and minds of organisation members when it is 'bottom up' rather than 'top down'.

3. Ways must be developed of competently facing member behaviours that indicate their membership of anti-cultures. The immediate priority seems to be accurately to diagnose such behaviours then attempt to teach different behaviours. Given the deep-seatedness in individuals of their attitudes, values and beliefs, this will not be easy to achieve, if, indeed, it is possible at all.

4. The loyalty and the evidence of effective and even innovative work identified in the fifth conclusion above should be rewarded if they are considered to be desirable employee traits. This needs to apply whether the employee is in a management grade or elsewhere in the hierarchy. Interview responses in chapter five that point to evidence of ritualised activity by managers need to be avoided. For example the sending out of 'thank you' notes which do not bear a personal signature seems to demotivate and render people cynical.

Summary and Chapter Conclusion

Discipline and control, accommodation and resistance seem to be key understandings that may be gleaned from the responses reported in chapter five and the mapping of them earlier in this chapter. It is proposed that if a four word summary of the relatively high volume of data in chapter five is possible, these four organisational insights may be pressed into service. However, this is not to oversimplify the notion of organisational culture. The concept is a complex one and the response-evidence eloquently bears testimony to that. Included in it, then, is a deal of management-supportive responses and behaviours that conflict with these reported understandings. There has been an honest attempt also to report that part of the data.

7   A Research Endpiece

This chapter seeks to update some of the theoretical threads of the study by recognising some of the new work in the field since this fieldwork and literature search was completed nearer to the middle of the decade than its turn. At the outset of this task, it is recognised that any attempt to develop and incorporate an account of the most recent thinking in the field is fraught with difficulties. One central difficulty is how best to 'set-off' the new ideas recognising both strengths and weaknesses. This requires some intellectual contexting that will inevitably demand a consideration of thinking published earlier. In so doing, there is a danger that the balance of what is intended to be a statement of most current thinking becomes stuck, and disturbed. If such a criticism as that could legitimately be made of this chapter, then that outcome would not be what was intended. So, the chapter contexts the findings from the empirical element of the research in this recent broader academic literature, and it has a number of strands developed from academic work-in-progress, and from already published work, that are interwoven in an attempt to deliver that objective. The key theoretical themes that have emerged, overall, from this study centre on the notions of discipline and control, accommodation and resistance, and so the examination of these ideas is continued here. This examination is conducted in the light both of the earlier discussion in chapter three and the empirical evidence already elaborated in chapter five.

Here, the strands comprise firstly a review of what is regarded as helpful thinking in the task of understanding the processes under analysis, and this is in two parts. The first part originates in recently published work from Stephen Ackroyd, of the Department of Behaviour in Organisations, within the University of Lancaster Business School. It is elaborated and then contrasted with what follows it. The second part of the review in the first strand is a brief consideration of the notion of 'trust' (Clark *et al.*, 1998). It will be argued that this idea is becoming an increasingly significant element in the debate about the social relations of organisations, in more recent literature. Its review is included here in recognition of the subtleties inherent in the relationships between organisational members and organisational seniors. It is to be regarded as a counterpoint to the consideration of the Willmott (1993) account of 'corporate culturism' that points up the in-built contradictions in the links between the notions of corporate culture and organisational change. There are both sharp differences, together with some more subtle resonances, compared with that adopted in the empirical phase of this study. The second strand of the chapter is also sub-divided. The first element deals with the debate about so-called 'strong' and 'weak' organisational cultures and examines some of this ground through the focus of a recently published text by Senior (1997). In so doing, it is proposed that the discussion rightly belongs in this final part of the study. The other part of the second strand is a consideration of Sackmann's (1997) recent contribution to the discussion about culture and organisation, on the basis of the collection of essays she edits. Of particular relevance to this part of the overall discussion in this chapter is the paper by McGovern and Hope-Hailey (1997). Their empirical approach takes a rather different emphasis to that of Senior (1997) and this is subsequently discussed.

Ackroyd, then, finds Atkinson's (1984) theorising about 'the flexible firm' as an inadequate account of the social reality it seeks to portray. There is, of course, a high degree of fit between the assumptions about labour flexibility that Atkinson makes, and a significant number of the reported responses in chapter five of this work, especially those originating in interviews with the more senior grades of managers who participated. For example, some interviews centred round the practical difficulties of hiring people whose jobs were recently made redundant. A number of these people were re-hired via an employment agency to do their old jobs, but as they were agency staff they were not directly employed by their old employer. Consequently, supervisors charged with the responsibility of managing the two groups working side by side found the unequal labour discipline and conditions of service challenging on a day-to-day basis. These processes may better be understood by Ackroyd and Proctor (1998) as a debate between the notions of what he re-labels the 'old flexible firm' to permit him to posit the existence of the 'new flexible firm'. The purpose of this element of the discussion is to illustrate how comfortably the evidence from the empirical enquiry in this study sits with the Ackroyd approach. The second strand of the chapter is an examination of some recent and largely managerialist thinking which culminates in what is argued to be an intellectual *cul-de-sac* when so-called 'strong' organisational cultures are identified and then compared with 'weak' ones. This strand challenges the entire basis upon which such thinking is constructed.

The case will be argued that there has been control exerted by organisational seniors in each of these manifestations of managerial strategic thinking, and this has separately been by Willmott (1993), Williams *et al.* (1992) and Foucault (1977), each identified in their different academic traditions. There are interesting links in particular between Ackroyd (1998) and the 'high surveillance firm' on the one hand and Foucault's concept of 'panopticism' on the other hand. An exploration of this linkage begins later in this chapter.

Over a decade ago, Pollert (1987) made a series of valuable criticisms of the notion of 'the flexible firm'. She argued persuasively that 'the model rests on an uncertain basis of confused assumptions and unsatisfactory evidence'. The assertion of a new polarization between core and periphery is misleading. So, it is clear that Ackroyd and Proctor have taken their places in a queue of writers presenting critiques of the flexible firm concept. He develops a model of the 'new flexible firm' ('the n.f.f.') as a culmination of theorising from a number of contributing models. All of his theorising is carefully confined to the context of manufacturing industry. Ackroyd has accumulated the 'Lancaster Archive of Large British Companies' through which it has been possible to identify the largest two hundred British firms, and within that number, further identify the sixty six largest manufacturing firms. His explanation for this surprisingly high fraction (1/3) of manufacturers over all large firms in Britain presently is interesting. He claims that his definition of a British firm is the reason; an enterprise needed to be quoted on the London Stock Exchange and have its Chief Office located in Britain to qualify for inclusion; naturally this excluded a significant number of private sector organisations which are manufacturing household names. However, they are not British by this definition.

Ackroyd recasts the Atkinson (1984) position as the 'old flexible firm', and uses this as a staging post *en route* to the 'knowledge intensive firm' and the 'high surveillance firm' before arriving at the already identified destination. The matrix below clarifies the relationships between these formulations. In the n.f.f. notion, Ackroyd identifies six features of note and these are subsequently discussed. Having established the importance of the sector both strategically and in quantitative terms, he carefully limits the context of his thinking to an industrial arena. However, this limitation is subsequently challenged.

The New Flexible Manufacturing Firm (n.f.f.); Summary of Features

1. The idea of the 'cell' explains how manufacturing workers are grouped. This permits an organisation of productive capacity which facilitates 'families' of components or other products. (i.e. related ones).

2. There is little use of advanced manufacturing technologies, partly through the cost in investment that may be regarded as prohibitive and partly through the concomitant requirement to train workers to operate effectively in such a high technology environment. Ackroyd observed that high technology may contribute as an adjunct to existing manufacturing equipment.

3. Flexibility is delivered via the work of teams of semi-skilled labourers. These have a limited on the job training so that they perform from a small repertoire different work tasks.

4. Unlike the Atkinson (1984) model, there is no core of key manual workers who enjoy a privileged status linked to high job security. Rather the existing labour force competes on price competitive terms with alternative, agency, labour suppliers and/or subcontractors and/or fixed contract labour for the opportunity to work and so earn income.

5. Through the 'cell working' principle already identified, each cell is segmented so that profit centres may be established and then the 'rigorous calculation' applied to them. Each centre is then an identifiable and hence dispensable element in the organisation overall.

6. The role for management in such an organisation is now clear: it minutely examines costs and this amounts to an intensive indirect control.

Source: Ackroyd and Proctor (1998) based on copyrighted material owned by Blackwell Publishers Ltd. and The London School of Economics and Political Science.

Ackroyd proposes two alternative constructs to the flexible firm of Atkinson (1984). These are the 'knowledge intensive firm' ('k.i.f.') and the 'high surveillance firm' ('h.s.f.'.). Neither is satisfactory. In the case of the former, Ackroyd argues that they are characterised by their highly technically sophisticated manufacturing. Yet, Ackroyd argues that the extensive Lancaster Archive of Large British Companies seems not to contain any real world examples of such organisations, so this formulation can hardly be seriously viewed as valuable in explaining the present conditions. Similarly, for Ackroyd, the 'h.s.f.' requires the 'last elements of effort that can be extracted from unwilling workers' (1998). Whilst this construct has an attraction in the light of the empirical evidence associated with this research project, Ackroyd asserts that it is typical only of electronics and other non-British owned manufacturing. At the pragmatic level, he identifies the substantial reductions in numbers of middle managers in such organisations who would presumably be tasked with the surveillance responsibilities. At this pragmatic level, it would then be difficult to sustain an argument that proposed that this the h.s.f. is an effective analysis of more than a tiny fraction of manufacturing in Britain. However such a perspective may miss the increasing impact of information technology upon the managerial surveillance of workers in the service sector. Certainly, the impact was significant on attitudes to work, job performance and work duties originating in computer software that had just become commercially available during the time this empirical enquiry was conducted. In the telecommunications company, the arrival of the 'WorkManager' package had just such a set of consequences. The software provides detailed tracking of the individualised progress of a telephone fitter's progress through a day's duties and this was introduced into one workplace during the time interviews were being conducted. According to the account of the supervising manager of such manual workers, those whose work was about to be managed in a different fashion greeted its arrival with anxiety and suspicion.

Those manufacturing firms that are high profit earners cannot best be modelled as either k.i.f. or as h.s.f. Ackroyd argues that 'the leading manufacturing firms in Britain are shy about challenges to their profit making capacity and keen to get in on others' [abilities to make profits]' (1998). The Lancaster Archive demonstrates that such organisations seek to find low capitalisation projects that will make the smallest possible investment demands in return for the largest possible short-term profits. The chief economic purpose of the n.f.f. is simply to reduce the risk that adequate returns on capital employed will not be achieved. So, the n.f.f. is a vehicle to achieve maximum profit from the organisation in the shortest time period available. In the service sector, typically the most expensive item on the balance sheet is the cost of labour, and so Ackroyd may also be able to explain why so many jobs are lost, through this analysis.

It may be, then, that there is a greater applicability of this modelling than initially appears possible. The two organisations at the centre of this research project are firmly located in the service sector of private enterprise and so are excluded from the Ackroyd area of interest - yet the idea of 'cell working' described above, to deliver service tasks rather than tangible goods, seems plausible. Secondly, the evidence gathered in this study about managerial parsimony in terms of investment in new, for example, telephone technology or desk top computer facilities sits comfortably beside the reasons advanced by Ackroyd (1998) for managerial lack of interest in purchasing advanced manufacturing technology. Similarly, the employee perceived lack of real commitment by their immediate and more senior managers to expensive staff development and training is also consistent with the tenets of n.f.f. Thirdly was the idea of team working and so-called 'dual-skilling' or even 'multi-skilling' which was the 'in-vogue' notion in the offices of the energy company examined in the empirical phase of this study. The idea was every bit as apparent in the retraining of telephone answering clerks also to deal with correspondence as Ackroyd (1998) found in the industrial context of his fieldwork. Fourthly, there is an increasing volume of evidence that has been derived both anecdotally from respondents and also on a whole organisation basis from published annual data. It indicates that the senior managements of each of the two organisations studied were increasingly moving to an employment settlement that destabilised job tenure. It also encouraged the recruitment of fixed term contract and employment agency employed people to work alongside existing and tenured staff groups. Fifthly, the large aggregates of staff and manual grades were increasingly subject to reorganisation into smaller and more localised teams (or 'cells' in Ackroyd's (1998) account). The notion of 'floating off' such teams (or 'cells') was increasingly passing into the general vocabulary of the people in the staff and manual grades that participated in the research. Finally, the interview evidence itself has remarks from heads of geographically localised teams which make clear their impatience to reduce costs by identifying the 'underperformance' so that it could be dealt with in an appropriate manner. As a result of all of this, there seems clear potential further to develop this model.

As a result of the foregoing, an initial and preliminary application of Ackroyd's (1998) thinking to the evidence and context of this research suggests that a fruitful avenue for further empirical enquiry is the relationship between non-manufacturing environments and his notion of the 'new flexible firm'. An ethnomethodological account of this might emphasise the ways in which social actors acting out roles in organisations may use the construct to underpin perceptions of the working realities in which they collectively collaborate to make sense of the social process. A positivist account in particular might seek to develop an early hypothesis that could be built around the idea that the new flexible firm extends well beyond the manufacturing sector, perhaps into the public services of the late century as well as the service sector element of private enterprise.

The Development of the New Flexible Firm in British Industry

Model	Staffing	Technology	Management Objectives/Strategy
Atkinson Model (o.f.f.)	**Requirements:** Highly skilled + low skilled.	Unspecified.	Policy and strategy unspecified.
Knowledge intensive firm (k.i.f.)	**Requirements:** Very highly skilled only.	High technology centred production only.	High quality, high specificity. Medium to large batch production. **Strategy:** high value added.
High surveillance firm (h.s.f.)	**Requirements:** Semi-skilled. **Policy:** progression through training.	Medium to high use of productive technology. **Policy:** routine IT surveillance.	**Objective:** reliable, high quality; large variety and volume production. **Strategy:** market penetration.
New flexible firm (n.f.f.)	**Requirements:** Some skilled but mostly unskilled. **Policy:** limited on the job training.	Low to medium technology. Cell working.	**Objective:** medium to large batches of related products for specific niches. **Strategy:** short-term profitability.

Source: Ackroyd and Proctor (1998).

Whether what Ackroyd has analysed and described amounts to the emergence of 'strong' organisational cultures which will then inevitably go on (in an almost Darwinian sense) to supplant 'weak' cultures is very much open to question, as indicated by the evidence already considered in preceding chapters of this study. Certainly, remembering its appearance in Peters and Waterman (1982) and Handy (1986), the analysis of so-called 'strong' cultures is a popular line of analysis in some parts of the academic

206 Organisational Culture: Organisational Change?

literature. It is conjectured that this is, perhaps, especially the case where such thinking is assisted by an investment of private sector capital as consultancy fees and associated expenses. Conducting the debate in terms of a language that identifies some cultures as 'strong' while others are 'weak' is another means of using language to hide competing perceptions of reality - that emanate, for example, from less powerful levels within the organisational hierarchies.

An examination of the idea of 'trust' as recently used in the academic literature will cast additional helpful light on the debate at this point and so it is to this area that the discussion now turns. The second part of the review of recent work was to be the consideration of the concept of 'trust'. In the context of a debate about the gender dimension within British higher education, Clark *et al.* (1998) observe:

> Commentators have borne witness to concerted attempts to rationalise higher education through an attack on the perceived inefficiencies of bureaucratic inertia and the tenacities of what have been seen as vested professional interests. A new managerialism, designed to deliver cost efficiencies and energise sinecured and moribund academics with aggressive entrepreneurial flair, has been in evidence in higher education... .

Here, there are strong echoes of attempts to uproot an existing organisational culture in British higher education and in some way or ways supplant it with a new one, based upon a formula developed and promulgated by the relevant senior management. No doubt part of this 'gap' between perceived reality and reality *per se* is the image of the university in British public life as meritocratic and collegial and the 'managerial masculinity' revealed to organisation members. Clark *et al.* (1998) argue that 'a 'hard' managerialism has displaced trust in higher education'. But, this particular type of cultural imperialism has the room for 'resistance to easy imbibing of commercial discourse'. It is in this space that their fieldwork is situated and it is interesting to note that their work attempts to address the perceived realities of organisation members in an empirical way. However, the present focus needs to be on their exegesis of 'trust'. Clark *et al.* (1998) propose that we should not:

> ignore the complex relationship between altruism...and control. After all, trust is what the professional seeks since the professional does profess, he [*sic*] asks that he be trusted;... In place of *'caveat emptor'* we have *'credat emptor'*... .

One insight is that the extent to which the professional control is the extent to which that person can act altruistically. The discussion turns on the role of the university lecturer as professional, but in the context of this study, the notion of 'professional' sits well with 'manager', especially that of 'senior manager'. There has been little evidence of altruism reported in the interview data in chapter five of this work; rather, there is better evidence for the classic Illich (1977) observation that 'the professions are a conspiracy against society'. He was pointing to the stark way in which professionals were (and indeed still are) able to maintain their hegemony through a series of strategies cloaked by an ideology of caring. Clark *et al.* (1998) go on to examine the work of Luhmann (1998) in order to elicit meaning from the links between 'trust' and 'confidence'. One similarity is that both ideas require a certain amount of risk to be accepted by the social actors concerned. However, in the case of trust, the actor will take a decision based upon that person's own best estimate of the outcome. The decision will typically be guided by the professional, but the person takes responsibility upon his/her self.

> The issue of confidence, deriving from expectation and shared assumptions underpins what has come to be called the new institutionalism or neo-institutionalism (Powell and DiMaggio, 1991, p.2; Lane and Bachmann, 1996, pp.370-371). Sociological in origin (with ethnomethodological and phenomenological roots) new institutionalism shows how taken for granted assumptions guide behaviour leading to the accomplishment of social relations and institutions - even if these sometimes work against the interests of those involved. (Powell and DiMaggio, 1991, p.26)

The key phrase in this quotation is, of course, the last phrase. It is an explanation of the trust exhibited by the more junior organisation members in respect of their dealings with their organisational seniors. It hints at the way that relations with, say practitioners of medicine, dentistry or chiropody may be transposed to the social and economic arena of workplace relations. It may be the case that trust is understood differently in each of these contexts. In the latter case there may be a tacit but quintessentially unexplored assumption that organisational juniors exhibit a preference for working long hours and in anxiety concerning their own job security in order further to develop the drive in favour of profit over the needs of labour. Here is another interesting overlap between empirical work examining culture and change - this study - and empirical work focussed upon gender and higher education.

Senior (1997) is also interesting. She provides a summary of available thinking in and around the area of organisational cultural change, and a debt is owed to this work for the insightful way that it summarises the intellectual background to the empirical evidence already discussed in this study. One of her main objectives is her attempt to examine how culture change in the literature is presently described and analysed, and another key theme for her is her examination of the structures, cultures, politics and leadership of change. Some of this is a useful broad focus for the framework of this part of this chapter. However, there are also significant weaknesses and shortcomings in the content and general approach of some of the Senior discussion, as well as strengths. Principal amongst these, perhaps, is the reification of the notion of organisation, and the reification of the concomitant notion of organisational management, with all that this implies. For example, there is an unmistakable feel of 'recipe knowledge' about the way that Child (1988) is cited in his listing of some of the results of the self-perceived inadequacies of organisation structures. He observes the following ingredients in the checklist:

> motivation and morale [of organisation members] may be depressed because... decision-making may be delayed and lacking in quality because...there may be conflict and a lack of co-ordination because... .

> an organisation may not respond innovatively to changing circumstances... .

> costs may be rising rapidly, particularly in the administrative area because... .

These may be useful common sensical insights into the ways that managers may be able to approach what they perceive as problems within their working lives. However, this overwhelmingly managerialist perspective effectively kills off the chance of the development of the provision of a hearing for any alternative accounts of the structure and nature of the essentially shared social reality of the workplace. A number of recently published works adopt this managerialist flavour, and the full titles of such works eloquently make that point. For example, Hampden-Turner's (1994) work *Corporate Culture* is subtitled *How to Generate Organisational Strength and Lasting Commercial Advantage*. Similarly, Hoecklin's work (1995) *Managing Cultural Differences* is subtitled *Strategies for Competitive Advantage*. Thirdly, and a little more chronologically distant although still very consistent with this theme, is Graves' (1986) work *Corporate Culture: Diagnosis and Change*. It is subtitled *Auditing and Changing the Culture of Organisations*. In each of these three books, the managerialist perspective could not be more explicit, and each appears to have its own, cosy moral justification for its position. In the case of Hoecklin, for example, she argues:

> Morality is a movable feast…values are relative…beliefs were based on the particular cultures they came from and each thought their own beliefs were correct. (Hoecklin, 1995, pp.10-11)

Such moral relativism probably has a place in academic discourse which is unrelated to the real world of the lives of organisational members as they negotiate through these times in which they are employed. However, such a perspective seems moderately slippery when used as a springboard to launch an analysis that seems to move inexorably towards the position: 'so why bother to try at all if it's not possible to achieve an absolute goodness in senior managements' dealings with staff groups?'

In contrast to all of this, an ethnographic methodology will suggest that the social reality of organisation membership and experience is collaboratively produced. As a result, it seems both contradictory and limiting that a significant body of the existing academic literature seems to celebrate the existence of the managerialist voice on the one hand and yet denies the authentic (and yet equally valid) voice of less high status organisation members on the other. It is the contention of this research that such checklists of organisational characteristics as earlier identified by Child (1988) offer little that is helpful to serious organisational analysis and that no matter how 'bespoke' such recipes may be, they cannot ever do justice to the rich complexities of organisational life. It is also the case that thorough empirical investigation may hardly achieve in terms of understanding that which an organisational membership may take years to understand. However such a direction seems to be more helpful than the alternatives.

This is an example of one *cul-de-sac* amongst many. It seems to be situated in that part of the academic literature that denies the legitimacy of some lower-placed members of the organisation to collaborate in defining the social processes experienced as part of their membership of their organisations. However, the Johnson and Gill (1993) approach seems better to capture the flavour of the evidence. They argue:

> Many of the prescriptions for cultural control through creating 'strong' cultures as a means of manipulating members is…somewhat crude, unsophisticated and touching only on the surface manifestations of

> organisational life. At worst, the management of culture emphasises the role
> that leaders and managers play when managing the socio-emotional
> domain...which is heavily dependent upon human relations assumptions,
> albeit it dressed up in new clothes. (Johnson and Gill, 1993, p.108)

This source is, then, clear that the real agenda of the proponents of organisational culture change is one that addresses control and perhaps even domination in the drive for super-normal profits. At an early stage in their argument they appear convinced that it is the superficial studies of 'organisation-culture-in-action' which are the managerialist ones. Most interestingly, the reference to the 'new clothes' in which the human relations assumptions are said to be dressed up touch upon a long and distinguished critical academic literature. This literature virtually spans the twentieth century. It originates in the debate begun by Frederick Winslow Taylor (1947 (3rd. edn.)) in his propositions about the efficacy of scientific management, it is then reincarnated in another suit of the 'new clothes' as 'the human relations school' (see Roethlisberger and Dickson, 1939). The most recent visit to the tailor seems to have produced what Willmott's (1992, 1993) polemic called 'corporate culturism'. Of course, what is in common between these notions is the consistent thread of management control over successively more and more of the lives of the organisation members in the context of their paid employments. At each spinning, the thread is manufactured as finer and finer yet stronger and stronger. This sub-strand of the literature is central to a complete reading of this study's contribution to the academic debate, and will shortly be considered in further detail, in the broader context of the Senior (1997) discussion about the structures, cultures, politics and leadership of change. Further elaboration of the Johnson and Gill (1993) argument is helpful at this point. They go on to assert:

> The main criticism of those who advocate cultural control is that it is not
> possible to manage and control cultures closely by their very nature and,
> further, that the more extreme and mechanistic prescriptions for managing
> cultures are, then, often the more manipulative, coercive and patronising
> and these are likely to be counter-productive in the longer term. (Johnson
> and Gill, 1993, p.108)

The evidence generated in this study seems to suggest that subtle processes are at work. This is in contrast to a rather crude view of conspiracy. Such a position supposes a liaison between the uppermost echelons of each organisation, each of which attempts to tread underfoot the needs and aspirations of its lower organisational hierarchy. This latter group amounts to a latter day kind of *lumpen proletariat*. Whether understood as subtle or crude, these processes may, nevertheless, have similar outcomes; each asserts as valid that organisational cultures can exert considerable control over organisational members.

What Johnson and Gill (1993) refer to as 'the management of meaning' is said to run parallel with the cultural apparatus which managements may seek to enshrine in the hearts and minds of their employees. Yet, this contrasts with evidence from this study revealed in a consideration of the impact of, say, the imposition of huge and open-plan office accommodation on employee groups. It is clear from the evidence that there was a sharply contrasting understanding of the agenda between the more senior and the more junior grades. This reveals the ambiguities. For example, the values of trust, openness and interpersonal communication of a real kind are said by the higher grades to be the reasons why such working arrangements have been established. This widely promulgated agenda seems to sit awkwardly as a gloss on a related agenda that emphasises what Johnson and Gill (1993) summarise as 'an emphasis on individual appraisal, secrecy about the level of rewards, and non-unionism' (1993, p.109).

They go on to add that what is good for the organisation is said also to be good for the employee and that this is managerial[ist], and that this has always been a feature of work organisations. The *raison d'être* for such thinking has already been identified above, namely the century of corporate control by organisational leaders over their employees. Johnson and Gill go on substantially to modify their position by making a reference to 'brain-washing and totalitarianism'. This mongrel of an idea that they themselves erect is then safely neutered with the remark 'however this may be an unduly pessimistic [set of] observation[s]' (1993, p.109). It is a contention of this study that some management behaviour is accurately described by Johnson and Gill (1993) as 'manipulative and insincere'. The related contention begins to emerge; that such behaviour possibly may be understood as part of a wider strategy to corral the non-work as well as the work behaviour in organisational life of a significant number of people in more junior grades. Furthermore, issue is taken with their assertion that follows the remark. They propose that 'cynical, pointed jokes are very powerful in helping to destroy the very practices to which they are directed'. They offer no evidence of their own in support, neither do they indicate a timescale during which such practices could be expected to be destroyed. This indifference seems not to be borne out by the empirically derived data from this study. Here, there is the evidence of the domain analysis already discussed. In contrast, this study points to concerns that are both contemporaneous and clearly expressed by organisational members interviewed. They focus on the position of people at a variety of points in their organisational hierarchies. We hear of their seeming lack of ability to stop the juggernaut of organisational change from steam-rollering them on the other side of the equation, in a number of what seem to be significant examples already cited in chapter five above. This contrasts with the complacency of Johnson and Gill (1993). They appear to mistake efforts by organisational members to produce effective strategies to combat unwelcome change with the 'cynical, pointed jokes that often amount to simple gallows humour'.

Issues about the 'strength' (or, indeed, the 'weakness') of each of the two organisation cultures examined seem to come nearer to the fore with such thinking, and further examination of this matter is appropriate. Consequently, it will be helpful to examine the literature to provide context and this will assist in making an assessment of the two cultures examined. Barbara Senior (1997) has a helpful insight. Quoting Brown (1995) 'Organisational cultures differ markedly in terms of their relative strengths', she goes on to comment:

> Whether defensive or supportive, intuitively, the existence of a strong culture implies a commonly understood perspective on how organisational life should happen, with most organisational members subscribing to it. Conversely, a weak culture implies no dominant pervasive culture, but an organisation made up of many different cultures, some of which will be in conflict with each other. (Senior, 1997, pp.137-138)

Both this study and Payne's (1997) thinking suggest that two sensible measures of the strength of an organisation's culture may be the degree of its widespreadness across its various boundaries and the intensity with which the culture is embraced by the organisational members.

According to Brown (1995), there are four consequences to having a strong or weak culture. These refer to the way that internal conflicts can be settled; in the Deal and Kennedy (1982) sense. This is about knowing about 'the way we do things round here'. Secondly, if the culture is said to be strong, it is supposed to help co-ordinate and control attitudes values and beliefs so that organisation members will all direct their energies towards achieving organisational goals. The third element is the uncertainty avoidance principal. Here, members new to the organisation will learn very quickly in a strong organisational culture what counts as a rational response to any eventuality and this rapidity will reduce the duration of the socialisation period of new members when such anxiety is most likely. Finally, the level of employee motivation is expected to be high as a result of their membership of a strong culture. This is to be understood as quite separate from pay rewards or other clear-cut means of measurement such as promotion through status (without pecuniary advancement).

An examination of these thoughts from Senior (1997) which she derives from Brown (1995) through the focus of empiricism in this study is revealing. The first assertion is that strong cultures resolve conflicts. If trades union membership is suppressed through management policies designed actively to discourage membership then both organisations studied had locales where this management policy was clearly evident. In the case of the energy company, there was one local manager who publicly espoused such principles. This person's arrival was recent at the time interviews were conducted at that location and so it is not possible to draw firm conclusions. However, it was apparent that resentment was caused amongst middle managers and supervisors at what were seen by them as attacks on their labour institutions. In the period of time between the interviews and the present, it is known that the local senior manager has left the place of work and a more ameliorative style of management replaced that which preceded it. In the telecommunications company, the central London locations where many of the chief office staff were based who were included in the sample had a significant number of management grade people who espoused views that were consistent with Senior and Brown. They seemed to be regarded as relatively out of touch with the views and attitudes of people on the ground in the regions and so in the other operating divisions of the company.

The second consequence of strong cultures concerns co-ordination and control. In the energy company location identified in the preceding paragraph, there is no doubt that that was the strongest culture observed. The incoming senior manager invested considerable financial resources in remodelling the premises and reorganising previously existing patterns of work and reporting relationships. In chapter five of this study, the comment that 'this is Year Nought', in the style of Pol Pot, was made by a person at this location. However, whether at the time of investigation this made everyone pull together was very much open to question. There was certainly much resentment, anxiety and anger, as judged by the comments made by people employed there. In the case of the telecommunications company, it is difficult to identify a suitable part of the organisation for an insight in this respect. The organisation as a whole was (and still remains) in search of a structure dynamic enough to grapple with change yet 'solid' enough to provide appropriate levels of support for its members. Consequently, there were no centres of 'new culture' that were observed and were effective enough to count here. However, in the parts of the country some hundreds of miles away from London, there was good evidence of 'old culture'. For example, the most outspokenly critical views of most senior management emanated from such locations. Criticisms centred on failures to communicate information and urgency to dismantle old structures before erecting new structures with which to replace them.

The third aspect of the Senior view originating in Brown's thinking is that of the reduction of uncertainty amongst organisation members. Neither organisation furnished new employees for interview purposes. This is hardly surprising since the focus for research was middle managers and both organisations were and still remain well known for promoting staff from within, when there were promotions to be made. Consequently, neither would have many people who were in promoted posts and were also newly appointed to the organisation. However, a significant proportion of people on both payrolls were in new parts of their organisations - some by request, but many more by transfer as a result of local or wider scale reorganisation. One respondent was comfortable with the word 'reorg.' as a means of succinctly expressing his recent experience within his organisation; he felt so busy - and pressurised that the tacit meaning he offered was that he was simply too busy to spend the time to speak the whole word! In such cases, there was a degree of mutual anxiety about the quality of the new working relationships that would result as a consequence of the organisational upheavals. No party to the research ever mentioned anything to do with reduction of uncertainty. It is contended that such linguistic constructions belong where they originate; in textbooks and in the minds of organisational historians who may choose to take *carte blanche* with the motives, purposes and intentions of social actors in a time period when the issues are of little importance to the protagonists.

The fourth element in the discussion about the most recent contributions to the debate about strong (and weak) cultures is that concerning motivation. It is clear from the evidence gleaned at both organisations that, overall, the sample identified with their organisation and with their work. Senior remarks:

> ...a culture which can offer employees a means of identification with their
> work, which can foster loyalty and assist their belief that they are valued,

will add to their motivation and presumably the overall organisational performance. (1997, p.101)

This is, no doubt, a valid point. However, it says little about which of the many prevailing cultures in an organisation will do this because this piece of wisdom misses all the richness of the variety that real organisations offer for analysis. This is especially pertinent at a time of great flux in both of the organisations investigated, when senior managements in each attempted to superimpose a new culture on top of a pre-existing one. The evidence is that at a time of rapid organisational change organisational members would be more likely to feel valued and motivated if they were left alone to achieve their pre-existing job objectives. This seems always to be regarded by post-holders as preferable to a job review - with all that that implies about the senior management perceptions of the value of their present duties and the consequent need to overturn those present duties in favour of new responsibilities. It must be remembered that, for some of the respondents, sometimes the old duties have been a responsibility for many years and so obliterating them spoke eloquently about their value in more recent times. This seems some distance away from the blanket prescription of Senior and Brown about the motivating and loyalty enhancing influences of organisational change on the people who undergo this. Theirs seems a rather pious and certainly managerialist perspective.

Senior concludes this section of her book by commenting that organisations with 'a weak dominant culture' may be advantageously situated compared with the strong:

> Strong, all-pervasive cultures can be a disadvantage when they become so controlling that there is little potential for the non-conformity that brings innovation and the capacity to adapt to change. (1997, p.138)

It is difficult not to be sympathetic with such a view, even though it is rooted in a social theoretical perspective that originates in the Mertonian functionalism of over forty years ago. It is mainly, but not entirely, for this reason that the 'strong versus weak' means of understanding the debate is identified as a *cul-de-sac*. Furthermore, on the basis of the evidence generated by this study, both of the senior managements within the two organisations studied would seem to disagree most strongly with the thinking that Senior elaborates. Each management tried to supplant 'weak' national level cultures with 'strong' ones, without allowance for the very many existing workplace organisational sub-cultural variations documented consistently as different in the various geographical locations where interviews and observation work was conducted as part of this study. The consequences of these management decisions to induce organisational culture change in the manner described and analysed amount to the contested terrain that forms the heart of this study, and about which Edwards (1971, p.131) wrote so convincingly. For him, an understanding of organisational culture involved the acceptance of a view that managements achieve domination in 'their' places of work through their frequently unchallenged right to manage the social and organisational structures within their companies.

The contribution of McGovern and Hope-Hailey (in Sackmann, 1997) that was identified in the opening paragraphs of this chapter is of interest here. Their empiricism produces this fascinating proposition:

> [Our] first [conclusion] concerns the introduction of a recent 'downsizing' program introduced by the [Hewlett Packard] company and employee responses to what was apparently the destruction of one of the central tenets of corporate philosophy: jobs for life. (McGovern and Hope-Hailey, 1997, p.188)

The anger detailed in so many of the interviews in chapter five of this study is tacit but still eloquent recognition of the power of their insight. The comfort of an implied 'job for life' would mitigate circumstances of relatively low pay over a number of years. The impact of the realisation of the fundamental emptiness of such an implied promise - that the sacrifices were all for nought as the job has disappeared anyway - is likely to generate the high level of anguish that chapter five of this study reveals in so many places. Their second conclusion joins together Edwards' idea (1971) of the power of bureaucratic control with their own perspective that emphasises that this occurs within the larger framework of a corporate culture; these pair of suppositions are said by them to exist in tandem.

Given the size and complexity of each organisation that had respondents in this study, the task assumed by the senior managements of reforming each culture is nothing less than audacious in its scope and scale. That each senior management has succeeded in effecting change is beyond doubt; whether this has all been intended outcomes of intended actions is - adopting the most optimistic interpretation possible rather than advisable - rather less clear. The rhetorical level of the debate is well captured by McGovern and Hope-Hailey. They contend that the culture of an organisation may be manipulated by use of mission statements and alterations to management styles:

> ...so that managements come to believe in profitability through people and employees come to believe in...being close to the customer, and the search for excellence becomes both a shared challenge and the means of boosting corporate profitability. (McGovern and Hope-Hailey, 1997, p.189)

Whom has benefited most from all the organisational stakeholders - employees, shareholders, neighbours and so on - is, as the above quotation suggests, rather less open to doubt. It is clear that equity values have moved ahead considerably in recent years, whilst numbers of people employed have fallen sharply, salary and wage costs have been tightly restrained for all but the very senior, board level groups, and environmental damage has been widely reported.

As indicated in the opening paragraphs, the final part of this chapter has sought to context the findings of the empirical enquiry within the most recent relevant academic literature. It is worthwhile to examine the way that the debate about power and control has been developed during the twentieth century, in the context of organisation, by pointing to the sympathies that exist between the outcomes of this study and their intellectual parents. Such parents are domiciled in the consequences of intellectual constructs such as mass production, Fordism, and the human relations management style. They are, perhaps, presently residing in the whole discussion about so-called 'strong' and 'weak' cultures and the general linkage between academe, management (that is, managerialist) consultancy initiatives and organisational leadership. This overarching framework is at its most visible when, as has been the case earlier in this work, the language of domination is considered. The final example of this is where managers choose to replace the word 'redundancy' with the idea of 'efficiency'.

Summary and Chapter Conclusion

This chapter has attempted to update the theoretical elements of the study by bringing into focus work written in the three years since the last empirical activity in this study was concluded. A number of different ideas are identified, and they are set in the context of the literature of the 1980s and 1990s. It is from there that much of the material in chapter three of this work is drawn, either as a consequence itself of earlier thinking, or as a new departure in terms of the hitherto existing literature.

Bibliography

Ackermann, F. (1995), *Graphics COPE Users Guide*, Banxia Software (University of Strathclyde), Glasgow.

Ackroyd, S. and Proctor, S. (1998), 'British Manufacturing Organisations and Workplace Industrial Relations, *British Journal of Industrial Relations*, vol. 36, no. 2, pp. 163-181.

Ackroyd, S. and Thompson, P. (1994), *Misbehaviour and Management in The New Organisations*, British Academy of Management, (September), Lancaster University.

Alvesson, M. (1993), *Cultural Perspectives on Organisation*, Cambridge University Press, Cambridge.

Argyris, C. (1964), *Integrating the Individual and the Organisation*, John Wiley, New York.

Argyris, C. (1991), 'Teaching Smart People How to Learn', *Harvard Business Review*, May/June.

Aron. (1965), *Main Currents in Sociological Thought*.

Atkinson, J. (1984), 'Manpower Strategies For Flexible Organisations', *Personnel Management*, April.

Bate, P. (1994), *Strategies For Cultural Change*, Butterworth Heinemann, Oxford.

Becker, H.S. (1963), *Outsiders*, Free Press of Glencoe, New York.

Beckhard, R. (1969), *Organisational Development: Strategy and Models*, Addison-Wesley, Reading, Massachusetts.

Belbin, M. (1993), *Team Roles at Work*, Butterworth Heinemann, Oxford.

Bendix, R. (1960), *Max Weber: An Intellectual Portrait*, Doubleday, New York.

Bendix, R. and Lipset, S.M. (eds.), (1967), *Class, Status and Power*, Routledge and Kegan Paul, London.

Bennis, W. (1959), 'Leadership Theory and Administrative Theory: Problems', *Administrative Science Quarterly*, vol. 4, no. 3.

Berger, P. and Luckmann, T. (1966), *The Social Construction of Reality*, Penguin, Harmondsworth.

Blake, R.R. and Mouton, J.S. (1964), *The Managerial Grid*, Gulf Publishing, Houston, Texas.

Blumer, H. (1962), 'Society as Symbolic Interaction', in A. Rose (ed.), (1962), *Human Behaviour and Social Processes*, Routledge and Kegan Paul, London.

Bott, E. (1971), *Family and the Social Network*, Tavistock, London.

Brake, M. (1980), *The Sociology of Youth Culture*, Routledge and Kegan Paul, London.

Braverman, H. (1974), *Labor and Monopoly Capital: The Degradation of Work in the Twentieth Century*, Monthly Review Press, New York.

Brown, A. (1995), *Organisational Culture*, Pitman Publishing, London.

Bryman, A. (ed.), (1988), *Doing Research in Organisations*, Routledge, New York.

Carr, E. (1964), *What is History?*, The GM Trevelyan Memorial Lectures, Penguin, Harmondsworth.

Carr, W. and Kemmis, S. (1986), *Becoming Critical: Education, Knowledge and Action Research*, Deakin University Press, Deakin.

Child, J. (1988), *Organizations: A Guide to Problems and Practice*, Paul Chapman, London.

Clark, H., Chandler, J. and Barry, J. (1994), *Organisation and Identities: Text and Readings in Organisational Behaviour*, Chapman and Hall, London.

Clark, H., Chandler, J. and Barry, J. (1998), *Scholarly Relations: Gender, Trust and Control in the Life of Organisations*, European Group For Organisation Studies, 14th Colloquium, Maastricht.

Clarke, L. (1994), *The Essence of Change*, Prentice Hall, Hertfordshire.

Corrigan, P. (1975), 'Doing Nothing', in S. Hall and T. Jefferson, (1975), *Resistance Through Rituals*, Hutchinson, London.

Corrigan, P. (1981), *Schooling The Smash Street Kids*, Macmillan, London.

Deal, T.E. and Kennedy, A.A. (1982), *Corporate Cultures: The Rites and Rituals of Corporate Life*, Addison-Wesley, Reading, Massachusetts.

Dennison, D. (1990), *Corporate Culture and Organizational Effectiveness*, John Wiley, New York.

Dreyfus, H. and Rabinow, P. (1982), *Michel Foucault: Beyond Structuralism and Hermeneutics*, Harvester Press, Sussex.

Durkheim, E. (1938), *The Rules of Sociological Method*, Free Press, New York.

Edwards, R. (1971), *Contested Terrain: Transformation of the Workplace in the Twentieth Century*, Basic Books, New York.

Elsmore, P.J.A. (1994), *Penetrating Large-Scale Organisations*, South Bank University Press, London.

Elsmore, P.J.A. and Jenkins, H. (1994), *Who Benefits From Changes in Organisational Cultures?*, British Academy of Management, September, Lancaster.

Fayol, H. (1930), *Industrial and General Administration*, Geneva International Management Institute, Geneva.

Filmer, P., Silverman, D., Walsh, D. and Phillipson, M. (1972), *New Directions in Sociological Theory*, Collier-Macmillan, London.

Foucault, M. (1977), *Discipline and Punish: The Birth of the Prison*, Penguin, Harmondsworth.

Furlong, V. (1975), *Towards a Study of Pupil Knowledge*, Open University Press, Milton Keynes.

Furlong, V. (1984), 'Interaction set in the Classroom: Towards a Study of Pupil Knowledge", in: M. Hammersley and P. Woods (eds.), *Life in School: The Sociology of Pupil Culture*, Open University Press, Milton Keynes.

Gambetta, D. (ed.), (1998), *Trust: Making and Breaking Co-operative Relations*, Sage, London.

Garfinkel, H. (1967), *Studies in Ethnomethodology*, Prentice Hall, Englewood Cliffs.

Gerth, H.H. and Mills, C.W. (eds.), (1948), *From Max Weber: Essays in Sociology*, Routledge and Kegan Paul, London.

Goffman, E. (1968), *Asylums*, Penguin, Harmondsworth.

Gramsci, A. (1971), *Selection From the Prison Notebooks*, Lawrence and Wishart, London.

Graves, D. (1986), *Corporate Culture: Diagnosis and Change*, Francis Pinter, London.

Hall, S. and Jefferson, T. (1975), *Resistance Through Rituals*, Hutchinson, London.

Hall, S., Critcher, C. *et al.* (1979), *Policing the Crisis*, Macmillan, London.

Hampden-Turner, C. (1994), *Corporate Culture: How to Generate Organisational Strength and Lasting Commercial Advantage*, Judy Piatkus, London.

Hammerslay, M. and Woods, P. (1976), *The Process of Schooling*, Routeledge and Kegan Paul, London.

Handy, C. (1985), *Understanding Organisations*, Penguin, Harmondsworth.

Handy, C. (1986), *Understanding Organisations*, (2nd edn.), Penguin, Harmondsworth.

Hannagan, T. (1995), *Management Concepts and Practices*, Pitman, London.

Hoecklin, L. (1995), *Managing Cultural Differences: Strategies for Competitive Advantage*, Addison Wesley, London.

Hofstede, G. (1984), *Cultural Consequences: International Differences in Work Values*, Sage, Beverley Hills.

Hofstede, G. (1988), 'Cultures and Organizations: From Fad to Management Tool', *University of Wales Review of Business and Economics*, vol. 9.

Hofstede, G. (1992), *Culture and Organizations: Software of the Mind*, McGraw Hill, Maidenhead.

Höpfl, H. (1990), 'The Making of the Corporate Acolyte - Charisma and Organisational Commitment', *Journal of Management Studies*, vol. 29, January.

Höpfl, H. (1992), 'Value and Valuation: Conflicts Between Culture Change and Job Cuts', *Personnel Review*, vol. 21, pp. 24-36.

Husserl, E. (1931), *Ideas*, Allen and Unwin, London.

Husserl, E. (1965), *Phenomenology and the Crisis of Philosophy*, Harper Torch Books, New York.

Illich, I. (1977), *Disabling Professions*, Marion Boyars, London.

Jacques, E. (1951), *The Changing Culture of the Factory*, Dryden Press, New York.

Johnson, P. and Gill, J. (1993), *Management Control and Organisational Behaviour*, Paul Chapman, London.

Jones, S. (1978), 'Choosing Action Research: A Rationale', in I.L. Mangham *et al.* (1978), *Interactions and Interventions in Organizations*, John Wiley, New York.

Katz, D. and Khan, R.L. (1966), *The Social Psychology of Organizations*, John Wiley, New York.

Keddie, N. (1971), 'Classroom Knowledge', in M.F.D. Young (ed.), (1971), *Knowledge and Control*, Collier-Macmillan, London.

Kilmann, R.H., Saxton, M.J. *et al.* (1985), *Gaining Control of the Corporate Culture*, Jossey Bass, California.

Kluckhohn, F. and Strodbeck, F. (1961), *Variations in Value Orientations*, Row-Peterson, Evanston, Illinois.

Kouter, R.M. (1984), *The Change Masters*, Allen and Unwin, London.

Kouter, R.M. (1989), *When Giants Learn to Dance: Mastering the Challenge of Strategy, Management and Careers in the 1990s*, Simon and Schuster, London.

Kroeber, A.L. and Kluckhohn, F. (1952), *Culture: A Critical Review of Concepts and Definitions*, Vintage Books, New York.

Lane, C. and Bachmann, R. (1996), *The Social Constitution of Trust: Supplier Relations in Britain and Germany*.

Levy, A. and Merry, U. (1986), *Organizational Transformations*, Praegar, New York.

Lewin, K. (1946), 'Action Research and Minority Problems', *Journal of Social Issues*, vol. 2, pp. 34-36.

Lewin, K. (1952a), 'Group Decision and Social Change', in G.E. Swanson, Newcom and Hartley (eds.), (1952), *Readings in Social Psychology*, Holt, Rinehart and Winston, New York.

Lewin, K. (1952b), *Field Theory in Social Science*, Tavistock, London.

Likert, R. (1961), *New Patterns of Management*, McGraw-Hill, Maidenhead.

Luhmann, N. (1998), 'Familiarity, Confidence, Trust: Problems and Alternatives', in D. Gambetta (ed.), (1998), *Trust: Making and Breaking Co-operative Relations*, Sage, London.

McRobbie, A. (1978), *Working Class Girls and the Culture of Femininity*, Centre for Contemporary Culture Studies, Birmingham.

McGovern, P. and Hope-Hailey, V. (1997), 'Corporate Culture and Bureaucratic Control', in S.A. Sackmann (ed.), (1997), *Cultural Complexity in Organizations: Inherent Contrasts*, Sage, Beverley Hills.

McNeill, P. (1985), *Research Methods*, Tavistock, New York.

Mangham, I.L. *et al.* (1978), *Interactions and Interventions in Organizations*, John Wiley, New York.

Manis, J. and Meltzer, B. (eds.), (1967), *Symbolic Interactionism*, Allyn and Bacon, New York.

Martin, J. and Siehl, C. (1983), 'Organizational Culture and Counterculture: An Uneasy Symbiosis', *Journal of Organizational Dynamics*.

May, T. (1993), *Social Research: Issues, Methods and Process*, Open University Press, Buckingham.

Mayo, E. (1960), *The Human Problems of an Industrial Civilization*, Harvard Business School Press, Boston.

Mead, G.H. (1934), *Mind, Self and Society*, C. Morris (ed.), University of Chicago Press, Chicago.

Merton, R. (1968), *Social Theory and Social Structure*, Free Press, New York.

Meyerson, D. and Martin, J. (1987), 'Cultural Change: An Integration of Three Different Views', *Journal of Management Studies*, vol. 24, no. 6.

Michels, R. (1949), *Political Parties: A Sociological Study of Oligarchy in Modern Democracy*, Free Press of Glencoe, New York.

Mills, C.W. (1959), *The Sociological Imagination*, Open University Press, New York.

Morgan, G. (1986), *Images of Organization*, Sage, London.

Morgan, G. (1993), *Imaginization: The Art of Creative Management*, Sage, London.

Murdock, G.P. (1949), *Social Structure*, Macmillan, New York.

Ogbonna, E. (1992), 'Managing Organisational Culture: Fantasy or Reality?', *Journal of Human Resource Management*, vol. 3, no. 2, pp.42-54.

Pacanowsky, M.E. and O'Donnell-Trujillo, N. (1982), 'Communication and Organizational Culture', *Western Journal of Speech Communication*, vol. 11, pp. 457-483.

Parsons, T. (1951), *The Social System*, Free Press, New York.

Patrick, J. (1973), *A Glasgow Gang Observed*, Eyre Methuen, London.

Payne, R.L. (1997), 'The Concepts of Culture and Climate', quoted in B. Senior, (1997), *Organisational Change*, Pitman, London.

Peters, T.J. (1978), 'Symbols, Patterns and Settings: A Case For Getting Things Done', *Journal of Organizational Dynamics*, vol. 3, no. 2, Autumn.

Peters, T.J. and Waterman, R.H. Jnr. (1982), *In Search of Excellence: Lessons From America's Best-Run Companies*, Harper Row, New York.

Pettigrew, A. (1990), 'Is Corporate Culture Manageable?', quoted in D. Wilson and R. Rosenfeld, McGraw-Hill, Maidenhead.

Pollert, A. (1987), 'The "Flexible Firm": A Model in Search of Reality (or a Policy in Search of a Practice?)', *Warwick Papers in Industrial Relations*, Warwick.

Pondy, L.R., Frost, P., Morgan, G. and Dandridge, T. (1983), 'Organizational Symbolism', *Journal of Administrative Management*, Greenwich, Connecticut.

Poulantzas, N. (1975), *Classes in Contemporary Capitalism*, New Left Books, London.

Popper, K. (1963), *Conjectures and Refutations*, Routledge and Kegan Paul, London.

Popper, K. (1966), *The Open Society and its Enemies*, Routledge and Kegan Paul, London.

Powell, W. and DiMaggio, P. (1991), *New Institutionalism in Organisational Analysis*, University of Chicago Press, Chicago.

Roethlisberger, F. and Dickson, W. (1939), *Management and the Worker*, John Wiley, New York.

Rose, A. (ed.), (1962), *Human Behaviour and Social Processes*, Routledge and Kegan Paul, London.

Rosenthal, R. and Jacobson, L. (1968), *Pygmalion in the Classroom*, Holt, Rinehart and Winston, New York.

Sackmann, S.A. (ed.), (1997), *Cultural Complexity in Organizations: Inherent Contrasts*, Sage, Beverley Hills.

Schattschneider, E.E. (1960), *The Semisovereign People: A Realist's View of Democracy in the USA*, Holt, Rinehart and Winston, New York.

Schein, E.H. (1985), *Organisational Culture and Leadership*, Jossey Bass, San Francisco.

Schein, E.H. (1990), 'Organisational Culture', *American Psychologist*, February.

Schein, E.H. (1992), *Organisational Culture and Leadership*, 2nd edn., Jossey Bass, San Francisco.

Schein, E.H. (1994), 'On Dialogue, Culture and Organisational Learning', *Journal of Organizational Dynamics*.

Schutz, A. (1972), *The Phenomenology of the Social World*, Heinemann, London.

Senior, B. (1997), *Organisational Change*, Pitman, London.

Silverman, D. (1972), 'Some Neglected Questions About Social Reality', in P. Filmer, D. Silverman, D. Walsh and M. Phillipson (1972), *New Directions in Sociological Theory*, Collier-Macmillan, London.

Smircich, L. and Morgan, G. (1982), 'Leadership: The Management of Meaning', *Journal of Applied Behavioural Studies*, vol. 18, pp. 257-273.

G.E. Swanson, Newcom and Hartley (eds.), (1953), *Readings in Social Psychology*, Holt, Rinehart and Winston, New York.

Taylor, F.W. (1947), *The Principles of Scientific Management*, 3rd edn., Harper Row, New York.

Taylor, J. (1988), *Mass Producing Fords*, Open University Press, Milton Keynes.

Thompson, E.P. (1994), *Writings on History and Culture*, New Press, New York.

Trist, E. and Bamforth, P. (1963), *Organisational Choice*, Tavistock, London.

Trompenaars, F. (1993), *Riding the Waves of Culture*, Economist Books, London.

Walsh, D. (1972), 'Sociology and the Social World', in P. Filmer, D. Silverman, D. Walsh and M. Phillipson (1972), *New Directions in Sociological Theory*, Collier-Macmillan, London.

Weber, M. (1964), *Theory of Social and Economic Organisation*, Free Press Glencoe/Chicago University Press, Chicago.

Wilkins, A.L. (1983), 'Organizational Stories as Symbols Which Control the Organization', in L.R. Pondy, P. Frost, G. Morgan and T. Dandridge, (1983), 'Organizational Symbolism', *Journal of Administrative Management*, Greenwich, Connecticut.

Williams, K. *et al.* (1992), 'Ford Versus Fordism', *Work, Employment and Society*, vol. 6, no. 1, pp.517-548.

Willmott, H. (1991), 'Strength is Ignorance: Slavery is Freedom: Managing Culture in Modern Organisations', *Proceedings From the Standing Conference on Organisational Symbolism*, Copenhagen.

Willmott, H. (1992), unpublished 2nd draft of 1993 paper.

Willmott, H. (1993), 'Strength is Ignorance: Slavery is Freedom: Managing Culture in Modern Organisations', *Journal of Management Studies*, vol. 30, no. 4.

Wilson, D. and Rosenfeld, R. (1990), *Managing Organisations*, McGraw Hill, Maidenhead.

Young, M.F.D. (ed.), (1971), *Knowledge and Control*, Collier-Macmillan, London.

Zuboff, S. (1988), *In the Age of the Smart Machine, the Future of Work and Power*, Heinemann, Oxford.

Appendix 1 Graphics COPE Maps

The Supermodel

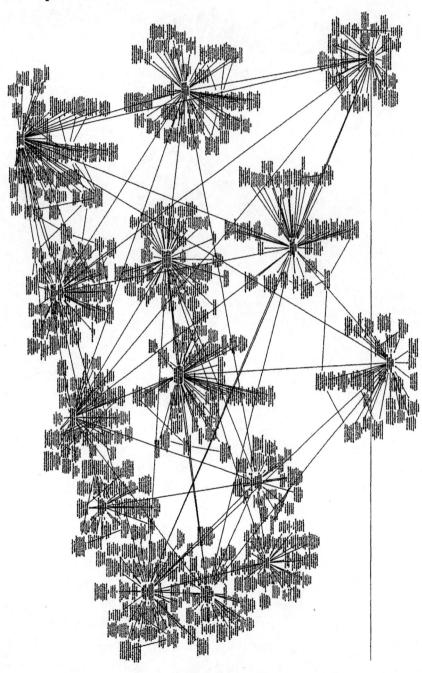

Map One

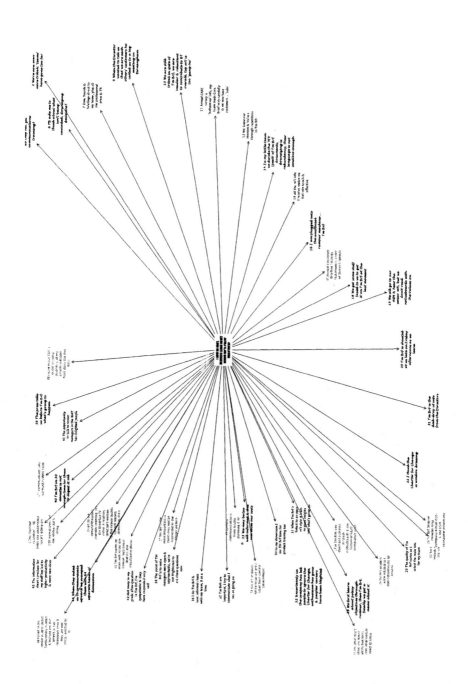

Map Two

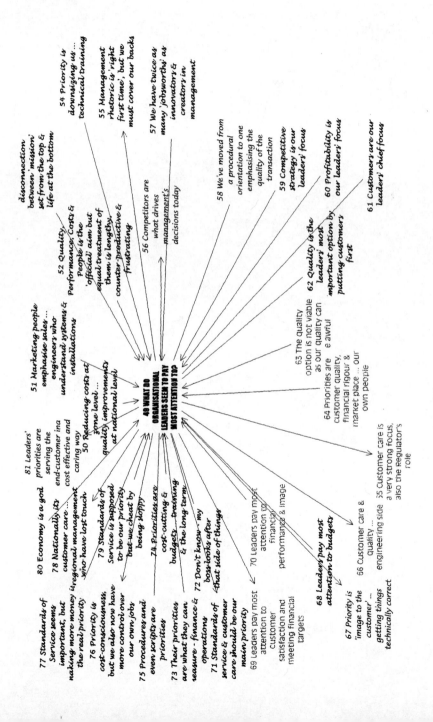

Map Three

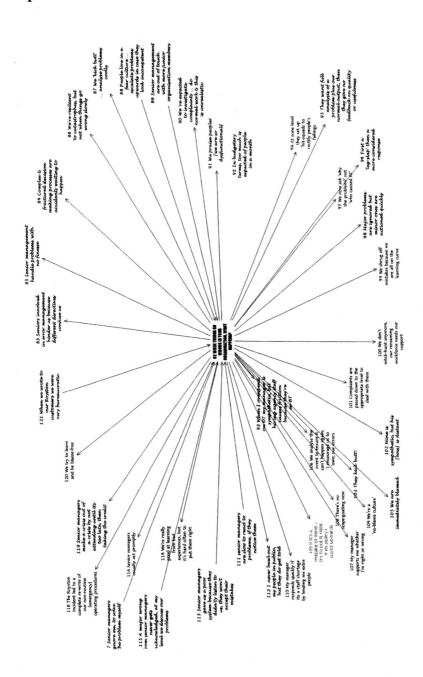

87 We 'kick butt'
...analyse problems easily

88 People live in a fear culture...
escalate problems
upwards in case they
look incompetent

86 We're resilient
to catastrophies, but
not when things go
wrong slowly

89 Senior management
are out of touch
with more junior
organisation members

90 We're expected
to investigate
complaints...its
normal work & this
is unrealistic

95 They want full
analysis of a
problem plus our
normal output, there
there's no
feedback on quality
or usefulness

84 Complex &
fractured decision-
making processes are
accidents waiting to
happen

91 We praise people!
(we are so
dysfunctional)

94 At zero level
they set up
'hit-squads' to
rectify people's
failings

96 First a
'tap-slap' then a
more considered
response

85 Senior management
handle problems with
no finesse

92 In budgetary
terms, too much is
expected of people
in a month

97 We now ask 'why
(the problem)' not
'who caused it!'

98 Major problems
are ignored but
minor ones are
actioned quickly

83 Seniors involved
in a crisis because
hinder us because
different directives
confuse us

99 We shrug off
mistakes because we
are all on the
learning curve

121 When we wrote to
our Royston
customers we were
very bureaucratic

100 We don't
witch-hunt anymore,
our remaining
workforce needs our
support

120 We try to learn
and be blame-free

101 Complaints are
passed down to the
appropriate level to
deal with them

119 Senior managers
make a crisis out of
not
attending until its
taking the credit

93 When I overspend,
one of my managers is
sympathetic but
hands out 'slaps'
because they're
angry.

102 Here is
sympathetic, but his
(boss) is distant

118 The Royston
incident led to a
complete rewrite of
our non-routine
(emergency)
operating procedures

106 We analyse the
event before
I encourage us to
own our errors

103 They kick butt!

7 Senior managers
ignore me, for when
the problem myself

116 Senior managers
usually act promptly

104 There's no
scape-goating now

104 We're a
'no-blame culture'

115 A major wrong
issue senior managers
never gets
acknowledged, at my
level we disguise our
problems

114 We're really
good at learning
from bad
experience, but
it's hard often to
put them right

109 If it's a
message or mine, I
try to put it right.
If it's policy I
blast upstairs

107 My manager
supports me whether
I'm right or wrong

105 We are
immediately blamed

113 Senior managers
have a poor
systems because they
didn't listen to
us, they won't
accept their
mistakes

112 I never break out
my people in public,
but they do get told

111 senior managers
are slow to react to
problems, if they
notice them

110 My manager
responds quickly if
its a staff shortage
by lending me extra
people

Map Four

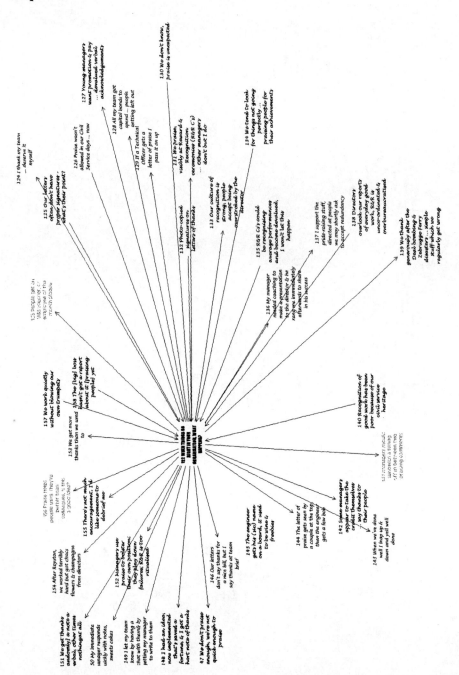

124 I thank my team ... deserve it myself

127 Young managers want promotion & pay ... devalued verbal acknowledgements

125 Our letters often about how people perform ... what's their point?

126 Praise wasn't allowed in our Civil Service days ... now

128 All my team got capital bonds to spend ... people getting left out

129 If a Technical Officer gets a letter of praise I pass it on up

130 We don't know, praise is unexpected

131 We praise, visibly at Reward & Recognition ceremonies (R&R C's) other managers don't but I do

134 We tend to look for things not going perfectly ... praising people for their achievements

123 People get an 'MBE award' or 'employee of the month' plaque

133 Our culture of recognition is strong, people accept being overlooked by the director

132 Photo-copied signatures on letters of thanks

135 R&R C's could be recognising average performances and become devalued, I won't let this happen

137 I support the pride-raising stuff, directed at people, we may shortly ask to accept redundancy

138 Directors overlook our reports of everyday good work, R&R is uncco-ordinated & overbureaucratised

136 My manager needed coaching to make a presentation to the director & he rang me immediately afterwards to share in his success

139 We thank generously after the Dunblane disaster & Zeebrugge Ferry disasters ... simple stuff which we regularly get wrong

157 We work quietly without blowing our own trumpets

158 The [big] boss hasn't got a report about it [praising people] yet

153 We get more thanks than we used to

121 WE'D THINK SO BUT IN THIS ORGANISATIONAL THAT MAPPED

140 Recognition of good work has been poor because of our civil service heritage

141 Managers include sandwiches & warmth in between two praising comments

156 Praise makes people think they're better than colleagues, is this a good idea?

155 There's not much encouragement, I'd like someone to debrief me

145 The employees get a list (sic) name on a board, it used to be wine & freebies

144 The letter of praise gets seen by a couple at the top, then the engineer gets a few bob

142 Some managers appear to take the credit themselves say thanks to their people

143 When we've done well I leap up & down and yell well done

154 After Royston, we worked terribly hard but got chocs, flowers & champagne from director

152 Managers use praise to bolster their own position, they play down failures, R&R is too ritualised

151 We get thanks randomly, a note a wash, other times nothing at all

50 My immediate manager responds quickly with notes, sweets cakes

149 I let my team know by having a chat with thumbs by getting my manager to write to them

148 I had an idea, now implemented, that's saved a fortune, & I got a hasty note of thanks

47 We don't praise enough, we're not quick enough to praise

146 Our letters don't say thanks for a nice bill, but I say thanks at team brief

Map Five

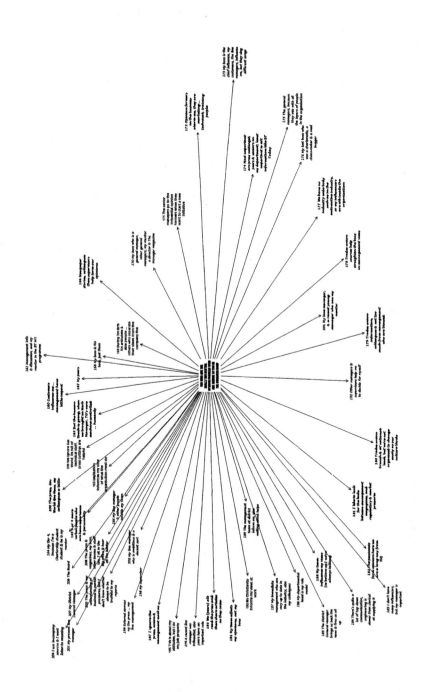

Map Six

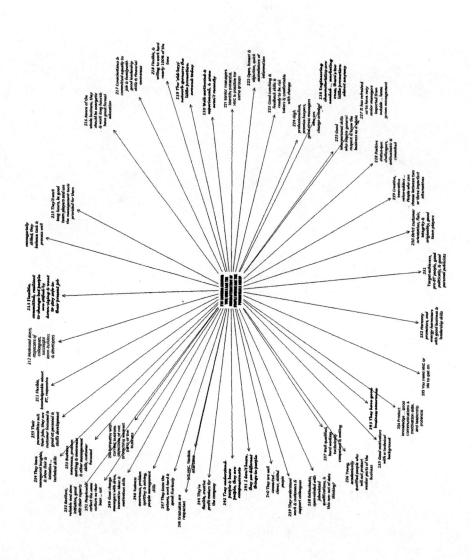

Map Seven

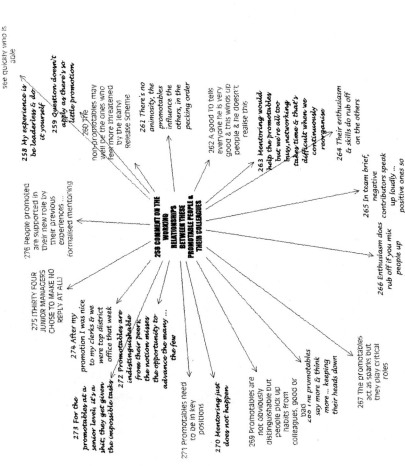

257 Relationships are hit & miss, you see quickly who is able

258 My experience is be leaderless & do it yourself

259 Question doesn't apply as there's so little promotion

260 The non-promotables may well be the ones who feel more threatened by the (early) release scheme

261 There's no animosity, the promotables influence the others, in the pecking order

262 A good TO tells everyone he is very good & this winds up people & he doesn't realise this

263 Mentoring would help the promotables but we're all too busy networking takes time & that's difficult when we continuously reorganise

264 Their enthusiasm & skills do rub off on the others

276 People promoted are supported in their new role by their previous experiences ... formalised mentoring

258 CONFLICT ON THE WORKING RELATIONSHIPS BETWEEN THESE PROMOTABLE PEOPLE & THEIR COLLEAGUES

265 In team brief, negative contributors speak up loudly ... positive ones so they need sitting on

266 Enthusiasm does rub off if you mix people up

275 [THIRTY FOUR JUNIOR MANAGERS CHOSE TO MAKE NO REPLY AT ALL]

274 After my promotion I was nice to my clerks & we were top district office that week

272 Promotables are indistinguishable from their peers the notion misses the opportunity to advance the many ... the few

273 For the promotables at a senior level, it's a shit, they get given the impossible tasks

271 Promotables need to be in key positions

270 Mentoring just does not happen

269 promotables are not obviously distinguishable but people pick up habits from colleagues, good or bad

268 The promotables say more & think more ... keeping their heads down

267 The promotables act as sparks but they play critical roles

Map Eight

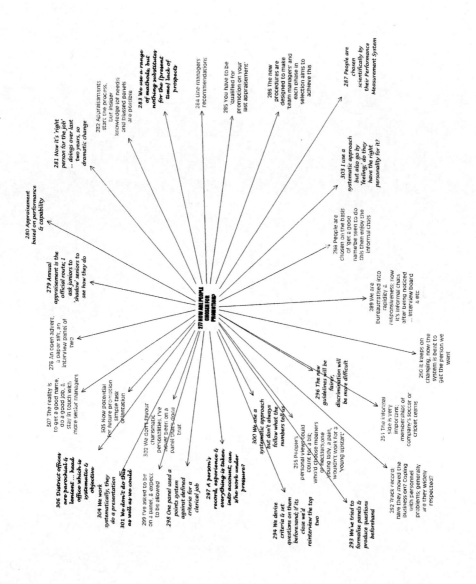

Map Nine

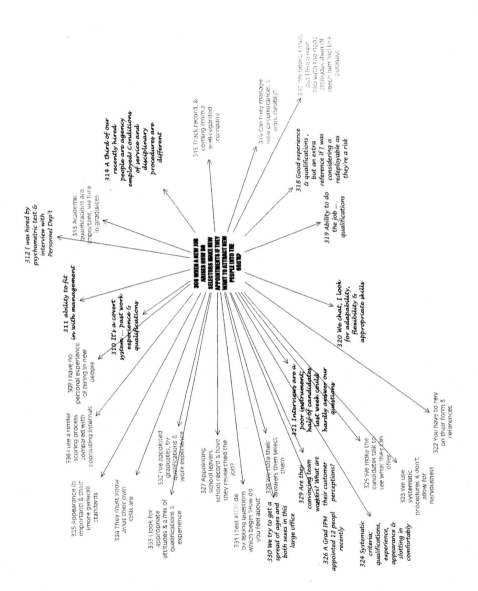

Map Ten

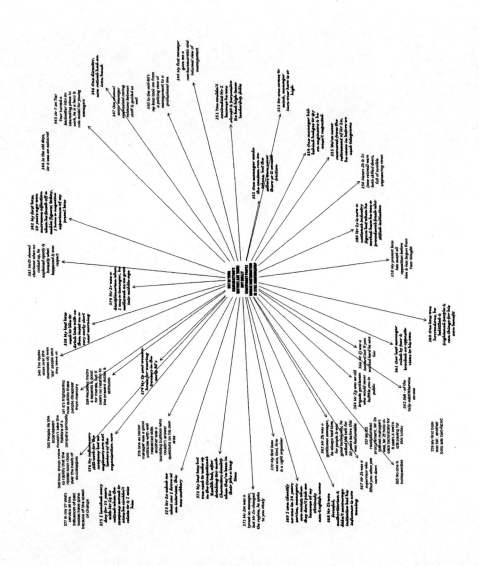

Map Eleven

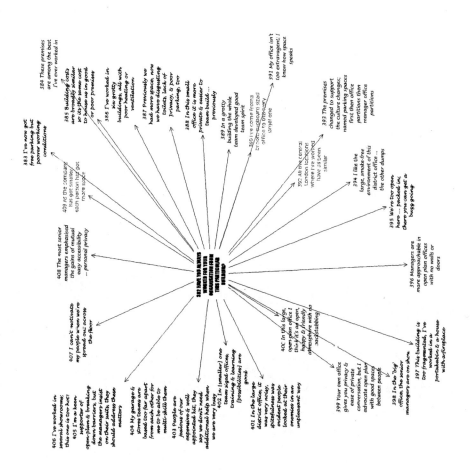

383 I've now got
free parking but
poorer working
conditions

384 These premises
are among the best
I've ever worked in

409 As the company
has got smaller,
each person has got
more space

385 Building costs
are brought similar
to its the same cost
to house us in good
or poor premises

386 I've worked in
six grotty
buildings, all with
poor heading or
ventilation

387 Previously we
had more space, now
we have disgusting
toilets, lack of
privacy, & poor
parking, too

408 The most senior
managers emphasised
the gains of mutual
easy accessibility
... personal privacy

388 In this small
office it is more
private & easier to
team build ...
previously

389 In a grotty
building the whole
team developed good
team spirit

390 I've come from a
broom-cupboard sized
office to an empty
large one

391 My office isn't
too extravagant; I
know how space
speaks

407 I can't motivate
my people when we're
spread out across
the floor

393 The premises
changed to support
the culture changes;
named parking spaces
first then office
partitions then
manager office
partitions

392 All the central
London locations
where I've worked
have all been
similar

406 I've worked in
several showrooms;
this one is too hot!

405 I'm a keen
supporter of
open-plan & breaking
down barriers, but
the managers insist
on their suits, they
should address these
matters

394 I like the
large, smoke-free
environment of this
district office ...
the other dumps

395 We're too open-
horn ... packed in,
there you can get a
bugg going

396 Managers are
more approachable in
open plan offices
with no walls or
doors

404 My garages &
stores teams are
based too far apart
from each other for
me to be able to
multi-skill them

403 People are
jealous of our
expansion & well
appointed kit; they
say we don't need
additional help when
we are very busy

402 In (smaller) one
team sized offices,
training & learning
[possibilities] are
good

401 In the large
district office, it
was very untidy,
spitefulness was
evident; people
looked at their
enemies in an
unpleasant way

40C In this large,
open-plan office I
think it's an open,
happy & friendly
atmosphere with no
backstabbing

399 Your own office
gives you privacy &
ease of private
conversation, but I
advocate open plan
with good spaces
between people

398 In the 'big'
office, the senior
managers are on show

397 This building is
too fragmented; I've
worked in a
portakabin & a house
with a fireplace

382 SOME TWO ALWAYS
WORKED FOR YOUR
ORGANISATION FROM
THIS PARTICULAR
BUILDING

Map Twelve

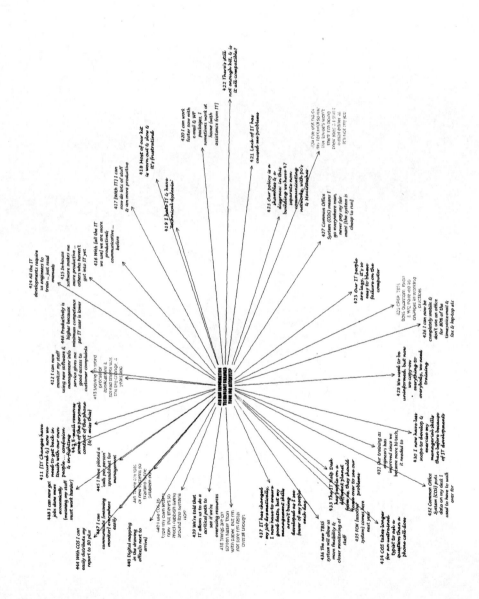

Map Thirteen

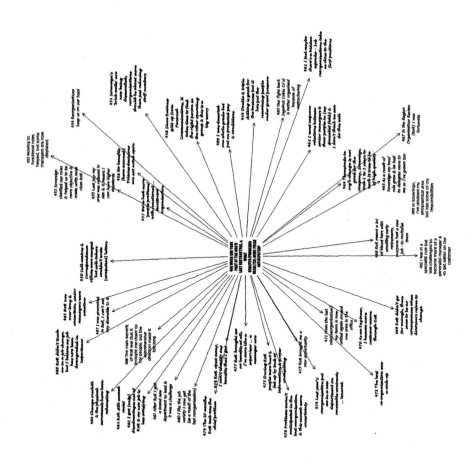

Map Fourteen

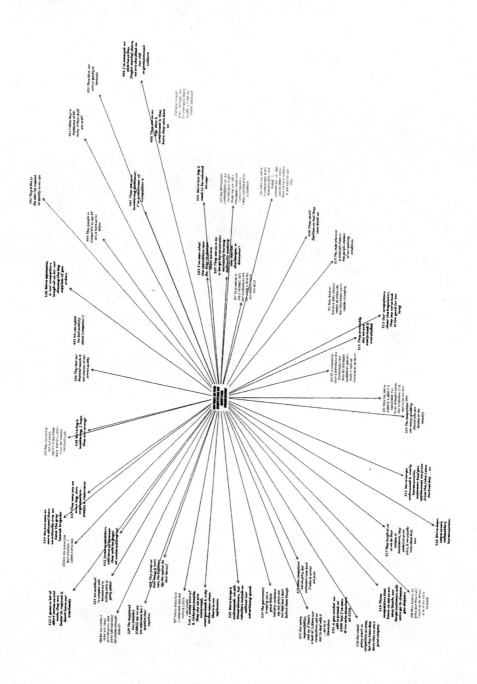

Appendix 2   Domain Analysis

The Top 29 Concepts in Descending Order of Value

49 links around:
159   "Who are the really influential opinion formers who are senior to you in the organisation?"

46 links around:
1   "How do members learn about senior management policy objectives?"

44 links around:
490   "What do your competitors say about your organisation?"
210   "Looking around you, what are the characteristics of people which are the promotable ones?"

39 links around:
82   "When things go wrong in your organisation, what happens?"

37 links around:
449   "When did your part of the organisation last restructure and what benefits/problems resulted; were these anticipated?"

36 links around:
337   "In your organisation's history, are there any really significant people whose contribution is still remembered?"

35 links around:
410   "Has information technology changed your job recently?"

30 links around:
122   "When things go right in your organisation, what happens?"

29 links around:
277   "How are people chosen for promotion?"

28 links around:
308   "When a new job arises how do selectors make new appointments if they want to attract new people into the organisation?"

27 links around:
49   "What do organisational leaders seem to pay most attention to?"

25 links around:
382   "Have you always worked for your organisation from this particular building?"

19 links around:
256   "Comment on the working relationships between those promotable people and their colleagues"

7 links around:
469   "RoR didn't go far enough, there seem to be no consequences when dinosaurs refuse to change"
499   "I'm amazed we still have this [high] market share, we are shackled in our old organisational culture"

5 links around:
423   "Our policy is a shambles and a disgrace: in this building we have 47 separate non-communicating networks, with PCs and Macintoshes"
485   "RoR was over-long and uncertain, senior managers were amateur"

4 links around:
263   "Mentoring would help the promotables but we're all too busy, networking takes time and that's difficult when we continuously restructure"
311   "Ability to fit in with management"
472   "The last re-organisation was a cock-up"
484   "Change overkill and the physical movements have been exhausting"

3 links around:
411   "[IT changes have occurred and] now we need to get back in touch with our own people ... confusion and in-fighting"

433 "The IT Help Desk has people on a different planet from us, they should come over to see our problems"

475 "During RoR people were hurt and fed up by lack of information and proper counselling"

478 "RoR upset many, I can't identify any benefits that I got"

488 "RoR didn't touch me in a job change, but I believe my job has now been downgraded in importance"

519 "Those competitors that know us see us as an easy touch, our large customers will soon go to cheaper gas shippers"

532 "Some competitors will love us because they will be great at undercutting us!"

Index of Authors

Index